Christian Literature in Chinese Contexts

Christian Literature in Chinese Contexts

Special Issue Editor

John T. P. Lai

MDPI • Basel • Beijing • Wuhan • Barcelona • Belgrade

Special Issue Editor
John T. P. Lai
Chinese University of Hong Kong
Hong Kong

Editorial Office
MDPI
St. Alban-Anlage 66
4052 Basel, Switzerland

This is a reprint of articles from the Special Issue published online in the open access journal *Religions* (ISSN 2077-1444) in 2019 (available at: https://www.mdpi.com/journal/religions/special issues/ Christian_Literature).

For citation purposes, cite each article independently as indicated on the article page online and as indicated below:

LastName, A.A.; LastName, B.B.; LastName, C.C. Article Title. *Journal Name* **Year**, *Article Number*, Page Range.

ISBN 978-3-03921-842-4 (Pbk)
ISBN 978-3-03921-843-1 (PDF)

Cover image courtesy of the Bodleian Library, University of Oxford.

Contents

About the Special Issue Editor

John T. P. Lai Having received his Doctor of Philosophy from the University of Oxford (2005), John T. P. Lai is currently Associate Professor at the Department of Cultural and Religious Studies, Chinese University of Hong Kong, and was Visiting Scholar of the Harvard-Yenching Institute (2015–2016). His research interests revolve around the interdisciplinary study of religion, literature, and translation, with a focus on Chinese Christian literature. He has published four monographs: *Negotiating Religious Gaps: The Enterprise of Translating Christian Tracts by Protestant Missionaries in Nineteenth-Century China* (2012); *The Afterlife of a Classic: A Critical Study of the Late-Qing Chinese Translations of* The Pilgrim's Progress (in Chinese) (2012); *Attuning the Gospel: Chinese Christian Novels of the Late Qing Period* (in Chinese) (2017); *Literary Representations of Christianity in Late Qing and Republican China* (2019). He obtained the "Research Excellence Award" (2011) and "The Faculty of Arts Outstanding Teaching Award" (for six times) from the Chinese University of Hong Kong. He has been awarded the "General Research Fund" from the Hong Kong Research Grants Council for four times.

Preface to "Christian Literature in Chinese Contexts"

Christianity in China has a history dating back to the Tang Dynasty (618–907 CE), when Allopen—the first Nestorian missionary—arrived there in 635. In the late sixteenth century, Matteo Ricci (1552–1610) together with other Jesuit missionaries commenced the Catholic missions to China. Protestant Christianity in China began with Robert Morrison (1782–1834), of London Missionary Society, who first set foot in Canton in 1807. Over the centuries, the Western missionaries and Chinese believers were engaged in the enterprise of the translation, publication, and distribution of a large corpus of Christian literature in Chinese. Apart from the direct reading of the Chinese translations of the Bible, the biblical stories and messages were more widely received among the Chinese audiences in a variety of modes, including hearing biblical stories paraphrased or recapitulated in sermons, singing of hymns and making use of liturgical texts, reciting catechisms and trimetrical primers, consulting Bible dictionaries and commentaries, reading or hearing the Christian novels read aloud, among others. While the extensive distribution of Chinese publications facilitated the propagation of Christianity, the Christian messages have been subtly re-presented, re-appropriated, and transformed by these works of Chinese Christian literature.

This Special Issue entitled "Christian Literature in Chinese Contexts" examines the multifarious dimensions of the production, translation, circulation, and reception of Christian literature (with "Christian" and "literature" in their broadest sense) against the cultural and sociopolitical contexts from the Tang period to modern China. The eight articles collected in this volume address an array of fascinating topics, including the political theology of Jingjiao Christianity in Tang China (by Chin Ken-pa); the introduction of European rhetoric to China during the late Ming and early Qing dynasties (by Sher-Shiueh Li); the Catholic reinterpretations of the *Yijing* (Classic of Changes) by both the Jesuit missionaries (by Sophie Ling-chia Wei) and Chinese believers (by John T. P. Lai and Jochebed Hin Ming Wu) in the Qing period; the intertextual theology of religions from the perspective of early 20th century Chinese religious periodicals (by Wai Luen Kwok); the missionary translation of Shakespeare as a piece of Chinese Christian literature (by Dadui Yao); the integration of Marxism into the biblical narratives of the life of Jesus (by Zhixi Wang); and the emergence of "spiritual writing" in contemporary Chinese literature (by Chloë Starr).

John T. P. Lai
Special Issue Editor

Article

Jingjiao under the Lenses of Chinese Political Theology

Chin Ken-pa

Department of Philosophy, Fu Jen Catholic University, New Taipei City 24205, Taiwan; kenpa.mnf@gmail.com

Received: 28 May 2019; Accepted: 16 September 2019; Published: 26 September 2019

Abstract: Conflict between religion and state politics is a persistent phenomenon in human history. Hence it is not surprising that the propagation of Christianity often faces the challenge of "political theology". When the Church of the East monk Aluoben reached China in 635 during the reign of Emperor Tang Taizong, he received the favorable invitation of the emperor to translate Christian sacred texts for the collections of Tang Imperial Library. This marks the beginning of Jingjiao (景教) mission in China. In historiographical sense, China has always been a political domineering society where the role of religion is subservient and secondary. A school of scholarship in Jingjiao studies holds that the fall of Jingjiao in China is the obvious result of its over-involvement in local politics. The flaw of such an assumption is the overlooking of the fact that in the Tang context, it is impossible for any religious establishments to avoid getting in touch with the Tang government. In the light of this notion, this article attempts to approach this issue from the perspective of "political theology" and argues that instead of over-involvement, it is rather the clashing of "ideologies" between the Jingjiao establishment and the ever-changing Tang court's policies towards foreigners and religious bodies that caused the downfall of Jingjiao Christianity in China. This article will posit its argument based on the analysis of the Chinese Jingjiao canonical texts, especially the Xian Stele, and takes this as a point of departure to observe the political dynamics between Jingjiao and Tang court. The finding of this paper does show that the intellectual history of Chinese Christianity is in a sense a comprehensive history of "political theology".

Keywords: Xian Stele; Jingjiao Christianity; Tang Dynasty; Political Theology; politics-religion relationship

---

1. Introduction

Conflict between religion and politics is a persistent phenomenon in history. In an introductory preface to Chen Yuan's (陳垣 1880–1971) *Mingji Dianqian Fojiao kao* 明季滇黔佛教考 [Late Ming Period Buddhism in Yungui Region], the prominent Chinese historian Chen Yinke (陳寅恪 1890–1969) claims: "General opinion has it that politics and religion are two different entities and should not be treated together. However, historical events suggest the opposite. Politics and religion are in indeed closely related. . . . When the Ming Dynasty fell, most of its literati royalists turned into avid Buddhist devotees in order not to serve the new dynasty. . . . In this context, religious history is nonetheless a political history"[1] (Chen 2002, pp. 235–36). In other words, Chen Yinke recognizes that Chen Yuan's historical survey on the propagation of Buddhism during the late Ming period also reflects the political condition of the Ming Dynasty. The author Chen Yuan himself wrote a postscript that reaffirmed Chen Yinke's statement when the book was reprinted in 1957 (Chen 2002, p. 480).[2]

---

[1]   Unless otherwise mentioned, all translation from the Chinese text in this article is by the author.
[2]   In this postscript, Chen Yuan has subtly made a critical allusion to the political-religion climate of his days.

A school of scholarship in Jingjiao (景教)[3] studies considers that the downfall of the Jingjiao-church in Tang China is the obvious result of its over-involvement in local politics.[4] However, the flaw of this assumption lies in the fact that it is not possible for Jingjiao, as a religious establishment, to avoid any interactions with the Tang court. In light of this notion, this article adopts Chen Yinke's view aforementioned and approaches the question of Jingjiao's downfall from the perspective of "political theology" instead. This paper argues that instead of over-involvement, it is rather the clashing of "ideologies" between the Jingjiao establishment and the ever-changing Tang court's policies towards foreigners that has caused the downfall of Jingjiao in Tang China.

In light of Chinese historiography, Chinese dynasties throughout the ages have always been a political domineering structure where the role of religion is subservient and secondary. When the Jingjiao-church first established itself in Tang China, official approval of settlement and royal patronage from the Tang imperial court were both crucial. From the moment Alouben and his missionary group entered Chang'an, they were well aware of the Tang court's "political theology". This awareness was explicitly but subtly revealed in Jingjiao's written records such as Xian Stele.

The Jingjiao establishment is often recognized as the beginning of the "political theology" awareness in the propagation history of Sino-Christianity. As one of the "three *yi*/barbarian religions" 三夷教 in the Tang Dynasty, the Church was inevitably subjected to the domineering cultural hegemony of the Tang court. According to Liu He, the concept of *yi* in viewing all foreigners as barbarian is "a Chinese classical theory of sovereignty imagination" (Liu 2004, p. 72). Liu argues that in classical Chinese view, this concept serves as an important figurative metaphor in the sovereign discourse of China imperial past viewing themselves as the center in the matter of both national administration and foreign relationships. As a discourse, *yi* serves the function of naming the boundaries of the imperial sovereign rule on the other's territories (Ibid.). In the Chinese context, the idea of sovereignty is closely associated with the view of *tianxia* (天下, literally "under heaven"). This is the figurative imagination of Chinese past dynasties which eventually turns into an imperial political discourse. In other words, in the traditional Chinese view, sovereignty is as much a matter of external recognition as one of domestic legitimacy, and it is the quest for such recognition that Chinese dynasties of the past often maintained a strict policy of *huayi zhi bian* (華夷之辨, distinction of Chinese against the foreign) in the coercion of foreigners. Segregating the Chinese from the barbaric foreigners is a projection of the classical Chinese imperial desire to dominate the others (Ibid., pp. 72–75). Hence, when Jingjiao first established itself in China, the institution was subjected to this domineering ideology of the Tang court.

The ego-centric world view of *tianxia* is the domineering political ideology that has shaped the foreign policies of ancient China towards its neighboring countries and other nationalities throughout the ages. Ancient imperial China referred to itself as *Zhongguo* (中國, the Centre State) and related to others as a suzerain would treat his vassals. Therefore, the demanding of tributes from the neighboring "barbarian" countries and treating all foreigners as "subjects" of the Chinese emperor were both justifiable and legitimate in the eye of Chinese sovereign rulers (Yu 2009, p. 221).

Within the conceptual framework of *tianxia* and *huayi zhi bian*, Jingjiao "political theology" needs to address two main issues: the sovereignty of *daotong* (道統 Chinese traditional orthodoxy) and the sovereignty of *zhengtong* (政統 political governance), i.e., *tianming* (天命, the Heavenly mandate) and *tianzi* (天子, the Son of Heaven-the emperor). Often, these two issues overlap with each other; they

---

[3] Jingjiao, the particular branch of Christianity which reached China during the Tang Dynasty, used to be commonly rendered as Nestorianism in English. However, the appropriateness of the term has recently attracted wide discussion in the scholarly circle East and West. Due to the limitation of capacity and scope, this paper will use Jingjiao 景教 instead of Nestorian to designate this particular religion, as this is the self-reference of the Jingjiao-church in Tang-China which is literally known as the "Luminous Religion".

[4] Representative scholars who hold this opinion includes Xu Zongze 徐宗澤, Yang Senfu 楊森富, Zhu Qianzhi 朱謙之, Jiang Wenhan 江文漢 etc. For general overview, ref. Ren Jiyu 任繼愈 ed. *Ershi shiji Zhongguo xueshu dadian: Zongjiaoxue* 20世紀中國學術大典：宗教學 (Fujian jiaoyu chubanshe, (Ren 2002)), pp. 274–75; Weng Shaojun 翁紹軍, Hanyu Jingjiao wendian quanshi 漢語景教文典詮釋 (Shanghai: Sanlian shuju, (Weng 1996)), pp. 9–10.

are the two sides of the same coin. To a certain extent, Tang Jingjiao priests might have noticed the potential problems which would arise out of the adherence of the two. Therefore, in the first part of the text inscribed (hereafter Inscription) on the Monument for the Propagation of Daqin Jingjiao in China (大秦景教流行中國碑, hereafter Xian Stele), an elaborated account of *daotong* (theology) is being given, while the second half of the Inscription is dedicated to the account of *zhengtong* (politics). The Inscription[5] reads: "But any (such) system without (the fostering of the sage (the sovereign),[6] does not attain its full development; and a sage (sovereign) without the aid of such a system does not become great" (惟道非聖不弘, 聖非道不大) (Legge 1966, p. 9). "None but the Illustrious Religion is observed; none but virtuous rulers are appointed" (法非景不行, 主非德不立) (p. 13). "There is nothing which the right principle cannot effect; and whatever it effects can be named. There is nothing which a sage (sovereign) cannot do; and whatever he does can be related" (道無不可, 所可可名; 聖無不作, 所作可述) (p. 19).

In other words, "foreign religions" and "barbarian temples" do need the Tang sovereign's patronage for their establishment in China. Even in such an underprivileged position, the Jingjiao clerics boldly declared the theological proposition of the Church that "politics cannot exist without the aid of religion" or "politics does need the support of religion". Obviously, the Jingjiao-church had attempted to strike a balance between their adherence to the "(Religion) system" and the "Sage (sovereign)". By implying the relationships to be mutual, Jingjiao in a way implied that both parties are "equal" in status. The aforementioned statement clearly shows that the most crucial problem Christianity encountered in Tang China is political theology in nature instead of a cultural-theology one. This issue remains unresolved until today. In fact, many of the challenges Jingjiao faced during the Tang Dynasty are not just religious or doctrinal in nature, such as *huayi zhi bian* which is partly ethnic in nature; *jingong* (進貢, paying tribute) which is political in nature, and *zhibai junqin* (致拜君親, worshipping the emperor and the ancestors) which is both cultural and religious in nature. As a "barbarian religion", Jingjiao had no alternative but to accept the assigned identity and designated naming of their establishment as stipulated by the Tang court. The Church was under the full governance of the national administrative system almost in every aspect, this is to demonstrate the encompassing Tang sovereignty towards foreign subjects. In this regard, the establishment of Jingjiao in Tang China involved not only the issue of keeping proper boundaries but also the shift of identity. By adhering to the requirement of *jingong* upon arrival and fully submitting to the Tang governance after its establishment, Jingjiao was shaped according to the cultural imagination and perceptions of the sovereign Tang. The submissiveness of the Jingjiao-church in accepting the designation of name and identity granted by the Tang court is the recognition of the full sovereignty of the Tang.

In traditional Chinese view, the power of state sovereignty is actualized through the integration of political and religious-cultural operations. Tang emperors turned this practice into a dominant political discourse to support royal legitimacy and the centralization of power. The history and destiny of the Jingjiao-church has clearly revealed the essentially subservient nature of Chinese political theology. In light of the stated observation, this paper intends to approach the issue of the down fall of Tang Jingjiao through the textual analysis of the Chinese Inscription on the Xian Stele, and takes this as a point of departure to observe the political dynamics between the Jingjiao establishment and the

---

[5] For the Inscription text of the Xian Stele, James Legge's English rendition is being used in this particular paragraph in order to stress the notion of "political sovereignty" in relation to the discussion of *daotong* 道統 and *zhengtong*. James Legge. *The Nestorian monument of Hsî-an Fû in Shen-Hsî, China relating to the diffusion of Christianity in China in the seventh and eighth centuries* (London: Trübner, 1888, New York: Paragon, 1966) Citations refer to the Paragon edition. For the rest of the article, the translation and commentary produced by L. Eccles and S. N. C. Lieu: *Stele on the Diffusion of the Luminous Religion of Da Qin (Rome)* in the Middle Kingdom 大秦景教流行碑 27 July 2016 is used, online at: https://bit.ly/2wdbNBv, accessed 14 April 2019.

[6] Legge has aptly translated *dao* (道, the Way) as the system, referring to the Illustrious Religion (*Jingjiao*) and the *sheng* (聖, the sage), referring to the sovereign.

Tang court so to prove the point that the intellectual history of Chinese Christianity is in a sense a comprehensive history of "political theology".[7]

2. Historical Background and Context

For extended periods of time, the Inscription remains as the sole documentary reference to Jingjiao until the discovery of other major manuscripts such as the *Daqin Jingjiao xuanyuan zhiben jin* (大秦景教宣元至本經)[8] in the beginning of the 20th century.[9] Although these manuscripts provide a clearer picture as regards to the theology of Tang Jingjiao, the bulk has not contributed much in the aspects of revealing Jingjiao propagation and activities in the Tang Dynasty.[10]

Therefore, the Inscription remains as most important historical archive in the intellectual history of Sino-Christianity. The discovery of the Xian Stele and the interest it has attracted from the scholarly circle is indeed a remarkable event in the studies of Tang Jingjiao. Fang Hao 方豪 (1910–1980) recognizes the Inscription as "The Champion of Chinese-Jingjiao text". When the Xian Stele was first discovered, its authenticity had been once questioned.[11] Such suspicion was soon dismissed. Historian Chen Yuan considers that it is the starting point of the history of Chinese Christianity. It is indeed the most substantial primary source text of Chinese Christian theology.[12]

---

[7] Rong Xinjiang 榮新江 is of the opinion that, "It has been a while since the research on Tang Jingjiao comes out with any groundbreaking discovery, ... Although the Stele with the inscription of 'The Propagation of the Luminous Religion in Daqin'—the most important substantiate written record on Jingjiao—should be taken seriously, it has already been studied over a span of three hundred years, not to mention the recent publication of Paul Pelliot's comprehensive commentary. One might wonder the justification of further study on this subject". Quoted from "Introduction" (導言) in *Tangdai zongjiao xinyang yu shehui* 唐代宗教信仰與社會 (Shanghai: Cishu chubanshe, (Rong 2003)), p. 10. Contrary to Rong's view, this paper attempts to offer an alternative approach to the interpretation of the Inscription.

[8] Scholars have varied opinions regarding whether the total number of chapters is 8 or 9; depending on whether *Xuanyuan zhibenjing* 宣元至本經 and *Xuanyuan benjing* 宣元本經should be treated as a single text or not. As for the authenticity of the text, Ref. Lin, Wushu 林悟殊, *Tangdai jingjiao zai yanjiu* 唐代景教再研究 (Beijing: Zhongguo shehui kexue chubanshe, (Lin 2003a)). Regarding the actual number of Jingjiao canons, Li (1628) Zhizhao 李之藻 (1571–1630) stated in the opening paragraph of *Tianxue chuhan* 天學初函 that quite a substantial number of these Jingjiao canons had been translated during Tang period. However, all of these texts were being collected into the anthology of *Beiye Cang* 貝葉藏, and therefore not properly categorized. Li further stated that the 27 Books of translated scriptural texts from Zhenguan 貞觀 period (627–649) might still be found in other Buddhist anthologies. Jingjing 景淨 (a Jingjiao Monk) was said to have translated 30 Books of Jingjiao Scriptures and that he was even being invited to translate Buddhist sutras. However, Jing unfamiliarity with Sanskrit was later being ridiculed.Scholars have varied opinions regarding whether the total number of chapters is 8 or 9; depending on whether *Xuanyuan zhibenjing* 宣元至本經 and *Xuanyuan benjing* 宣元本經should be treated as a single text or not. As for the authenticity of the text, Ref. Lin, Wushu 林悟殊, *Tangdai jingjiao zai yanjiu* 唐代景教再研究 (Beijing: Zhongguo shehui kexue chubanshe, (Lin 2003a)). Regarding the actual number of Jingjiao canons, Li (1628) Zhizhao 李之藻 (1571–1630) stated in the opening paragraph of *Tianxue chuhan* 天學初函 that quite a substantial number of these Jingjiao canons had been translated during Tang period. However, all of these texts were being collected into the anthology of *Beiye Cang* 貝葉藏, and therefore not properly categorized. Li further stated that the 27 Books of translated scriptural texts from Zhenguan 貞觀 period (627–649) might still be found in other Buddhist anthologies. Jingjing 景淨 (a Jingjiao Monk) was said to have translated 30 Books of Jingjiao Scriptures and that he was even being invited to translate Buddhist sutras. However, Jing unfamiliarity with Sanskrit was later being ridiculed.

[9] (Deeg 2006), pp. 92–93).

[10] The research on Jingjiao is far from seeing its end. Scholars around the world are showing greater interest in the studies of Jingjiao than the Chinese academics. The Monumenta Serica Institute in Salzburg, Germany holds special international conference regarding this topic triennially. The Initial Conference: "Jingjiao: The Church of the East in China and Central Asia" was held in 2003, followed by "Research on the Church of the East in China and Central Asia" in 2006. In China, research has been reactivated after the new discovery of the Luoyang jingchuang 洛陽經幢. See Ge Chengyong 葛承雍 ed. *Jingjiao yizhen —Luoyang xinchu Tangdai Jingjiao jingchuang yanjiu*景教遺珍—洛陽新出唐代景教經幢研究 (Beijing: Beijing Wenwu chubanshe, (Ge 2009)). Apart from that, an important breakthrough has been attained in the research of Yuan Jingjiao stele inscriptioninscriptions. Ref. Niu Ruji 牛汝極, *Shizi lianhua —Zhongguo Yuandai Xuliya wen Jingjiao bei wenxian yanjiu*十字蓮花—中國元代敘利亞文景教碑文獻研究 (Shanghai: Guji chubanshe, (Niu 2009)).

[11] For detail discussion on the queries, Ref. Erica C.D. Hunter (2010). "Syriac Onomastica in the Xian Fu Inscriptions". *Parole de l'Orient* 35: 357–69.

[12] The first person who has annotated the Xian Stele Inscription is the Portuguese Jesuit Emmanuel Diaz Jr. (1574–1659). *Jingjiao liuxing Zhongguo beisong zhengquan*景教流行中國碑頌正詮 was inscribed in the 17th year of Ming Chongzhen 明崇禎 (1644 A.D). The text was later compiled into *Tianzhujiao dongchuan wenxian xubian*天主教東傳文獻續編 (Taibei: Taiwan Xuesheng shuju, (Diaz 1966)). One of the earliest translated versions (the Shaanxi陜西version) of the Inscription was done by the Italian Jesuit Missionary Nicolas Trigault (1577–1628) with the help of Wang Zheng王徵 (1571–1644) and Zhang Xunfang 張纘芳. Another early translated version (The Hangzhou 杭州 version) was done by the Portuguese Jesuit Missionary Alvaro de Semedo (1585–1658), collected in his work *Da Zhongguo zhi*大中國志. It is noteworthy that Li Zhizao 李之藻has

Why was the Xian Stele installed in the first place? It is widely recognized as a "monument" (碑) which commemorates certain occasion or event, but early Chinese Scholar Feng Chengjun馮承鈞 (1887–1946) believes that it is a tombstone instead (Feng 1931, p. 69).[13] Feng contends that Jingjing 景淨 (also known as Adam, a Jingjiao priest) ordered the Xian Stele to be made in order to commemorate and give credits to the merits and works of Yisi伊斯 (Iazedboujid): " ... to engrave a grand tablet, in order to set forth a eulogy of such great deeds ... " (顧刻洪碑, 以揚休烈) (Eccles and Lieu 2016, p. 7).[14] However, Paul Pelliot disagrees with this notion. Instead, Pelliot contends that the stele was "simply" set up during one of the annual gathering banquets of Jingjiao clerics for the purpose of documenting the history of Jingjiao in China.

However, the events inscribed on the Xian Stele covers a span of over 150 years of Jingjiao history in China, ranging from the ninth year of Tang Zhenguan 貞觀 (635 CE) when Alouben arrived in the imperial capital Chang'an till the date when the stele was set up in the second year of Tang Jianzhong 建中 (781 CE) under Dezhong's 德宗 (742–805 CE) reign. From this perspective, the installation of the stele and its occasion should not be taken lightly. As one among the "three barbarian religions", the Jingjiao-church is the only one which had received such a favor, the reason behind needs to be further investigated. In Chinese history, the Tang Dynasty is one of the extra-sensitive periods in regard to the relationships between politics and religion. In this context, the favoritism received by Jingjiao is exceptional and almost impossible without the patronage of the Tang court. Jingjiao indeed acquired the legitimacy of its establishment in China under the sovereign recognition of the Tang court. Such an insight should not be ignored by those who are acquainted with the complicated relationships between politics and religion in Tang China. Therefore, the occasion of installing the stele should be viewed as a more solemn and significant event than what has been suggested by Pelliot.

Nevertheless, as the most important text of Jingjiao, the Inscription has fully revealed that the installation of the Xian Stele was the result of an important military operation by the Tang court to suppress the An-Shi Rebellion (安史之亂) in which the prominent Jingjiao priest Yisi made a tremendous contribution. The whole affair therefore is political in nature. According to the Inscription, Yisi " ... was the Duke's right-hand man (lit. 'claw and fang') and was the eyes and ears for the army" (為公爪牙, 作軍耳目) (Ibid., p. 6). Therefore, the imperial Tang court conferred to Yisi a purple priestly gown. On top of that, Emperor Suzong (肅宗) further rewarded Yisi by granting him the favor of "rebuilt the Luminous temples in Lingwu and four other commanderies"[15] (於靈武等五郡, 重立 景寺) (Ibid., p. 5). Based on Yisi merits, Jingjiao finally gained the precious opportunity to reaffirm

---

played a significant role in influencing Alvaro de Semedo's study and translation of the Inscription. There is a speculation on whether Li is in fact the real author of this work attributed to Emmanuel Diaz. Fang Hao方豪has denied this possibility. According to Emmanuel Diaz, when the Xian Stele Inscription was first discovered, Li commented that "From now on, people in China can no longer blame the holy teaching for arriving so late! The sages in the past have started the cause, and it has flourished within the imperial court and among the commoners. They have all glorified the teaching. Moreover, the believers of such great teachings are still existing right here and right now". Ref. "Preface" to *Tang Jingjiaobei Song Zhenquan*唐景教碑頌正詮 in Xu Zongze ed. 徐宗澤 *Ming Qing jian Yesu huishi yizhe tiyao*明清間耶穌會士譯著提要 (Shanghai shudian chubanshe, (Diaz 2006)), p. 178. After Li studied the Inscription, he commented, "It is surprising to know that this religion already existed in China since 990 years ago". Ref. Li Zhizao 李之藻, "Du Jingjiaobei Shu Hou" 讀景教碑書後, in *Tianxue Chuhan*天學初函 (Taibei: Taiwan Xuesheng Shuju, (Li 1965)). In *Tang Huiyao* 唐會要Vol. 49 the followings are recorded: "Alouben" 阿羅本, "establishing a "temple" in Yi-Ning Ward 義寧坊建寺" "Persian sutras and religion 波斯經教" and "Daqin Temple大秦寺". See Xu Zongze ed. 徐宗澤*Zhongguo Tianzhujiao Chuanjiaoshi Gailun* 中國天主教傳教史概論, (Shanghai: Shanghai shudian, (Xu 1992)), pp. 76–78.

13 Later Chinese scholarship considers Feng's statement to be inaccurate. See Wu Changshing 吳昶興, *Zhenchang zhidao*：*Tangdai Jidujiao lishi yu wenxian yanjiu* 真常之道：唐代基督教歷史與文獻研究 (Taiwan Jidujiao wenyi chubanshe, (Wu 2015)), pp. 46–47.

14 From this point onwards, unless otherwise mentioned, the Eccles and Lieu English translation text will be consistently used for the contemporariness of language. (Ref. Footnote No. 5).

15 It is widely acknowledged that Yisi伊斯 (Iazedboujid) is a doctor as well. His medical expertise is described as "the best among those in the three dynasties and good in treating all illness". He is a well praised philanthropist who "fed the hungry; clothed the naked; cured the sick; and buried the dead". Iazedboujid was probably a coadjutor bishop, therefore not an ordinary priests. As for his political standing, Iazedboujid survived three Tang emperors and was a close ally of Guo Ziyi 郭子儀. See Duan Qing 段晴. "Tangdai Daqinsi yu Jingjiaoseng xinshi" 唐代大秦寺與景教僧新釋, in Rong Xinjiang 榮新江 ed. *Tangdai zongjiao xinyang yu shehui*唐代宗教信仰與社會 (Shanghai: Cishu chubanshe, (Duan 2003)), pp. 463–66.

its establishment, and to recount the favorable treatments from a list of successive Tang emperors, meanwhile also not forgetting to praise the virtuous rule of the stated emperors. In view of this, the Inscription has on one hand expounded the doctrines and theological belief of Jingjiao from its very beginning, but also recounted over 150 years of its history. The purpose was obviously to "legitimatize" the status of Jingjiao-church establishment in Tang history.

From the ninth year of Zhenguan to the fifth year of Huichang 會昌 (845 CE), the Jinjiao-church was at the pinnacle of its establishment for a period of nearly 200 years. However, this does not mean that the church had not faced any challenges during this period of time. The Tang Jingjiao establishment had at least undergone three critical moments concerning its establishment during the stated period. When Tang Wuzong's 武宗 (814–846 CE) suppression of the Buddhist establishments reached its climax in the fifth year of Huichang, Jingjiao was also not exempted from this ordeal and suffered from the impact of this operation. All the Jingjiao monasteries were being destroyed, and the believers were either forced to renounce their faith or retreated to remote borderlands of Tang territories. Since then the Jingjiao-church was detached from the politics of the Tang Dynasty. All the Jingjiao foreign missionaries were expelled and Tang Jingjiao seemingly never recovered from this heavy blow. Over two centuries of missionary work had ended up pathetically described by the poet Yang Yunyi楊雲翼when he visited the Daqin Temple: "The temple is collapsed; only the ruins remain. All the people had left; the place is laid waste" (寺廢基空在，人歸地自閑).[16]

Chinese scholars with "ecclesiastic background" have always attributed the fall or failure of Jingjiao mission in China to its over-emphasis on indigenization (Song 1978, p. 41; Fang 1983, p. 424). This school argues that on one hand, the Jingjiao priests appropriated too much of the Buddhist and Taoist terminology in translating the Jingjiao canons, and therefore compromises in their theological stance (Yang 1968). On the other hand, the Jingjiao establishment depended too heavily on the patronage of the Tang court, and therefore subjected the Church's autonomy to the mercy of the Tang sovereign (Yang 1968; Zhu 1993; Zhu 2009).[17]

From the perspective of historical context, the first cause as regard to the fall of Jingjiao seems to be a misjudgment due to the lack of historical insights. Those who hold this opinion have overlooked the social-political setting of the Tang Dynasty where the Jingjiao priests had little other option but to appropriate existing Buddhist and Taoist terminology in their translation of scriptures. As a foreign religion which entering Tang China, it is quite feasible that Jingjiao doctrines and theological teachings would first undergo a process of language and cultural appropriation. The canons needed to be rendered into local language and dictions familiar to the locals in order to propagate. When Jingjiao founders first settled in Tang China, the domineering religious terminology and dictions were those of the Buddhism and Taoism. If the pioneering Jingjiao priests wished to propagate their faith in Tang China, they would have had no other alternatives but to appropriate the terminology used by the two established religions in the rendition of Jingjiao canons and liturgies. Unless the initial Jingjiao establishment only intended to serve the Tang Assyrian community exclusively, the clerical group would have needed to appropriate the existing local religions for their translation endeavor. Since the Chinese Republic era, Chinese intellectuals have been deeply concerned about the issue of so call "Christianity indigenization" (or "practicality" as what Cai Hongsheng 蔡鴻生 refers to). They have deemed the Tang Jingjiao clerics' appropriation exercise as erroneous and a gesture of compromise to the local beliefs, especially to Buddhism in particular. What the "indigenous" school in the past overlooked is the fact that their interpretation is anachronistic. Tang Jingjiao clerics did not enjoy the

---

[16] Yang, Yunyi (2019), *Daqingshi* in *Qingding Siku quanshu* 欽定四庫全書, digital version available at Ctext Repository, Url: https://ctext.org/wiki.pl?if=en&chapter=779959 (accessed on 16 April 2019).

[17] For an overview of the representative Chinese scholars who hold this view, see Sun Shangyang 孫揚, N. Standaert 鐘鳴旦, *1840 nianqian de Zhongguo Jidujiao* 1840年前的中國基督教 (Xueyuan chubanshe, (Sun and Standaert 2004)), pp. 42–46; Gu Weimin 顧衛民. *Jidujiao yu jindai Zhongguo shehui* 基督教與近代中國社會 (Shanghai renmin chubanshe, (Gu 2010)), pp. 23–24. For linguistic discussion, refer to Nie Zhijun 聶志軍, *Tangdai Jingjiao wenxian ciyu yanjiu* 唐代景教文獻詞語研究 (Hunan renmin chubanshe, (Nie 2010)).

many advantages and benefits of multi-languages learning in a modern society. The appropriation of local religions terminology seemed to be the most natural and reasonable decision for them. At least such an adaptation indeed provided room for Jingjiao to thrive under the prevailing mainstream Tang discourse of *huahu jingshuo* 化胡經説 [Laozi[18] has converted the barbarians]. Therefore, the root cause of the downfall of Jingjiao is more political than cultural in nature.

Scholars, with or without an "ecclesiastic background", who contend that the perishing of Tang Jingjiao from an appropriation perspective have overlooked the context of political theology.[19] In Tang history, religion and politics were inseparable. Therefore, religious establishments must serve the purpose of a political end i.e., to pacify the people and maintain the stability of the social structure.[20] In other words, as far as the Tang court was concerned, religious institutions were only allowed when the institutions served the political agenda of its governance. Jingjiao was obviously not exempted from this governing principle. The notion is presented in the stele inscription:

> Though elevated he (Emperor Dezhong) is humble and because of his inner tranquility he is merciful and rescues multitudes from misery, he bestows blessings on all around. The cultivation of our doctrine (Illustrious Religion) gained a strong basis by which its influence was gradually advanced. If the winds and rains come at the right season, the world will be peaceful; people will be reasonable, the creatures will be clean; the living will be prosperous, and the dead will be at peace. When thoughts echo their appropriate response, affections will be free, and the eyes will be sincere; such is the laudable condition which our Luminous Religion labor to attain. (Eccles and Lieu 2016, p. 6)

> 廣慈救苦，善貸被生者，我修行之大猷，汲引之階漸也。若使風雨時，天下靜，人能理，物能清，存能昌，歿能樂，念生響應，情發目誠者，我景力能事之功用也. (Ibid., p. 6)

From this perspective, the rise and fall of religious institutions in Tang China was indeed completely subjected to the encompassing control of the central political administrative system. In other words, the propagation and diminishing of Tang religious institutions was a matter greatly affected by the active interference and close management of the imperial policies. Many Jingjiao scholars, including Saeki Yoshiro (1871–1965), were oblivious to this historical context. Such oversight is the result of underestimating the impact and the inseparable political-religious dynamics in Tang China. A comparative study on Tang Buddhism and Taoism will clearly reveal the political challenges faced by religion institutions from which the Jingjiao-church was not exempted.

Cai Hongsheng once commented on this situation, "(In China) Manichaeism gradually heads toward heresy, Zoroastrianism gives in to populism while Jingjiao inclines to pragmatism" (Lin 2003b, p. 359 ff.). Manichaeism had gone underground and Zoroastrianism integrated itself into the local religions. As a result, these religion institutions had both disassociated themselves from the political arena of the host country. In contrast, Jingjiao adopted a pragmatic strategy instead. The Jingjiao-church actively engaged in the Tang court's affairs and practically earned the official recognition of the Church's social-legal status from Tang authorities. In other words, Jingjiao had aligned its political theology with the mainstream political-religious discourse. For this was the only possible way to ensure the success of the Church establishment in Tang society. As a result, since the reign of Tang Taizong Li Shimin 唐太宗李世民 (598–649 CE), Jingjiao was always very supportive and cooperative to the Tang administration, a gesture of goodwill and friendliness to its host country.

Apart from that, a noteworthy point of Tang administration is its double-edged religious policies, which on one hand was rigorously domineering and on the other hand dependent. In the Tang court, the power struggle within the imperial establishment often involved religious institutions. This

---

[18] Laozi 老子 is the founder of Taoism.
[19] Ref. Footnote No. 17.
[20] (Daoxuan 655).

particular historical reality during the Tang Dynasty again points to the fact that the Jingjiao-church did not have the convenience to decide on its own political stance. Autonomy was next to impossible. The best illustration is the case of changing the name of the Jingjiao monasteries from "*Bosi si*" (波斯寺) to "*Daqin si*" (大秦寺). The change of name could only be carried out with the agreement of the emperor and officiated by a nation-wide imperial edict (Li 2003, p. 1405).

Since the founding of the Tang Dynasty, the involvement of religious institutions in the political struggle of the imperial court was a norm. Taizong ascended to the throne with the help of the Taoist group led by Wang Yuanzhi王遠知 (528–635 CE) while Taizong's brother Li Jiancheng李建成 (589–626 CE) was supported by the Buddhist group led by Falin 法琳 (572–640 CE). When Taizong Li Shimin won out in the end and ascended to the throne, he arrested Falin on the ground that Falin had criticized Laozi's teachings in *Bianzheng lun* 辯正論 [On true orthodoxy]. This is overtly a political backlash and indeed has little to do with religious beliefs. From this point onwards, though Confucianism, Taoism and Buddhism co-existed, but Taoism became the most distinguished. Taken at face value, Taoism became the most prestigious religious establishment during the Tang Dynasty because the Tang royal family considered themselves as Laozi's decedents as they shared the same surname Li (李) with Laozi. However, a closer investigation shows that in actual fact the Tang emperors had established Taoism as the "state religion" of Tang imperial out of their political concerns. This was a political strategy to suppress Buddhism. When Gaozong 高宗 (628–683 CE) was at his death bed, he reiterated to his Taoist courtiers and royalists that the legitimate rulers of the Tang imperial must came from the "Li" family instead of the "Wu". Gaozong's last words indicated his strong will in preventing Wu Zetian武則天 (624–705 CE) from usurping the throne (Kou 1998, pp. 69–77).

The Tang Jingjiao clerics were indeed well aware of this political reality. Their establishment and success in propagation was at the mercy of the Tang rulers. This notion is implied clearly in the Inscription which reads, "But any (such) system without (the fostering of the sage (the sovereign), does not attain its full development; and a sage (sovereign) without the aid of such a system does not become great" (Legge 1966, p. 9), "None but the Illustrious Religion is observed; none but virtuous rulers are appointed" (Ibid., p. 13). "There is nothing which the right principle cannot effect; and whatever it effects can be named. There is nothing which a sage (sovereign) cannot do; and whatever he does can be related" (Ibid., p. 19). The Inscription has represented the goodwill of the Jingjiao-church in maintaining a favorable and cordial relationship with Tang court as well as its succession of emperors. Apart from that, these statements also reveal the honorable and exclusive role played by Jingjiao in the arena of Tang politics. In this context, the fact that the destiny of Jingjiao in Tang China was actually decided by the Tang court's political agenda more than any other thing else is conclusive. The reception of a religious establishment in Tang China was almost exclusively dependent on its political stance rather than its doctrine and liturgies. The Inscription is a convincing proof of the political theology issue in the Chinese context, i.e., the domination of political sovereignty over religious orthodoxy. Religion is subservient to politics.

Therefore, the Inscription should be read and understood as a discourse of political theology. The Xian Stele is a sign which represents the political reality of the Tang Dynasty. The Inscription states the fact that *zhengtong* ("sage") and *daotong* ("orthodoxy") are inseparable. As far as the Jingjiao-church is concerned, "a sage (sovereign) without the aid of such a system does not become great". "None but the Illustrious Religion is observed". However, for the Tang rulers, "any (such) system without the fostering of the sage (the sovereign), does not attain its full development". "There is nothing which a sage (sovereign) cannot do; and whatever he does can be related" (Legge 1966). Either party could interpret from the perspective of their respective "ideologies", but the ultimate and sole authoritative interpretation came from the *zhengtong* representative—the emperor. All theological ideas at the end are subjected to political interpretations, for the power of interpretation and discourse was in the hands of the Tang rulers instead of the clerics. Hence, it is conclusive that in the discussions of Jingjiao, the political agenda of the Tang court: "the government establishes temples for the purpose of pacifying the country" should prevail, and that religion indeed was subservient to Tang political sovereignty.

3. Political Theology in Chinese Context

The first paragraph of the Inscription expounds the Jingjiao theological stance and its doctrinal belief, after that a long account of the history of the Church follows. A noteworthy point in the historical narration is the stressing of the cordial relationships between a succession of Tang emperors and the Jingjiao-church. This cordial relationship implies the harmonious relationship between the church and the "State", one that is based on mutual trust. As a result, "While this doctrine (the Illustrious Religion) was established in the Ten Provinces, the State became rich and tranquility abounded. Because every city was full of monasteries, the (ordinary?) families enjoyed 'luminous' (or illustrious) (jing) fortune". (Eccles and Lieu 2016, p. 4) The most extraordinary gesture of the imperial court in showing royal favor is by sending the portraits of various emperors to the Jingjiao monasteries—a significant sign of political symbolism:

> The virtue of the house of Zhou had come to an end, and the black chariot has ascended into the western heaven. The way of the great Tang dynasty shone forth, and the Luminous teachings spread into the East. It was decreed that the Emperor's portrait should be copied onto the temple wall. His celestial image radiated light, giving a heroic aspect to the luminous portal. His sacred countenance brought blessings upon it and cast glory upon the learned company. (Ibid., pp. 3–4)

> 宗周德喪，青駕西昇。巨唐道光，景風東扇。旋令有司將　帝寫真轉摸寺壁。天姿汎彩，英朗景門。聖騰祥，永輝法界。. (Ibid.)

The then newly constructed Jingjiao Monastery (named "Persian Temple" at that time) received a gift from the Tang court, a painted portrait of Taizong. The proper officers were further decreed to have the portrait copied and transferred to the walls of the monastery. This is a significant sign of recognition of the Tang court to the Jingjiao-church. The Inscription also mentions that "In the early Tianbao period (742 CE) the great general Gao Lishi had received royal instructions to send (a) sacred portrait(s) of the five sages (emperors) and have it (them) placed in the temple ... " (Ibid., p. 4–5). This is an event in which Emperor Xuanzong 玄宗 (685–762 CE) had the portraits of the five emperors (Gaozu 高主, Taizong 太宗, Gaozong 高宗, Zhongzong 中宗 and Ruizong 睿宗) sent as a gift to the Jingjiao Monastery situated in Chang'an Yi-ning Ward, so that the monastery monks could "honor this picture of wisdom (the emperors portrait(s)" 奉慶睿圖, and the Priest Jihe 佶和"following the sun, came to pay court to the most honorable (i.e., the Emperor) 望日朝尊" (Ibid., p. 5). This particular description which implies the notion of "emperor Worship" is full of figurative images of the sovereign. The expressions such as *qingruitu* 慶睿圖 (the picture of wisdom), *longran* 龍髯 (beard of the Dragon (emperor)), *tianyan* 天顏 (celestial visage (the emperor's countenance)), etc. are figurative imagination referring to the sovereign throne and its ruler. The rhetorical imagery reflects the political theological intentions of the Inscription.

It is crucial to understand that portraits of the emperors were hung in the Jinjiao monastery for worshipping purposes (Lei 2009, p. 101ff). When Alouben arrived at the capital of Tang China, he had brought " ... scriptures and images from afar and presented them at the capital" (遠將經像來獻上京) (Ibid., p. 3). However, he immediately gauged the social-political reality of his host country and therefore accepted the fact that " ... the Emperor's portrait should be copied onto the temple (the Jingjiao Monastery) wall". (帝寫真轉摸寺壁) (Ibid., p. 3). During the Tang Dynasty, the emperors gave out their portraits as gifts to be *chaobai*朝拜 (worshipped) by the recipients as a sign of royal favors to the recipients. To a certain extent, this is a representation of "the cult of emperor worship" which existed in the Tang Dynasty under the principle of *zhibai junqin*致拜君親 (worshipping the emperor and one's parents).

Zhibai junqin comes from the idea of being loyal to the emperor and paying respect to one's parents which originates from Confucianism since the period of the Six Dynasties. At some point, Taoism adopted this particular idea and transformed it into a Taoist religious ethic. Scholarship on

Tang religions is well aware of the strife between Buddhism and Taoism over the question of *zhibai junqin*.[21] Tang emperors were closely attached to Taoism. From Gaozu to Xuanzong, numerous conflicts had risen between the throne and the Buddhist Sangha. There were a few specific royal edicts commanding all the religious personnel regardless of their orders to "worship" their parents (ancestors).[22] Obviously in Tang Dynasty the principle of *zhibai junqin* had been implemented as an imperial policy and represented an indispensable element in political-religious conflicts. In other words, the root course of those conflicts is "political theology" in nature. To the Taoists, practicing *zhibai junqin* is the proper adherence to the mainstream "political-religious" discourse. The Taoist establishment was under the royal patronage of the Tang court—the sovereign recognition of their religious establishment to the effect of becoming state-religion. On the occasion that Gaozong set up a Taoist Temple *Haotian Guan* 昊天觀 for the specific purpose of conducting the ritual of commemoration and reverting blessings to Taizong, the prestigious status of Tang Taoism was obvious. Taizong's portrait was placed in the temple. When the royal family and all the Taoist priests bowed down to the portrait and performed the ritual of worship, the notion of imperial ritualistic worship was established. In this regard, the sovereign throne became the subject of religious worship (Tonami 2004; Wu 2009).

The practice of "state-emperor" worship was indeed established by the Tang Taoists. As mentioned earlier, the Tang sovereign honored Laozi, claiming that he is the distant ancestor of the Tang emperors based on sharing the same surname of "Li". Apart from that, Taoism venerates Laozi as Taishang xuanyuan huangdi 太上玄元皇帝 [Ultimate and Primordial Emperor] and Dashengzu 大聖祖 [The Great Sage Ancestor] which verifies that Taoism is indeed an "emperor worshipping cult", or rather it is the cult of "emperor worship" which successfully integrated with Taoism and formed a new Taoist religious model in Tang Dynasty. Since Taishang Xuanyuan huangdi was the ancestor of the Tang emperors, all the successive emperors were his descendants. Taoism had therefore naturally become the State-religion. In addition, when the royal family worshipped Xuanyuan huangdi, they (the Tang emperors) were implying that they were indeed the most distinguished descendants of Xuanyuan huangdi.[23] This is the imagination that had ensured the political legitimacy of the Tang royal family to the throne. In this regard, installing the portraits of the emperors in all the temples and shrines was an act of orthopraxy. During Tang era, religious practice became an integrated part of the imperial ritualistic structure. When portraits of the emperors were installed in every imaginable worship venue, the imagination of the emperor's "divinity" was stressed and effectively communicated to the common people during the open imperial sacrificial and ritualistic ceremonies.[24]

The cult of emperor worship encouraged the general public to worship the emperor portraits while worshipping other gods and deities. The death anniversaries of all the deceased emperors would have been commemorated with full ritualistic religious ceremonies during Tang era. These ceremonies were

---

[21] For a comprehensive overview of the discussion see Wu Zhen 吳真. "Daojiao xiudao shenghuo de zhong yu xiao—Yi chu Tang zhibai junqin lunzheng wei zhongxin" 道教修道生活的忠與孝—以初唐「致拜君親」論爭為中心. *Journal of Modern Philosophy* of Sun Yat-sen University 105 (2009): 111–16.

[22] "Ling sengni daoshi nuguan bai fumu chi" 令僧尼道士女冠拜父母敕 [The royal edict on commanding the Buddhist monks, nuns, Taoist male and female priests to worship their parents] and "Sengni bai fumu chi" 僧尼拜父母敕 [The royal edict on commanding the Buddhist monks and nuns to worship their parents], in Song Minqiu 宋敏求 ed. *Tang dazhaoling ji* 唐大詔令集 [Collection of Tang Dynasty Imperial Edicts and Orders]. (Beijing: Zhonghua shuju, 2008), pp. 588–89; "Ling sengdao zhibai fumu zhao" 令僧道致拜父母詔 [The royal edict on commanding the Buddhist monks and Taoist priests to worship their parents], in Li Ximi 李希泌 ed. *Tang Dazhaoling ji bubian* 唐大詔令集補編 [Collection of Tang Dynasty Imperial Edicts and Orders (Suppliments)] (Shanghai: Guji chubanshe, 2003), p. 1358.

[23] See several representative royal edicts which imply this notion, such as Zhuizun Xuanyuan huangdi zhi 追尊玄元皇帝制 [The Edict of honor the Ultimate and Primordial Emperor] (cf. Song 2008, pp. 442–43) and Chongsi Xuanyuan zhongdi zhi 崇祀玄元重帝制 [The Edit of worshiping Xuanyuan zhongdi] and Chongfeng Daojiao zhao 崇奉道教詔 [The Edict of honoring Taoism]. (cf. Li 2003, pp. 1378, 1383).

[24] It is a common practice to hang portrait for of Xuanyuan huangdi 玄元皇帝. See Wei Xuanyuan huangdi shexiang zhao 為玄元皇帝設像詔 [The Edict for the portrait installation of Xuanyuan huangdi] (cf. Li 2003, p. 1374). See also Ji Yuanqiu mingtang bingyi Gaozu Taizong pei zhao 祭圓丘明堂並以高祖太宗配詔 [The Decree on conducting rites at the Round Altar and Bright Hall and making offerings to Gaozu and Taizong] and Jiaoli weitian haocheng Tian wudi zhicheng di zhi 郊禮唯天昊稱天五帝只稱帝制 [The Decree of addressing the Lord of Heaven as such and the Five Emperors as emperors in the suburb rites] (cf. Song 2008, p. 376).

performed either in Buddhist or Taoist rituals, and sometimes both. According to *Tang Huiyao* 唐會要 [Notabilia of Tang], religious activities and ceremonies in regard to "state-emperor" worship were active and frequent. In a way, frequent and repetitive ceremonies refreshed the imagination of emperor worship, and reminded the public that the link between politics and religion was inseparable. The sovereign was pursuing the public recognition of its legitimacy. On the other hand, public ritualistic performances carried out in those commemoration ceremonies were signs of recognition of the imperial sovereignty (Lei 2009, pp. 72–76). In this context, the emperor "deified" himself by installing his portrait in temples and worship venues, and made himself the subject of public worship.

In this context, though the Jingjiao monasteries had no alternative but to receive the portraits of the emperors and hence in a subtle way accepted the reality of the state-emperor worship, its establishment had as a result received the patronage of the Tang court. Portraits of the emperors placed in the Jingjiao monasteries were worshipped. The acceptance of portraits in which "his (the emperors) celestial image radiated light, giving a heroic aspect to the luminous portal. His sacred countenance brought blessings upon it and cast glory upon the learned company" (Eccles and Lieu 2016, pp. 3–4) by the Jingjiao establishment ensured and secured the Church propagation in Tang China. The gestures of portrait donation suggest that the ethnic identity of the Jingjiao Syriac community was being "recognized" by the host country which generally despised the "Others".

"Barbarians come from the four directions to subject themselves to the king: This is what the sagely ancestors have desired and the outcome of the ultimate Way".[25] In the Inscription, it was said that Xuanzong once issued an order: "The Emperor commanded the priest Luohan (Abraham), the priest Pulun (Paul), and others, seven in all, together with the great virtuous (i.e., bishop) Jihe, to perform a service of merit in the Xingqing palace". (詔僧羅含僧普論等一七人, 與大德佶和, 於興慶宮 修功德) (Eccles and Lieu 2016, p. 5). What does a "service of merit" refer to? What kind of a place is Xingqing Palace 興慶宮?[26] (cf. Lin 2006, p. 114) By the context of the description, Xingqing Palace was definitely one of the palaces within the compound of the Imperial palace. Most probably the portraits of all the emperors were kept in this great hall. Though it is unclear whether "the service of merit" was a common religious ritualistic ceremony, it is definitely not a Jingjiao worship ceremony. It seems like the ceremony Xuanzong conducted was the ritualistic ceremony of ancestral worship.

Indeed, public performance of sacrificial ritual was crucial in the state's civil religion structure. After indoctrinating and formalizing the worship of state-emperor through the installation of emperors' portraits in all religious establishments proper, the imperial court had effectively—especially through Buddhism and Taoism—imprinted the ideology of a civil religion into all spheres of life. The comprehensive ceremonious performance, which included incense offerings and bodily gestures of kneeling/bowing down to the emperors' portraits, reinforced the solemnity and religious notion of orthopraxy. In Tang era, State sacrificial rite had partially replaced the traditional Confucians rites of paying respect to the deceased rulers and sages. The ritualistic civil religious structure was a form of cultural hegemony with an underlying state political agenda. Performing sacrificial rituals for the remembrance of previous emperors became in essence a "cult" of emperor worship instead of simply a commemorating ceremony of paying respect to bygone sages and ancestors. In this context, politics integrated with religion and formed a civil religion discourse that promotes the theology of the triune "state-emperor-deity". From this perspective, the political theology issue that Jingjiao faced was not merely the 'worship' of emperors' portraits along with God but the encompassing orthopraxy imposed by the imperial religious establishment. The royal sovereign was the civil religion itself. As the Inscription phrases: "The way of the great Tang dynasty shone forth, and the Luminous teachings spread into the East" (Eccles and Lieu 2016, p. 3). The integration of *zhengtong* and *daotong* was crucial

---

[25] Refer to "Zhuizun Xuanyuan huangdi fumu bing jiashi yuanzu zhi" 追尊玄元皇帝父母並加諡遠祖制 [The decree for honoring the Ultimate and Primordial Emperor's parents and to name them as distant ancestors]. (Li 2003, p. 1381).

[26] Presumably a *neidaochang* 內道場 [inner court worship hall] refers to a Buddhist or Taoist temple situated within the royal palace compound where the emperor and the royal family attend and perform religious ceremonies.

in the Tang court establishment. The Inscription shows the awareness of the Jingjiao-church to the encompassing control of the imperial court in religious matters. As a response, Jingjiao-church stepped up to the challenge by adapting itself positively and actively to the civil religious structure established by Tang administration. The history of Jingjiao in Tang China as narrated on the Xian Stele is a history of making compatible the Church's political theology in Tang China,

Apart from the Xian Stele, another primary text of Jingjiao: *Xuting mishisuo jing* 序聽迷詩所經 [The Jesus Sutras] (hereafter *Xuting*)[27] is especially noteworthy in the investigation of Jingjiao political theology. The author of this manuscript consistently insists on the virtue of filial piety, as well as respect for the emperor, indicating a conscious adaptation to the traditional Chinese values which emphasizes *zunjun shiqin* 尊君事親 [loyalty to the emperor and servitude to the parents].[28] It is clearly a teaching which has infused and integrated with the ideology of Tang civil religion. In the stated sutra, *shiyuan* 十願 [ten vows][29] are listed. In the very first vow *shengshang* 聖上 [emperor] is being regarded as an equal to *tianzun* 天尊 [God].[30] The text reads, "The fear (of God) is like the fear of the Emperor. The Emperor is who he is because of his previous lives which have led to his being placed in this fortunate position. He is chosen by God, so cannot call himself God, because he has been appointed by God to do what is expected. This is why the people obey the Emperor, and this is right and proper" (Palmer 2001, p. 163). (眾生若怕天尊，亦合怕懼聖上。聖上前身福私天尊補任，亦無自乃。天尊耶屬 自作聖上，一切眾生，皆取聖上進止) (CBETA, p. 2. L5–L7). This paragraph implicitly refers to the Confucians teachings of *weitianming* 畏天命 (fearing the command of Heaven) and *weidaren* 畏大人 (fearing those in authority). The seeming exegesis and rendition of the Christian Ten Commandments which has added in "the Emperor" reveals a genuine appropriation of Christian text on the part of Jingjiao author.

In *Xuting*, a true believer must be a person who is conscientious in serving God, the Emperor and one's parents. The reason is given below:

> The whole Heaven and Earth follow this way. Everything follows this way of respecting parents; throughout the world everything owes its existence to parents. The sacred spirits have ordained that the Emperor is born as Emperor. We should fear God, the Sacred One, and the Emperor. And fear your parents and do good. If you understand the Law and precepts, do not disobey, but instead teach all people true religion". (Palmer 2001, p. 163)

> 為此普天在地，並事父母行，據此聖上皆是神生，今世雖有父母見存，眾生有智計，合怕天 尊，及聖上，並怕父母，好受天尊法教，不合破戒。. (CBETA, p. 2. L12–L14)

The passage implicitly refers to the dominant Confucian ideologies of *daotong* and *zhengtong* again by mentioning "the Way" and "the Emperor". Read within the framework of the Tang context, the impact of the imperial religious policy of integrating politics and religion is quite obvious. Disobedience to or rebellion against the Emperor is regarded as "sinful" as the disobedience to God. Based on the text of *Xuting*, the Jingjiao-church seems to have created a new "triune" of God, the Emperor, and one's parents in the process of appropriation, placing the latter two as subjects equal to God and worthy of being worshipped. Recognizing the Emperor's ordination as mandated by God bears the Chinese notion of referring to the Emperor as *tianzi* 天子 [the Son of Heaven]. In the light of this Jingjiao

---

[27] Hereafter, *Xuting*.

[28] The text is reproduced in Saeki (1937, pp. 13–29). Takakusu Junjirō 高楠順次郎 bought the original manuscript of this text from a Chinese seller in 1922. Saeki (1937, pp. 113–17) argued that this text is produced by Aluoben before 638. Saeki (1937, p. 147) suggested that *Xuting* 序聽 is a Chinese approximation of 'Ye-su' (Jesus). *Mishisuo* 迷詩所 is a scribal error for *Mishihe* 迷詩訶 or 'Messiah' (Haneda 1958, vol. 2, p. 250). See (Kotyk 2016).

[29] A parallel to the Christian Ten Commandments.

[30] For English translation of *Xuting mishisuo jing* 序聽迷詩所經 [The Jesus Sutras], the rendition by Martin Palmer is used. Ref. Martin Palmer. *The Jesus sutras: Rediscovering the lost scrolls of Taoist Christianity*. (Wellspring/Ballantine, 2001), pp. 159–68. The Chinese text of *Xuting mishi suo jing* is cited from Taisho shinshu daisokyo Vol. 54 No. 2142 *Xuting mishi suo jing*, digital copy provided by CBETA, available at https://bit.ly/2Ela0z2, accessed 18 April 2019.

"triune", the Emperor and one's parents have implicitly become deified. It is in this implication that "to serve" became an act of presenting an offering which bears a religious connotation. In a sense, only God, deities and other spiritual beings are the subjects of *jisi* 祭祀 [sacrificial rites]. Only those are liable of receiving sacrificial offerings. Therefore, implying that the service due to the Emperor and one's parents are the same as the service due to God is subtly deifying the Emperor and parents. From this perspective, the connotation of "emperor worship" and "ancestral worship" is being explicitly demonstrated. Jingjiao's incorporation of the traditional discourse of loyalty to the emperor and obedience to the parents into its teaching was an adherence to the civil political theology of the imperial Tang. However, rather than contending that the proposition in *Xuting* as appropriation of the Chinese *daotong* of loyalty (忠) and faithfulness (誠) (common elements uphold by the three main local religions) by the Jingjiao-church which ultimately tampers its unique theological stance, it is more appropriate to see that the Jingjiao-church has no other alternatives but to compile a grand discourse of the imperial civil religion constitution.

4. Discussion

The Jingjiao-church was established at the most glorious period of the Tang Dynasty. However, that was also the period when religious establishments were most tightly controlled. In the Tang context, religion was an integrated part of the state establishments and therefore subjected to the full supervision of the imperial court. In other words, the Tang court's religious policy was intentionally a civil religion system meaning that all religious establishments were "owned" by the state. The stated policy was implemented through the establishment of ritualistic public religious performances and active intervention in all levels of the constitution of the religious institutions (Zhou 2005).

During the Tang period, a large corpus of written law was in effect. According to the Tang Code唐律疏義 (*Tanglü shuyi*, [Tang Code and commentaries]), these rules and regulations were categorized into four divisions: the Codes (*lü*律), the Statutes (*ling*令), the Regulations (*ge*格), and the Ordinances (*shi*式).[31] Apart from those mentioned, there were also the Imperial Edicts (Decrees) (*chi*敕) promulgated by the emperor at his discretion (Xiong 2009, p. 335). "At times the Lord of Men finds it fitting to use his power to make judgments by an imperial decree or an imperial edicts, he weights the circumstances in making decisions by the time ... " (Johnson 1979b, p. 556) (事有時宜, 人主權斷, 制敕量情處分) (Zhangsun et al. 1983, p. 562). Although in principle, Edicts were only case specific in nature, and could not overwrite the Codes, Statutes, Regulations and Ordinances, it is noteworthy that they could be all encompassing at times. For example, edits that were directed to specific groups: such as "Ling sengni daoshi nuguan bai fumu chi" 令僧尼道士女冠拜父母敕 [The royal edict on commanding the Buddhist monks, nuns, Taoist male and female priests to worship their parents]; "Sengni bai fumu chi" 僧尼拜父母敕 [The royal edict on commanding the Buddhist monks and nuns to worship their parents], etc. These were apparently the emperor's sole discretion when he saw it "fitting to use his power to make judgments" (Ibid.). At times, Edicts could also function as a supplementary to the four divisions of regulations. Particularly in the context of revising and amending existing law articles, the impact of the Edict could be enormous.

The core maxim of Tang court political theology was: "The way does not have a constant name, and the holy does not have a constant form. Teachings are established according to the locality, and their mysteries aid mankind" (道無常名, 聖無常體, 隨方設想, 密濟群生) (Eccles and Lieu 2016, p. 3).[32] From the investigation of the large corpus of rules and regulations that governed religious matters, Tang court religious administration focused on three main aspects: controlling the number of votaries,

---

[31] For Tang Code, the English translation produced by Wallace Johnson is used throughout this article. Ref. Wallace, Johnson. *The T'ang Code, Volume I: General Principles.* (Princeton, New Jersey: Princeton University Press, Johnson 1979a), p. 5

[32] This is taken from a Tang decree which was recorded in *Tang Huiyao* (Wang 1955, p. 864), also quoted in the Inscription.

restricting the construction and renovation of temples, and preempting the potential threats posed by Buddhists and Taoist communities (Zhou 2005, pp. 17–18).

Monitoring the number of religious personnel was administrative in nature. The Inscription records the number of Jingjiao clerics. When Daqin Temple was built in Yi-Ning Ward, there were "twenty-one priests". There were "seven in all who was called to the Xingqing Palace to perform a service of merit" (Eccles and Lieu 2016, p. 5). At the end of the Inscription, sixty-seven Jingjiao priests had signed their names in Syriac.[33] It was also recorded that every year Yisi (Iazedboujid) "assembled the monks from the four temples, and provided for them for fifty days" (每歲集四寺僧徒) (Ibid., p. 7).

In the first year of Huichang (841 CE), Tang Wuzong decreed a campaign of suppressing Buddhism.[34] The related edicts detailed the number of the temples and shrines affected, especially specified the number of monks and nuns mandated to revoke their votary vows. Since the underlying agenda of this suppression was to appropriate war funds and to eliminate foreign influence, other religions including Jingjiao were also affected (Foster 1939, pp. 121–25). According to the edicts, over 3000 priests from Jingjiao, Zoroastrianism and other religions were commanded to revoke their religious vows and left China, in order to maintain Chinese traditional orthodoxy and culture (Zhang 1977, pp. 127–28). According to *Zizhi tongjian* 資治通鑑 [Comprehensive mirror to aid in government] Book 248 on Tang Dynasty: "All the priests of Daqin (Jingjiao) and Zoroastrism all revoked their votary vows" (餘僧及尼並大秦穆護，襖僧皆勒歸俗) (Sima 1086, 248:36).[35] In *QuanTangwen* 全唐文 [Complete History of Tang Dynasty] Book 967: "Since Buddhism has been eradicated, the other heretic teachings should not exist either. The priests should be ordered to revoke their religious vows. These personnel shall be sent back to their hometowns and become tax-paying citizens. The foreigners shall be sent back to their home country" (釋教既已厘革，邪法不可獨存。其人並勒還俗，遞迴本貫充稅戶，如外國，送還本國收管) (QTW 1819, 967:60).[36]

Tang China used to be a place where "monks can be seen in every village of ten households and towns of a hundred families. It is even more so in the recent years of our dynasty. Various barbarians also came: Manicheans, Daqing people (Jingjiao), and Zoroastrians. However, all the temples of the three barbarian religions put together, the number is not as numerous as the number of Buddhist temples in one small county" (故十族之鄉，百家之閭，必有浮圖，為其粉黛。國朝沿近古而有加焉，亦容雜夷而來者，有摩尼焉，大秦焉，襖神焉。合天下三夷寺，不足當吾釋寺一小邑之數也) (Yao 1986).[37] From the description, it is known that the actual number of foreign monks and clergies was relatively small as comparing to Buddhist monks and nuns. While during that period over 260,000 Buddhist monks and nuns were commanded to revoke their votary vows and resumed the status of secular civilians, the whole population of foreign monks and clergies from the three "barbarian religions" only amounted to 3000 as noted in *Tang huiyao*. The number of Jingjiao clerics was already relatively small; after the impact of Wuzong persecution, Jingjiao was almost wiped out from Tang China.[38]

During the Tang Dynasty, the number of religious personnel was controlled by the Department of Religious Establishments (*cibu*祠部) of the Ministry of Rites (*libu* 禮部). During the Huichang

---

33 For the discussion on the Syriac names, Ref. Erica C.D. Hunter (2010), "Syriac Onomastica in the Xian Fu Inscriptions", *Parole de l'Orient* 35: 357–69.

34 Huichang Suppression of Buddhism會昌毀佛, also known as The Great Anti-Buddhist Persecution initiated by Tang Emperor Wuzong reached its height in the year 845 CE. The purpose of this campaign was to appropriate war funds and to cleared China from foreign influences. As such, the persecution was directed not only towards Buddhism but also towards other religions, such as Zoroastrianism, Jingjiao Christianity, and Manichaeism. See Philip, T. V. *East of the Euphrates: early Christianity in Asia* (Kashmere Gate, Delhi: CSS et ISPCK, (Philip 1998)), p. 125. See also John, Foster. *The church of the T'ang dynasty*. (London: SPCK, 1939).

35 The Chinese text of *Zizhi tongjian* 資治通鑑 (*ZZTJ*) is cited from Ctext Repository, available at https://bit.ly/2VXytVD, accessed 18 April 2019.

36 The Chinese text *Quan Tangwen* (*QTW*) is cited from Ctext Repository, available at https://bit.ly/2YFJ3h2, accessed 18 April 2019.

37 Also recorded in *QTW* 727:57, available at https://bit.ly/2WYtd0p, accessed 19 April 2019.

38 See Yule, Henry. *Cathay and the Way Thither: Being a Collection of Medieval Notices of China*. ed. Henri Cordier. Chinese translation by Zhang Xushan (Kunming: Yunnan Renmin Press, (Yule 2002)), pp. 83–100.

Persecution, although Buddhism was the main target, all the other religious establishments were not exempted from the impact. Religious personnel (including monks, nuns, Taoist priests and priestess, and religious personnel from all other religions) were forced to *huanshu*還俗 (literally return to secular), which was to revoke their votary vows and resume a secular life. The Tang court viewed monks and nuns as the pillars of the Buddhist establishments (likewise other religious personnel to their respective establishments). The increasing and numerous religious votaries could pose a potential political threat to the imperial court. On top of that, one of the reasons why Wuzong persecuted the Buddhist establishments and temples in the imperial domains was related to economic matters. Monks and nuns once ordained would cease to contribute to the labor force, i.e., production activities such as agricultural farming and weaving. In addition temples and religious establishments were exempted from tax. Therefore, the persecution in actual fact sought to restore the monks and nuns to become tax-paying commoners and be economically productive again (Reischauer 1955, p. 221 ff.). Suppressing the scale of religious establishments therefore bears an economic notion. It was an effective economic measure to elevate labor productivity and effective land-use. Monastery economics had had a great impact on the state establishment in the Tang Dynasty. The financial autonomy and ever increasing clerical population of the religious establishments had indeed become a threat to the imperial court. The religious establishments had in a way become "states within a state".[39] The whole dynamics of political and economic concerns ultimately culminated in the Grand persecution during Huichang period and made the Tang era one of the most religiously sensitive periods in Chinese history.

The sensitivity and delicate nature of the Tang religious situation had driven the Tang court to implement a strict religious policy. The ideologies of *daotong* and *zhibai junqin*[40] were actively promoted. The orthopraxy of *Zhibai junqin* had become a yard stick to test the political stance of the religious establishments. The abolishing of the Buddhist temples (and all other religious establishments) was an effective measure in killing off the Buddhist religious development by taking away their economic support. In the light of the Grand Buddhist persecution, the dilemma of the Jingjiao community is clearly revealed. Indeed, the greatest concern of all the Tang rulers was the stability and security of their sovereign throne. "The way does not have a constant name, and the holy does not have a constant form. Teachings are established according to the locality, and their mysteries aid mankind" (Eccles and Lieu 2016, p. 3) serves as the ultimate guideline for the Tang religious administration. Under the surface of religious freedom, there was always an effective regulating institutional structure which was in control. In this context, the establishment and propagation of Jingjiao, likewise many other religions, during the Tang era was unquestionably fragile and restricted. Even the indigenous religions were not exempted from state persecution, let alone the "barbarian" religions. On top of that, the occasional social turmoil during Tang era had further pressurized the fragile establishment of the Jingjiao-church. Scholarship which sees the downfall of Jingjiao during the Tang era from the perspective of overtly political involvement and too much appropriation might widen their scope of investigation and consider the whole matter in the context of Tang religious policy. Perhaps in the light of the long established traditional Chinese political theology based on *daotong* and *zhengtong*, the history of Jingjiao can be understood more correctly, and serve as an allegorical prophecy on the fate of Christianity in Modern China. The root cause of the rise and fall of Jingjiao during the Tang era might be varied. However, the emphasis of the discussion should not only focus on Jingjiao's agency alone such as failure in indigenization, over appropriation, etc. but on the wider social and political context in which Jingjiao had to face the formative political theology of the Tang civil religion. This might be a more inclusive scope in the discussion of the Tang Jingjiao.

According to a narration of the Northern Wei period (386 to 534 CE) historian Yang Xuanzhi 楊炫之, *Siyi guan* 四夷館 [The Four Foreigners/Barbarians residences] were established. The establishments were

---

[39]   Xie, Chongguang. *The Monk-Official System and Social Life in the Mid-Ancient Times* (Beijing: The Commercial Press, (Xie 2009)), pp. 419–40.

[40]   Ref. Discussion of this idea in Section 1 of this paper.

situated at both sides of the imperial main street between the Yi River and the Luo River. Additionally, at the Westward lane, there were the establishments of *Siyi li*四夷里 [The Four Foreigners/Barbarians Quarters], named *guizheng*歸正 [Adapt to orthodoxy], *guide*歸德 [Adapt to virtue], *muhua*慕化 [Aspire to culture], and *muyi*慕義 [Aspire to righteousness] (Yang 2006, p. 120).[41] The domineering Chinese mainstream discourse of *huayi zhi bian* (cf. Liu 2004, p. 72) again was clearly illustrated. This Chinese traditional idea holds that the main difference between *hua* (Chinese) and the *yi* (barbarians/foreigners) is that the Chinese are civilized and the foreigners are not, therefore all foreigners are barbarians. All non-Chinese were treated with contempt and were despised. *Hua* was superior over the inferior *yi*. Thus arise the terms of *rangyi* 攘夷 (drive out the barbarians) and *zhiyi* 治夷 [control the barbarians]. The Tang legend of Laozi converting the barbarians apparently emerged from this Chinese cultural superiority complex. In short, all tribes beyond the Tang imperial territories were considered as barbarians. Therefore, they were expected to either comply or to be submissive to the Chinese culture and ruling; the essential sentiments of *gui* and *mu* (to acknowledge the political status quo and resume a right political identity).

As a *yijiao*—barbarian religion—all the Jingjiao priests and their followers inevitably had to acknowledge their appointed barbarian identity. These people had to abandon their native "barbaric" attire and put on proper Chinese attire. The shift of attire is both a physical and metaphorical sign of submission. The school of scholarship which contends that the failure of Jingjiao is due to its inherent heretic inclination has truly underestimated the power of the deep rooted Chinese tradition of *daotong* and *zhengtong*, as well as the cultural hegemony of *huayi zhi bian*. These are the two pillars of Chinese imperial ideologies reinforced throughout the ages. In other words, the Jingjiao-church and community was facing an extremely powerful "political theology" from its host country. Therefore, the contingency plan of the Jingjiao-church was inevitably to acculturate in nature: the explicit expressions of similarities must be shown while all the differences must be eradicated; emphasizing the commons and getting rid of the odds.

5. Conclusions

In the contention of how to relate and appropriate Jingjiao in Tang China, the majority of the existing scholarship has taken a cultural approach; stressing on the negative impacts of appropriating too much Buddhist and Taoist terminologies. Thought part of the scholarship might have noticed the social-political dilemma Jingjiao had faced during the Tang Dynasty, yet the deep underlying political theology root of Tang civil religion structure at work is generally over-sighted (Chen 2012). Indeed, few people have recognized the political theology notion revealed in the Inscription. When Yisi was contributing extensively to the successful suppression of the An-Shi Rebellion, his purpose was to show the functionality and allegiance of him and his religion to the Tang court. Underlying this allegiance, the legitimacy of the Jingjiao establishment was at stake. Therefore, it is more appropriate to base the discussion of the demise of Jingjiao-church from a political-religious point of view instead of a purely cultural one. At the end of the day as informed by history, the Tang sovereign did have the last say in affecting the rise and fall of a religion, local or foreign. In light of this, the setting up of a stately and solid monument could not be considered as light and trivial as suggested by Pelliout. On the contrary, this was a solemn occasion which represented the rare opportunity to dignify recognition and patronage granted by the imperial court to a foreign community. The Jingjiao clerics attached to the Jingjiao community had met the basic expectations of the imperial authorities. Their efforts of making positive contributions in maintaining the social stability of the imperial power and defending the throne were appreciated, therefore their religion was being officially recognized.

For Yisi "the white-robed Luminous priest" (白衣景士) (Eccles and Lieu 2016, p. 7), had earned the trust of the imperial court towards the Jingjiao community by making crucial contributions in the

---

[41] Referring to the details of the '*yi*'—foreigner/barbarian concept discussed earlier in this article. (cf. Liu 2004).

successful suppression of the An-Shi Rebellion. Not only had he with his priestly status represented the loyalty and services rendered by the Jingjiao community to the imperial court but he also demonstrated the orthopraxy of the community. To the Tang rulers who were always alert and sensitive to religious matters, the Jingjiao-church was eager to show their loyalty in order to secure the royal patronage. This would ensure a better prospect for the Jingjiao religious community to propagate in Tang China. In other words, the Jingjiao-church was seeking earnestly for the cultural recognition of its host country as well as the imperial power's political recognition. The latter is obviously more urgent and crucial than the former: "the pure, bright Luminous Religion was being introduced to (us) Tang" (明明景教, 言歸我唐) (Ibid.).

Looking from this perspective, the Inscription is indeed a written manifesto in terms of political theology. The historical narrative of the inscription has duly described the beginning of the Jingjiao establishment in Tang China that was closely related to the Tang political establishment. In a sense the history of Jingjiao was also shaped by politics. When the Jingjiao monk Alouben first reached China, he had duly followed the rules of the Chinese "tributary system". He came with tributes (gifts) and presented them to the imperial court. The tributary system was a pattern of interaction between the imperial authorities and their foreign counterparts. Although under the lenses of traditional Chinese imperial world view, this is a kind of suzerainty relationship between the empire and its colonies.[42] The Inscription mentions that the Jingjiao Abbot Lohan and priest Gabriel came with precious gifts and paid tributes to the court as a way of retaining cordial relationship. The Inscription reads: "At that time there was the Abbot Lohan, the Bishop Jilie (i.e., Gabriel), both noble sons from the golden regions (i.e., the West), unworldly senior monks, who harmoniously restored the mystic order and tied up the broken knot" (有若僧首羅含, 大德及烈, 並金方貴緒, 物外高僧, 共振玄網, 俱維絶紐) (Eccles and Lieu 2016, p. 4).

Apart from the tributary system, there was a top down title conferring system. The conferring of title represented a master-servant relationship between the suzerain and the vassal. In Jingjiao case, the conferring of title to the Bishop Alouben represented an imperial gesture of recognition to the "barbarian religion".[43] The Inscription illustrates one such incident: "He (Gao Zhong) also honored Alouben by making him the great master of doctrine for the preservation of the State" (仍崇阿羅本為 鎮國大法主) (Ibid., p. 4). In fact, when Alouben arrived China during the Zhengguan period under Taizhong's reign, he had paid tributes to the Tang court and therefore had in a way demonstrated the submissive and subservient stance of Jingjiao establishment to the Tang Empire. The inscription describes this clearly:

> In Syria there was a man of great virtue (bishop), known as Aluoben, who detected the intent of heaven and conveyed the true scripture here. He observed the way the winds blew in order to travel through difficulties and perils, and in the ninth year of the Zhenguang reign (635 CE) he reached Chang'an. The emperor (Taizhong) dispatched an official, Duke Fang Xuanling as an envoy to the western outskirts to welcome the visitor, who translated the scriptures in the library. [The emperor] examined the doctrines in his apartments and reached a profound understanding of their truth. He specially ordered that they be promulgated. (Eccles and Lieu 2016, p. 3)

> 大秦國有上德。曰阿羅本。占青雲而載真經。望風律以馳艱險。貞觀九祀至於長安帝使宰臣 房公玄齡總仗西郊賓迎入內。翻經書殿。問道禁闈。深知正真。特令傳授. (Ibid.)

From this description, the influence of *daotong* and *zhengtong* in Tang imperial administrations is clearly illustrated. When Alouben reached China, he was first met up by a high ranking court official,

---

[42] See Zheng, Yongnian. *China and international relations: the Chinese view and the contribution of Wang Gungwu* (London: Routledge, (Zheng 2012)), p. 103.

[43] Yu, Yunguo. "The Ancient Chinese View of the Neighboring Countries: as Seen in 'On the Barbarians' of *General History of Institutions and Critical Examination of Documents and Studies*". pp. 222–23.

the Prime Minster Fang Xuanling 房玄齡 (579–648 CE), who was appointed by Emperor Taizong. Then Alouben discussed in length with Taizong. The emperor questioned Alouben regarding the doctrinal teachings of Jingjiao and read the translated Jingjiao Sutras provided by Alouben in his own private quarters. After seeing the similarities of the Jingjiao doctrines to that of the Taoist thought, the emperor was convinced that this faith was a "harmless" religion (to the state). Therefore, it was allowed to propagate in Chang'an. The Inscription describes Jingjiao doctrine as understood by the emperor as such:[44]

> Having carefully examined the scope of his (Alopen) doctrines, we find them to be mysterious, admirable, and requiring nothing special to be done; principal and the most honored having looked at the points in them, they are intended for the establishment of what is most important. Their language is free from the troublesome verbosity; their principles remain when the immediate occasion for their delivery is forgotten; their system is helpful to all creatures, and profitable to men. Let it have free course throughout the empire. (Legge 1966, p. 11)

> 詳其教旨。玄妙無為。觀其元宗。生成立要。詞無繁説。理有忘筌。濟物利人。宜行天下. (Ibid., p. 10)

However, it is noted that from the time Alouben arrived at the imperial capital city of Chang-an in 635 CE to the actual establishment of the Jinjiao monastery with proper personnel in 638 CE, there was a three-year gap. Presumably, certain official procedures concerning religion establishments still needed to be processed. Only after three years, Taizong issued the edict which allowed the Jingjiao-church to conduct liturgical services and engage in missionary activities. It is interesting to observe how Taizong "interpreted" Jingjiao doctrine and defined the religion as a religion of "requiring nothing special to be done" (*wuwei*無為, literally "doing nothing"). *Wuwei* is the core teaching of Taoism. Whether Taizhong's interpretation of Jingjiao theology was proper and agreed by Alouben or not was uncertain. However, in a social cultural milieu in which Taoism was the civil religion, the adherence of Jingjiao theology to that of the Taoism as understood by the emperor fully expresses the imperial attitude towards religion: it must be practical and functional. The religion must be "helpful to all creatures, and profitable to men" (Legge 1966, p. 11) and therefore beneficial to the *zhengtong* (political administration) of the imperial court.

The translation of the Jingjiao canons is another important aspect worth discussion. According to *Junjing*[45] 尊經, Alouben had brought numerous books that he intended to translate into Chinese to Chang'an. Later Jingjing (Adam) brought more. It was said that thirty of those books had been translated, while most were "still in the leather folder to be translated".[46] Judging from the political climate and strict religious control during the Tang era, there is a high possibility that those Jingjiao canons were not rendered into Chinese due to political reasons. Considering the close examination Alouben had to undergo, this proposition is quite possible. In the light of this possibility, one cannot take it for granted that the inquiries of Taizong and his administration were "friendly" or just for the sake of learning new ideas.

Xiang Da, an expert of Tang history, contends that the splendor of Tang Dynasty is manifested in its active communications with foreign cultures:

> The power of China extends beyond its western border. It reaches its peak in the Han and Tang Dynasties. During Tang Dynasty, Chinese are referred to as "Tang people" in central

---

[44] The translation of James Legge is quoted in this context for its clarity in the doctrinal exposition.

[45] *Zunjing* 尊經 is an anonymous work from the early tenth century. It provides the names of saints such as David, Hosea, Peter, and Paul. It lists several presently non-extant texts including the *Book of Moses* 牟世法王經 *Zechariah* 刪河律經 *Epistles of Saint Paul* 寶路法王經 and *Revelations* 啓真經 (Foley 2009: 7–8). It mentions the aforementioned clergyman Jingjing (Adam), stating that he translated thirty texts listed therein. See (Kotyk 2016).

[46] *Jingjiao sanwei mengdu zan* 景教三威蒙度讚 [Nestorian Hymn of the Three Majesties for Obtaining Salvation], digital copy taken from CBETA, available at https://bit.ly/2JCLP3e, accessed 18 May 2019.

Asia. This is how powerful Tang China was. Since Zhenguan period, royal families from the neighboring countries had to send their princes to live in Tang court as hostages. There were also countless foreigners from various countries that had made Chang'an their home. This group of people has greatly contributed to the dissemination of the Western territories culture to Chang'an. [47]

中國國威及於西陲，以漢唐兩代為最盛；唐代中亞諸國即以「唐家子」稱中國人，李唐聲威之宣赫，於是可見也。貞觀以來，邊裔諸國率以子弟質于唐，諸國人流寓長安者亦不一而足，西域文明及於長安，此輩蓋預有力焉. (Xiang 1988, p. 4)

Therefore, the perishing of the three "barbarian religions" in China could not be taken for granted as just a common phenomenon in the history of East West cultural exchange and communications. In fact, looking from the perspective of *huayi zi bian*, it is the ability to sinicize and acculturate the barbarians which forged the Chinese Empire. The Middle Kingdom world view of *tianxia* is the fundamental essence of imperial China sovereignty. *Huayi zhi bian* ultimately bears the connotation of differentiating "those who are of us" and those "who are against us". In such, the tributary system becomes the signifier of an inequality relationship between the imperial and its colonies.

It is not necessarily true that when an empire becomes more powerful, it will be more confident in the reception of anything foreign and therefore become more open and lenient in its foreign policy. On the same basis, the seemingly openness of Tang Dynasty towards the reception of foreign cultures and influences does not necessary represent that the Tang imperial court is less suspicious of the "Others". Instead this might be a reflection of the imperial court's confidence in its tight administrative system which is capable of handling any undesirable situations or threats posed by foreign cultures.[48] In other words, the openness of Tang Dynasty in its reception of foreign cultures does not represent that the empire is more lenient and welcoming than its predecessors in handling foreign relationships. Underlying that seemingly openness is the stronghold of a political structure formed by the integration of *daotong* and *zhengtong* which represents an imaginative "civil religion". Under this notion, it is right to conclude that the deep rooted traditional Chinese imperial ideologies and its conception of "State sovereignty" have always been a form of political theology, and this is the kind of political theology that Jingjiao encountered in Tang China.

The majority of Chinese Jingjiao scholars such as Fang Hao, Gu Weimin, Zhang Xinlang, etc. have looked at the downfall of Jingjiao from the perspective of cultural exchange between China and the West. In the discourse of cultural exchange, many have concluded that the downfall of Jingjiao was caused by its inherent inclination of appropriating Buddhist and Taoist terminologies. In short, the Jingjiao downfall may be considered to be due to the agency of its clerics from within. This assumption falls short of presenting a comprehensive picture of the whole issue. The underlying imperial "political theology" formed by the integration of *zhengtong* and *daotong* has been almost completely ignored. The significant role played by the deep rooted traditional Chinese concept of sovereignty affecting Tang Jingjiao is mostly overlooked. The greatest fault of the scholarship which overlooks the political theology aspect of Jingjiao downfall is perhaps their exclusion of the Tang court's crucial and active agency in this whole matter. As has been discussed in this paper, it might be more appropriate to consider the downfall of Jingjiao in the context of Tang sovereign "political theology" which will give a more accurate picture of the propagation and demise of Jingjiao in Tang China.

Funding: This research received no external funding.

Conflicts of Interest: The author declares no conflict of interest.

---

[47] In Chinese History, East West Cultural Communication is always a significant phenomenon and a popular topic for scholastic inquiries.

[48] Ke, Wen 柯文. (Paul A. Cohen) contends that Modern China has developed four types of anti-foreignism based on wrath, fear, contempt, and shame. See Ke (1989). *Discover History in China*. Beijing: China Press, 1989. pp. 36–37.

References

Primary Sources

Ji Yuanqiu Mingtang bingyi Gaozu Taizong pei zhao 祭圓丘明堂並以高祖太宗配詔, and Jiaoli weitian haocheng Tianwudi zhicheng dizhi 郊禮唯天昊稱天五帝只稱帝制. 2008. In *Tang dazhaoling ji* 唐大詔令集. Edited by Minqiu Song. Beijing: Zhonghua shuju, p. 376.

Jingjiao sanwei mengdu zan 景教三威蒙度讚 [Nestorian Hymn of the Three Majesties for Obtaining Salvation]. Digital Copy Available at CBETA. Available online: https://bit.ly/2JCLP3e (accessed on 18 May 2019).

Liangjing Bosisi Gaiming Da Qin Si Zhao 兩京波斯寺改名大秦寺詔. 2003. In *Tang Dazhaoling ji bubian* 唐大詔令集補編. Edited by Ximi Li. Shanghai: Guji chubanshe, p. 1405.

Ling sengdao zhibai fumu zhao 令僧道致拜父母詔. 2003. In *Tang Dazhaoling ji bubian* 唐大詔令集補編. Edited by Ximi Li. Shanghai: Guji chubanshe, p. 1358.

Ling sengni daoshi nuguan bai fumu chi 令僧尼道士女冠拜父母敕. 2008. In *Tang dazhaoling ji* 唐大詔令集. Edited by Minqiu Song. Beijing: Zhonghua shuju, p. 588.

Sengni bai fumu chi 僧尼拜父母敕. 2008. In *Tang dazhaoling ji* 唐大詔令集. Edited by Minqiu Song. Beijing: Zhonghua shuju, p. 589.

Wei Xuanyuan huangdi shexiang zhao 為玄元皇帝設像詔. 2003. In *Tang Dazhaoling ji bubian* 唐大詔令集補編. Edited by Ximi Li. Shanghai: Guji chubanshe, p. 1374.

Zhu zhi chi duan zui 諸制敕斷罪. 1983. In *Tanglu shuyi (juan) 30* 唐律疏議 卷30. Edited by Wuji Zhangsun, Ji Li, Zhining Yu, Lin Tang, Baoxuan Duan, Yanke Liu and Minxing Jia. Beijing: Zhonghua shuju, p. 562.

Zhuizun Xuanyuan huangdi fumu bing jiashi yuanzu zhi 追尊玄元皇帝父母並加諡遠祖制. 2003. In *Tang Dazhaoling ji bubian* 唐大詔令集補編. Edited by Ximi Li. Shanghai: Guji chubanshe, p. 1381.

Zhuizun Xuanyuan huangdi zhi 追尊玄元皇帝制, and Chongfeng Daojiao zhao 崇奉道教詔. 2003. In *Tang Dazhaoling ji bubian* 唐大詔令集補編. Edited by Ximi Li. Shanghai: Guji chubanshe, pp. 1378, 1383.

Secondary Sources

Chen, Yuan. 2002. *Mingji dianqian fojiao kao* 明季滇黔佛教考. Beijing: Fu Jeng Daxue, Reprint Shijiazhuang: Hebei jiaoyu chubanshe. Citations refer to the Hebei edition.

Chen, Huaiyu. 2012. *Jingfeng fansheng* 景風梵聲. Beijing: Zongjiao wenhua chubanshe.

Daoxuan (596–667). 655. *Xu gaoseng zhuan* 續高僧傳. Book 25, digital Version Available at CBETA Repository. Available online: https://bit.ly/2ExzzwR (accessed on 16 April 2019).

Deeg, Max. 2006. The 'Brilliant Teaching': The Rise and Fall of 'Nestorianism' (Jingjiao) in Tang China. *Japanese Religions* 31: 91–110.

Diaz, Emmanuel, Jr. 1966. Jingjiao liuxing Zhongguo beisong zhengquan 景教流行中國碑頌正詮. In *Tianzhujiao dongchuan wenxian xubian Vol. 2* 天主教東傳文獻續編 (二). Edited by Xiangxiang Wu. Taibei: Taiwan Xuesheng shuju, pp. 653–754.

Diaz, Emmanuel, Jr. 2006. Tang Jingjiaobei song zhengquan 唐景教碑頌正詮序. In *Ming Qing jian Yesu huishi yizhe tiyao* 明清間耶穌會士譯著提要. Edited by Zongze Xu. Shanghai: Shanghai shudian, pp. 178–79.

Duan, Qing. 2003. Tangdai Daqinsi yu Jingjiaoseng xinshi 唐代大秦寺與景教僧新釋. In *Tangdai zongjiao xinyang yu shehui* 唐代宗教信仰與社會. Edited by Xinjiang Rong. Shanghai: Cishu Chubanshe, pp. 434–72.

Eccles, L., and Sam Lieu. 2016. *Stele on the Diffusion of the Luminous Religion of Da Qin (Rome) in the Middle Kingdom* 大秦景教流行碑. July 27. Available online: https://bit.ly/2wdbNBv (accessed on 14 April 2019).

Fang, Hao. 1983. *Zhongxi jiaotongshi* 中西交通史. Changsha: Yuelu shushe.

Feng, Chengjun. 1931. *Jingjiaobei kao* 景教碑考. Shanghai: Shangwu yinshuju.

Foster, John. 1939. *The Church of the T'ang Dynasty*. London: Society for Promoting Christian Knowledge (SPCK).

Ge, Chengyong, ed. 2009. *Jingjiao yizhen—Luoyang xinchu Tangdai Jingjiao jingchuang yanjiu* 景教遺珍—洛陽新出唐代景教經幢研究. Beijing: Beijing Wenwu chubanshe.

Gu, Weimin. 2010. *Jidujiao yu jindai Zhongguo shehui* 基督教與近代中國社會. Shanghai: Shanghai renmin chubanshe.

Haneda, Tōru. 1958. *Haneda Hakushi shigaku ronbunsh* ū 羽田博士史學論文集. Kyōto: Tōyōshi Kenkyū kai.

Hunter, Erica C.D. 2010. Syriac Onomastica in the Xian Fu Inscriptions. *Parole de l'orient* 35: 357–69.

Johnson, Wallace. 1979a. *The T'ang Code, Volume I: General Principles*. Princeton: Princeton University Press.

Johnson, Wallace. 1979b. *The T'ang Code, Volume II: Specific Articles*. Princeton: Princeton University Press.

Ke, Wen (Paul A. Cohen). 1989. *Zai Zhongguo faxian lishi* 在中國發現歷史. Translated by Tongqi Lin. Beijing: Zhongguo shuju.

Kou, Yanghou. 1998. Tangchu Sandi De Sanjiao Gongcun Yu Daoxian Fohou Zhengce 唐初三帝的三教共存與道先佛後政策. *Wen Shi Zhe* 4: 69–77.

Kotyk, Jeffrey. 2016. Nestorian Christianity in China 景教. In *Digital Dictionary of Buddhism*. Edited by A. Charles Muller. Available online: https://bit.ly/2YF4K0L (accessed on 20 April 2019).

Legge, James. 1966. *The Nestorian Monument of Hsî-an Fû in Shen-Hsî, China Relating to the Diffusion of CHRISTIANITY in China in the Seventh and Eighth Centuries: With the Chinese Text of the Inscription, a Translation, and Notes and a Lecture on the Monument; with a Sketch of Subsequent Christian Missions in China and Their Present State*. London: Trubner & Co., Reprint New York: Paragon Book. Citations refer to the Paragon edition.

Lei, Wen. 2009. *Jiaomiao Zhiwai: Suitang Guojia Jisi Yu Zongjiao* 郊廟之外：隋唐國家祭祀與宗教. Beijing: Sanlian shudian.

Li, Zhizhao. 1628. *Tianxue chuhan* 天學初函. Taiwan: Xuesheng shuju.

Li, Zhizao. 1965. Du Jingjiaobei Shu Hou 讀景教碑書後. In *Tianxue chuhan* 天學初函. Edited by Zhizao Li. Taibei: Taiwan Xuesheng Shuju, pp. 77–92.

Li, Ximi, ed. 2003. *Tang dazhaoling ji bubian* 唐大昭令集補編. Shanghai: Shanghai Guji chubanshe.

Lin, Wushu. 2003a. *Tangdai jingjiao zai yanjiu* 唐代景教再研究. Beijing: Zhongguo shehui kexue chubanshe.

Lin, Wushu. 2003b. Tangdai Sanyijiao de Shehui Zouxiang 唐代三夷教的社會走向. In *Tangdai zongjiao xinyang yu shehui* 唐代宗教信仰與社會. Edited by Xinjiang Rong. Shanghai: Cishu Chubanshe, pp. 359–84.

Lin, Xilang. 2006. *Tangdai Daojiao guanli zhidu yanjiu* 唐代道教管理制度研究. Sichuan: Bashu shushe.

Liu, Lydia He. 2004. *The Clash of Empires: The Invention of China in Modern World Making*. Cambridge: Harvard University Press.

Nie, Zhijun. 2010. *Tangdai Jingjiao wenxian ciyu yanjiu* 唐代景教文獻詞語研究. Changsha: Hunan renmin chubanshe.

Niu, Ruji. 2009. *Shizi lianhua—Zhongguo Yuandai Xuliya wen Jingjiao bei wenxian yanjiu* 十字蓮花—中國元代敘利亞文景教碑文獻研究. Shanghai: Guji chubanshe.

Palmer, Martin. 2001. *The Jesus Sutras Rediscovering the Lost Scrolls of Taoist Christianity*. New York: Ballantine Wellspring.

Philip, T. V. 1998. *East of the Euphrates: Early Christianity in Asia*. Kashmere Gate: CSS et ISPCK.

Quan Tangwen (QTW) 全唐文. 1819. Available online: https://bit.ly/2YFJ3h2 (accessed on 18 April 2019).

Reischauer, Edwin O. 1955. *Ennin's Diary: The Record of a Pilgrimage to China in Search of the Law*. New York: Ronald Press.

Ren, Jiyu, ed. 2002. *Ershi shiji Zhongguo xueshu dadian: Zongjiaoxue* 20世紀中國學術大典：宗教學. Fuzhou: Fujian jiaoyu chubanshe.

Rong, Xinjiang. 2003. Daoyan 導言. In *Tangdai zongjiao xinyang yu shehui* 唐代宗教信仰與社會. Edited by Xinjiang Rong. Shanghai: Shanghai Cishu chubanshe, pp. 1–12.

Saeki, Yoshirō. 1937. *The Nestorian Documents and Relics in China*. Tōkyō: Maruzen.

Sima, Guang. 1086. *Zizhi tongjian* 資治通鑑. Available online: https://bit.ly/2VXytVD (accessed on 18 April 2019).

Song, Lanyou. 1978. Jingjiao youguan 'Tianzhu' de fanyi 景教有關「天主」的翻譯. *Shenxue niankan*, 41–54.

Song, Minqiu, ed. 2008. *Tang da zha ling ji* 唐大詔令集. Beijing: Zhonghua shuju.

Sun, Shangyang, and Nicolas Standaert. 2004. *1840 nianqian de Zhongguo Jidujiao* 1840年前的中國基督教. Beijing: Xueyuan chubanshe.

Tonami, Mamoru. 2004. *Sui Tang fojiao wenhua Part. 1* 隋唐佛教文化 (上篇). Translated and Edited by Sheng Han. Shanghai: Guji chubanshe.

Wang, Pu, ed. 1955. Daqinshi 大秦寺. In *Tang Huiyao* 唐會要. Beijing: Zhonghua shuju, Volume 49, p. 864.

Weng, Shaojun. 1996. *Hanyu Jingjiao wendian quanshi* 漢語景教文典詮釋. Shanghai: Sanlian shuju.

Wu, Zhen. 2009. Daojiao xiudao shenghuo de zhong yu xiao—Yi chu Tang zhibai junqin lunzheng wei zhongxin 道教修道生活的忠與孝—以初唐「致拜君親」論爭為中心. *Journal of Modern Philosophy of Sun Yat-sen University* 105: 111–16.

Wu, Changshing. 2015. *Zhenchang zhidao: Tangdai Jidujiao lishi yu wenxian yanjiu* 真常之道：唐代基督教歷史與文獻研. Xinbei shi: Taiwan Jidujiao wenyi chubanshe.

Xiang, Da. 1988. *Tangdai Changan yu Xiyu wenming* 唐代長安與西域文明. Taibei: Mingwen Shuju.

Xie, Chongguang. 2009. *Zhonggu Fojiao sengguan zhidu he shehui shenghuo* 中古佛教僧官制度和社會生活. Beijing: Shangwu yingshuguan, 2009.

Xiong, Victor Cunrui. 2009. *Historical Dictionary of Medieval China*. Lanham: Scarecrow Press.

Xu, Zongze. 1992. *Zhongguo Tianzhujiao chuanjiaoshi gailun* 中國天主教傳教史概論. Shanghai: Shanghai shudian. First Published 1938.

Yang, Senfu. 1968. *Zhongguo Jidujiaoshi* 中國基督教史. Taibei: Taiwan shangwu yinshuguan.

Yang, Xuanzhi. 2006. Longhuashi 龍華寺. In *Luoyang Galanji yizhu* 洛陽伽藍記譯注. Nanjing: Jiaoyu chubanshe.

Yang, Yunyi. 2019. Daqing si 大秦寺. In *Qingding Siku quanshu* 欽定四庫全書. Available online: https://bit.ly/2M9e2AV (accessed on 16 April 2019).

Yao, Xuan, ed. 1986. *Tang Wencui* 唐文粹. Hangzhou: Zhejiang Renmin chubanshe, Book 2. Volume 65.

Yu, Yunguo. 2009. Gudai Zhongguoren de zhoubian guozuguan 古代中國人的周邊國族觀. *Zhonghua wenshi lunchong* 93: 215–396.

Yule, Henry. 2002. *Dongyu jicheng lucong* 東域紀程錄叢. Translated by Xushan Zhang. Kunming: Yunnan renmin chubanshe.

Zhang, Xinglang. 1977. *Zhongxi jiaotong shiliao huibian Vol. 1* 中西交通史料彙編 (第一冊). Beijing: Zhonghua shuju.

Zhangsun, Wuji, Ji Li, Zhining Yu, Lin Tang, Baoxuan Duan, Yanke Liu, and Minxing Jia. 1983. *Tanglu shuyi (juan) 30* 唐律疏議 卷30. Beijing: Zhonghua shuju.

Zheng, Yongnian. 2012. *China and International Relations: The Chinese View and the Contribution of Wang Gungwu*. London: Routledge.

Zhou, Qi. 2005. *Tangdai zongjiao guanli yanjiu* 唐代宗教管理研究. Ph.D. dissertation, Department of History, Shanghai Fudan University, Shanghai, China.

Zhu, Qianzhi. 1993. *ZhongguoJingjiao: Zhongguo gudai Jidujiao yanjiu* 中國景教：中國古代基督教研究. Beijing: Renmin chubanshe.

Zhu, Xinran. 2009. *Ansheng yu limin: Dongfang jiaohui zaihua xuanjiaoshi* 安生與立命：東方教會在華宣教史. Hong Kong: Jinhui chubanshe.

Article

Rhetorica and *Exemplum*: The Genesis of Christian Literature in Late Imperial China

Sher-Shiueh Li

Institute of Chinese Literature and Philosophy, Academia Sinica, Taipei 11529, Taiwan;
shiueh@gate.sinica.edu.tw

Received: 7 June 2019; Accepted: 1 August 2019; Published: 5 August 2019

Abstract: This paper offers a survey of how European rhetoric reached China in the transitional period between the Ming and the Qing dynasties. The focus of my paper is how a verbal *ars* is transformed into the written *ars*, thus inaugurating the Christian literature in late imperial China.

Keywords: rhetoric Jesuits Sino-Western literary relations; comparative literature; translation history in China

1. Why Did the Ming Chinese Forget Rhetoric?

Most students of late Ming and early Qing Jesuit writings (1583–1805) have reached the somewhat dubious conclusion that the Chinese converted to Catholicism because they were tempted by the excellence of European science and technology (Gernet 1986, pp. 15–24; Fan 1992; Chu 1996, pp. 47–97; Liu 2018; Han 2019).[1] This traditional view, however, has been interrogated intensively ever since some twenty years ago (e.g., Zürcher 1996, pp. 331–60). One reason to doubt the standard interpretation is that conversion is commonly, though also with exceptions, the result of *chuanhua* 勸化or "persuasion," the ultimate purpose of rhetoric according to Aristotle (Kennedy 1991, 1.2.1). If the missionary works concerned have to rely greatly on writing, the act of persuasion may in fact have been more strategic and therefore rhetorical in nature. Its literariness, in fact, almost equals its religiosity if one agrees that rhetoricity is part of this quality. As scholars such as Billings (2009) and Redaelli (2007) have done, my investigation of the Ming and Qing Jesuit writings in Chinese finds that they, indeed, are comprised of a large amount of material that can be properly qualified as literary, including dialogues, hagiography, and collections of maxims, fables, and anecdotes.

Among these Jesuit works of seemingly apologetical nature, a special genre stands out: *exemplum*. An *exemplum* has been defined as a short narration given as truthful and intended to be inserted into a speech, usually a sermon, to convince an audience by means of a salutary lesson (Gregg 1997, pp. 11–16). To the best of my knowledge, works under this generic rubric have attracted few critical attentions in literary history, even though they contributed greatly to the masterpieces of such well-known authors in the West as Geoffrey Chaucer (1343–1400) and John Gower (c. 1330–1408). *Exemplum* is also a critical rhetorical device in the catechetic works of such important Ming Jesuits as Matteo Ricci (利瑪竇, 1552–1610) and Diego de Pantoja (龐迪我, 1571–1618). When it comes to rhetoric, let me begin with a short story about Ricci, the most important and famous figure in the first generation of Jesuits in China.

Before Ricci died in 1610, he had been harshly attacked once by Zou Weilian 鄒維璉 (d. 1636), one of the activists of the Dongling Party renowned in the political society of late-Ming China. Zou

---

[1] For discussions in Western languages, see the titles listed in Zürcher 1991, pp. 101–24, or its expanded version by Nicolas Standaert, in Standaert 2001, pp. 238–45, and 936–41. On mathematics, there is one book worthy of our special mention: Engelfriet 1998. But studies on humanities also began long ago. For discussions particularly on literary works, see selected titles in Li and Lam 2014.

---

criticized Ricci by saying that "as to that monster Li (Ricci), his tongue is as fast as the lightning, and his oration is as powerful as the waves. He is truly a Zhang Yi or a Su Qin in our times" (若乎利妖，電光之舌，波濤之辯，真一儀秦; Zou 2001, 3:198a).[2] Zhang and Su were two orators in the period known as Warring States of the Zhou Dynasty, also two figures about whom Zou Weilian knew quite well. The same remarks as Zou's made at the turn of the sixteenth century on Ricci's eloquence can be found in, for one more instance, Xie Zaozhe's 謝肇淛 (1567–1624) *Wu zazhu* 五雜組 (Xie 1959, juan 4, 1:120), regardless of those of other literati contemporizes of Ricci's. But Zou and Xie might not be aware that Ricci's eloquence, famed during the life span of his stay in China, was the result of his familiarity with European "rhetoric," the kind of verbal art that, to the best of my knowledge about China, had long been forgotten ever since Confucianism became dominant in the Hang Dynasty.[3] With the exception of Liu Xie's 劉勰 (*c.* 465–521) *The Literary Mind and the Carving of the Dragon* (文心雕龍), nearly no theoretical work on verbal art ever appeared before the modern era. Ricci, as were most of other Jesuits who came to China during the transitional period between the Ming and the Qing dynasty, was well trained in this particular art of effective speaking.

The reasons why the Chinese "forgot" their interest in rhetorical discourse, in my humble view, can be divided into several ones: First of all, the Confucian rejection of beautiful but not kind speech in the *Analects*, such as "one's cunning words and fawningly expression" (巧言令色) going in full support of the idea that this kind of person must have his "benevolence remain with only a small part" (鮮矣仁; Zhu 1997, p. 62). Other accounts for the Ming ignorance of public speaking include what is more institutional than individualistic: beginning with town examination and ending with capital or palace ones, none of the different levels of the imperial examination required oral presentations. Whereas I do not know in what language Zou Weilian talked with Ricci, that which lies at the bottom of the above "ignorance" in traditional Chinese society is the lack of a sort of "common language" or "*lingua franca*," with which people from all regions of the empire were allowed to communicate without oral interpretation. The worst is, as Joseph Edkins (艾約瑟, 1823–1905), a Protestant missionary who spared no effort to promote rhetoric and Cicero in the late-Qing dynasty, pointed out at that time that in later times there were no such institutions as assemblies and councils (*yihui* 議會) in China that could continue the ancient legacy of rhetoric (Ai 2006, p. 523). George A. Kennedy keenly observes in his *Comparative Rhetoric* that, in sharp contrast to Western rhetoricians, Chinese rhetors, called pejoratively as *chushi* 處士 or *zhonghen jia* 縱橫家, if not cunningly, then surely were reactionary (Kennedy 1998, p. 143).

2. European Jesuits and the Appearance of Western Rhetoric in China

This notwithstanding, what concerns me in recollecting Ricci's story with reference to Zou Weilian, especially, is a question rarely raised by modern specialists in the field of Jesuit writings: To what degree was European rhetoric introduced by early Catholic missionaries in China? It is self-evident that Ricci's *Western Mnemonics* or *Xiguo jifa* 西國記法 is itself the outcome of his reworking on medieval rhetoric.[4] Whereas the idea of rhetoric in *Xiguo jifa* is most likely Ciceronian, it does not mean that the Ming Jesuits knew this particular typology of rhetoric only. In his *Xixue fan* 西學凡 (1623) or the *General Introduction to Western Learning*, Julius Aleni (艾儒略, 1582–1649) has highlighted the three types of Aristotelian rhetoric by paraphrase: Deliberative speaking is employed "in times when the gentry cannot make a decision about things important, or to persuade people to shun from bad things or evil ways of life (衿紳偶有大事難決者，或民習於陋業，沉於邪俗者)." Epideictic oratory is employed "in

---

[2] For a biography of Zou Weilian, see Chen 1991, comp., *juan* 18, in Zhou 1991, 6:231. For Su and Zhang, see the discussion of them in Xing 1998, p. 87.

[3] Not until the Song and the Ming, those Neo-Confucians, for teaching purposes, began to deliver longer speeches as we understand them today, although they were still not the outputs of an art equaled to the Greco-Roman art of speech. See Song and Huang 1991, pp. 166–259.

[4] For the text of *Xiguo jifa*, please refer to Wu 1964, 1–70. For a recent study on *Xiguo jifa*, see Ahn 2017, "On *Xiguo jifa* (『西國記法』) of Matteo Ricci (1552–1610)," pp. 99–121.

times when one is to talk about the merits of the virtuous or to criticize those whose behavior is vicious (或當誦説聖賢之功德，或當譏彈不肖之惡行)." Forensic speaking is employed "to demand redress for a grievance, to make the cunning submitted, and to punish the mischievously sinned (枉者伸，詐者服，凶頑者罪; Ai 1964, p. 30)."

Another connection between the Ming Jesuits and Classical rhetoric lies in their meticulously clever use of *exemplum*, a specific genre that, as suggested above, comes from Aristotelian theory of *pisteis*. Most of the *exempla*, pursuant to Aristotle's *Rhetoric*, are "embodied in art" (2.2.1–2.2.3). One of the earliest Jesuit *exempla* concerns St. Augustine of Hippo (354–430), and appears in Michele Ruggieri's (羅明堅, 1543–1607) *Tianzhu shengjiao shilu* 天主聖教實錄 (1584), which can be taken here for an exemple:

> ...... [嘗] 聞古有一賢士，欲盡明天主之説，晝夜尋思。一日在於海邊往來，遇一童子，手執漏碗，望海而行。士問曰：『子將何往？』童子曰：『吾執此碗，欲汲盡此海水。』士笑曰：『欲以漏碗而汲盡滄海，子言謬矣。』童子曰：『爾既知漏碗不能汲竭海水，而顧勞神殫思，求知天主之説，豈不大謬？』須臾，童子不見。士大驚，悟知其為天人也。

> ... [I] was told that there was a virtuous scholar who would like to know all about God, thinking about Him all day long. One day, as he was walking along the seashore, he met a child, who hold a bowel with cracks and walked toward the sea. The scholar asked the child, "Where will you go?" The child replied, "I like to put all the water of the sea into this bowel." The scholar laughed, "You are wrong if you want to put the entire sea into this bowel." The child answered, "Since you have known that I can't exhaust the sea by using this bowel with cracks, isn't it ridiculous for you to exhaust the knowledge about God by sparing no effort to do so?" The child then vanished in no time, and the scholar was so surprised that he was illuminated to knew that the child was an angel.[5]

This story was likely the most famous *exemplum* in the Ming and the Qing dynasties. Several known and unknown authors of this period quoted it intensively in their respective texts.[6] Although Ruggieri tells a complete story in his book, the European originals of his story, the one in the Iberian *Libro de los enxienplos por a.b.c.* for instance, relates that virtually, St. Augustine, while writing a book on the Trinity, was admonished by a cherubic child he encountered along the seashore that the endeavor was as futile as trying to put all the ocean into a small hole in the sand one spoonful at a time.[7] Famous as this "Vision of St. Augustine" may be, it is not found in any of Augustine's works, including his well-known *Confessions*. In addition to indicating the exact source of this *exemplum*, one should know that, in the context of Ruggieri's catechism, it is enlisted to demonstrate that God is totally beyond human knowledge. The child's analogy is nothing short of an apocalypse for Augustine the "*shengren* 聖人," a term for "saint" appropriated in the revised, 1630 version of the *Tianzhu shilu* (Luo 1966, 2:769–770), in that it reveals to him human smallness and divine grandeur. This story, generally attributed to Augustine of course, not only has the intrinsic interest of all good tales and the concreteness of all analogies, but it also functions as authorities (St. Augustine as a "*shengren*," for whom Confucians show great respect), not merely because it quotes the "life" of an authoritative figure, but also because it itself is truth and thus authority incarnate (cf. Gregg 1997, pp. 11–16).

---

[5] My translation. For the Chinese text of the story, see Luo 2002, 1:14–15. For the nature of *Tianzhu shilu*, see Front 2019, pp. 201–25.

[6] So far as I know, the anonymous Chinese authors of *Xingmi pian* 醒迷篇 (2002), *Tianzhu shengjiao koduo* 天主聖教口鐸 (2013), *Lun fuli xiushi* 論輔理修士 (2013), and *Shanyi shengxue* 三一聖學 (2009) all quote the "Vision of St. Augustine" in their respective titles. See Zhong et al. 2009, 9:268–269; 9:268–269; Zhong et al. 2009, 3:428–430; Zhong et al. 2013, 20:130. For known authors' citations, see Li 2009; Zhou 2013, 27:148.

[7] See Sánchez 1992, p. 277. Ricci, in his *Tianzhu shiyi* 天主實義, offers the first "correct" version as paraphrased in the text. See Li 1965, 1:395.

3. Ciceronian Rhetoric and Its Representation in Ming China

When one considers the settings and origins of *exempla* or the European cautionary stories as a whole, one finds that they can be roughly divided into two categories, as suggested earlier: classical and Christian types. The supposedly biographical tales in what St. Jerome (340–420) calls *Vitæ patrum* (third century) and in Jacobus de Voragine's (1230–1298) *Legenda aurea* (*c.* 1260) generally have been thought of as typical sources of Christian type of exemplum.[8] As for the classical species, fable and anecdotes are the most prominent typologies (Kaufmann 1995, pp. 66–93; Carter 1928, pp. 7–8). *Exemplum* is therefore one of the effective rhetorical devices, a literary *ars* that not only makes its way into China before any other literary genres from the West but is no doubt a subject also related to the problems of language.

It requires little imagination to see that once the Jesuits recognized that there was no standardized Chinese in its spoken form (or even in its colloquial, written form), they were confronted with the necessity of adjusting their concept of European rhetoric. In the period when Ruggieri and Ricci sailed eastbound, rhetoric had already become part of Jesuit curricula (Ganss 1996, p. 296; Fitzpatrick 1993, pp. 208–16).[9] It was, however, by no means what is known as the sacred oratory of the Renaissance, which features expository and exegetical allegiance to Roman orthodoxy (McGinness 1995, pp. 3–8). Judging from the contents of the Jesuit texts in Chinese, one may conclude that what Ricci and his Jesuit fellows had been trained to do in such Jesuit institutes as the Collegio Romano and Coimbra University falls into the category of medieval *ars praedicandi*. I am of this opinion because the use of *exempla* had been condemned harshly ever since the Council of Trent (1545–1563), and also because only in such medieval artists of preaching as Alan of Lille (d. 1202) can one find the firmest support of the use of the classical type of sermon *exemplum*—under the aegis of the rhetoric of exemplification. Medieval though Alan might be, he and his preaching theory were well known in the Renaissance (Walsh 1977, pp. 117–36; Wilks 1977, pp. 137–57), and they might have stimulated the formation of Jesuit sacred lectures, in all likelihood through indirect sources.

As is the case with classical rhetoric, the medieval art of preaching is indeed no more than an *ars* of religious oration, with greater emphasis on oral training than on writing (O'Malley 1993, pp. 94–95). This can be seen clearly by a glance at Cypriano Soarez's (1524–1593) *De arte rhetorica* (Soarez 1955), a textbook of rhetoric widely used in the Jesuit educational institutions of the Renaissance.[10] Although Soarez wrote the book to "assist the young men to read the learned books of Aristotle (384–322fli BCE), Cicero (106–43 BC), and Quintilian (*c.* 35–*c.* 100 AD) wherein lies the well-springs of eloquence," "he argues that eloquence is no more than a means to the higher end of a more virtuous life on earth as preparation for a fuller existence in another, better world." To "draw greater profit from eloquence," one therefore must "carefully purify it by Christian teaching" (Soarez 1955, p. 113). The Ciceronian tasks of rhetoric, namely (1) *inventio*, (2) *dispositio*, (3) *elocutio*, (4) *memoria*, and (5) *actio* (*pronouncio*), are the major parts in the structure of *De arte rhetorica*.

Oration is the science of efficient and successful speech, but the Ciceronian parts of rhetoric might have to undergo an essential metamorphosis in Ming China due to the latter's different definition of its "common language." Aleni's *Xixue fan* has been generally conceived of as the first introduction to Ciceronian rhetoric in China,[11] but this is a long-standing, serious mistake; Aleni's formulation of the five procedures actually bases itself on Alfonso Vagnone's (高一志, 1566–1640) paraphrase of them

---

8 For the texts where Christian type of *exemplum* was often made of, see Rosweyd 1864, in J.-P. Migne, ed. 1862–1864, vol 73; Waddell 1987; and Voragine 1993. It is said that it was partially for the latter collection that Ignatius of Loyola made up his mind to be a priest (Tylenda 1985, p. 12). Ignatius's dramatic decision had itself become a Christian *exemplum* in Alfonso Vagnone's work in Chinese before 1628 (Gao, in Zhong et al. 2002, 1:367–68). For a modern discussion on the rhetoricity of this episode in Ignatius's autobiography, see Boyle 1997, pp. 5ff.

9 For more discussions, see Grendler 1989, pp. 377–81; and Lang 1952, pp. 286–98.

10 Most of the important texts concerning the medieval art of preaching can be conveniently found in Miller et al. 1974. For an excellent survey, see Murphy 1974, pp. 269–355.

11 For a discussion on this subject, see D'Elia 1950, pp. 58–76. For Aleni's text, see Ai 1964, pp. 27–30.

in his 1615 treatise written to describe "Western learning" (西學).[12] Vagnone's paraphrase, in turn, is developed from the related passage in Soarez's *vade mecum* of religious rhetoric, though Soarez bases his discourse on Cicero:

> [此五法者] 先究事物人時之勢，而思具所當言之道理，以發明其美意焉。次貴乎先後布置有序，如帥之智者節制行伍：勇者置於軍之前後，而懦者屯之於中。次以古語美言潤飾之。次以所成議論嫻習成誦，默識心胸，終至於公堂或諸智者之前辯誦之。(Gao 1995, 1:371–372)

> [The five parts of rhetoric] begin with the study of things, events, persons, and the conditions of times before one speculates on the cause of delivering one's speech for the presentation of one's proper intention. What is important next is the deployment [of materials and arguments.] This has to be made in good order, in the way as a wise commander would do with his troop: the brave will be deployed in front and at the back of the troop, while the cowardly will be placed in the middle. And then one adorns one's speech with antique gems and beautiful diction. And then one commits to memory the finished discourse by recitation. Finally one delivers it in a public hall or disputes it with wise persons.[13]

The related comparison made by Soarez is of course taken from Cicero's *De oratore* and Quintillian's *Institutio oratoria* (Cicero 1996, I. xxxi. 143–147; Quintilian 1993, III. iii. 1-iv. 15; also see Cicero 1989, I. ii. 3). *De oratore* was a common text for rhetoric classes in the schools of the Renaissance and the Reformation as well. Removing the troop comparison from this context, Aleni elaborates on Vagonone's idea as follows:

> [西人]議論之法，大約必由五端：一先觀物觀事，觀人觀時勢，而習覓道理以相質，所謂種種議論之資料是也。二貴乎先後布置有序而不紊。三以古語擷華潤色。四將所成議論嫻習成誦，默識心胸。其人靈悟善記，則有溫養之法；其人善忘難記，則有習記之法。終至於公所主試者之前誦說之，或登高座與諸智者辯論焉。蓋議論本欲破人之疑而發其志，以善處其事，不能通人之心，感人之情，無益也。故言語之輕重疾徐，以至容貌顧眄，舉手順目，皆有其法，俾聽者之愛惡悲喜，言下即觸，不徒浮言散於空中而已。

As for the method of discourse, there are five steps. First, to observe things, events, persons, and the conditions of the times, and to seek the causes behind them; such are called materials for discourse. Second, to deploy [materials and arguments] in good order: first this, then that. Third, to adorn with gems from ancient writers. Fourth, to commit to memory the finished discourse. If a student is intelligent and good at memory, there is method for keeping his memory fresh. If the student is forgetful, there is the art of memory. Finally, the student appears in a public hall in front of the examiners to recite his discourse or mounts a platform for a disputation with wise and learned persons. Now the purpose of discourse is to pierce the doubts and guide the will of the listened, for it does little benefit if one is capable of handling affairs but incapable of moving the hearts and emotions of others. Hence, there is a method, too, in the stress and speed of delivery, in the facial expressions, and in the movements of the

---

[12] For the year the chapter on Western learning was completed, see Mei 2017, p. 216n2.

[13] My translation here is done partially by following Bernard Hung-kay Luk's rendition of Aleni's version, with different wording and diction, in *Xixue fan*. See Luk 1977, p. 70. Unfortunately, Luk is ignorant of Aleni's borrowing from Vagnone, nor is he aware of Vagnone's borrowing from Soarez. He thus comes to the misleading conclusion that the Ciceronian parts of rhetorical formation "are quite obviously derived from Cicero's *De oratore*." I agree that Soarez's source is Cicero, *De Oratore*, 1.31.142–143, but it is clear that Vagnone's source is *De Arte rhetorica*. An obvious evidence of Vagnone's borrowing from Soarez lies in their shared emphasis on the simile of the commander and his troop. Soarez's original in this context, to quote Flynn's translation, reads, "The calibre of a distinguished commander is not better discerned from his selection of the brave and the spirited soldiers for war, than from posting an army for battle" (Soarez in Flynn 1955, p. 209). Elsewhere, Soarez uses the same figure of idea once more, although not so relevant to my argument: "The army that has a wise commander is governed more satisfactorily in all respects than one ordered by some rash and stupid person" (Soarez in Flynn 1955, p. 240).

hands and eyes, of the speakers, so that the words will touch the listeners' loves and hates, sorrows and joys and do not merely disperse in the air.[14]

Despite Vagnone's use of such words as "dispute" and "recitation," he paradoxically designates the result of these steps as "the *essay* of the Far West" (太西之文), rather than as its "speech" or "oration." Such designation, in other words, has laid bare Vagnone's intention to accommodate European rhetoric to Chinese literary culture, which generally bases itself on writing rather than on speaking. I believe that what had motivated Vagnone to make the designation must have been greatly influenced by his understanding of what the "language" commonly shared by the Ming Chinese was: it is the so-called *wenyanwen* 文言文 or literary Chinese. Aleni's elaboration upon Vagnone in his *Xixue fan* reflects even more the same understanding. He identifies *leduolijia* 勒鐸里加 (*rhetorica*) as the "science of literature" (文藝之學) and specifies its contents as "proverbial sayings of the ancient sages" (古賢名訓), "books on history of different nations" (各國史書), "poetry and prose of different kinds" (各種詩文), and "essays and argumentative articles written by individuals" (自撰文章、議論) (Ai 1964, p. 28). Obviously, here, the study of oration has been turned to become that of the written, literary language. To put it one more step further and, therefore, more precisely, through the joint efforts of the late-Ming Jesuits, the late-Qing Protestant missionaries like Joseph Edkins, and some Ming-Qing Chinese scholars such as Yang Tingyun (楊廷筠, 1562–1627) and Wei Yuan (魏源, 1794–1857), the "wen" in Vagnone's translation would later undergo an essential transformation from rhetoric into a Sino-European "wenxue文學" or literature, as I have indicated elsewhere (Li 2017, pp. 29–34). Such a transliterated transmutation of *rhetorica* into *leduolijia*, one should also note, had already been foreshadowed by an observation Ricci made some twenty years earlier. Ricci wrote in his *Storia dell'Introduzione del Cristianesimo in Cina* that all Chinese "*rettorica et eloquentia*" were to be found "in their writings rather than in the spoken word, in which they resemble Isocrates, who had a reputation among the Greeks for the eloquence of his writings."[15]

4. European and Chinese Rhetoric Compared

Chinese, in fact, is by no means lacking in "*rettorica*" or "*rhetorica*," albeit of a different nature.[16] Texts which teach debate or verbal discourse have been found in works spanning from *Xunzi* 荀子 through *Hanfeizi* 韓非子 to *The Literary Mind and the Carving of the Dragon*.[17] Authors of especially pre-Qin times (pre-221 BCE), however, were born in different kingdoms and thus might speak different languages. What they talked about in their individual works on "rhetoric," i.e., *bian* 辯, *shuo* 說, *yi* 議, *dui* 對, or *lun* 論, might thus vary to a certain degree, especially in oral presentation (Lu 1998, pp. 468–93). In addition, in this period, the Chinese idea of persuasion might lack "the connotation of artistic composition or style, which 'rhetoric' often carries in the West," and it henceforth, is replete with political imports. By the standards of Aristotle's *On Rhetoric* or Alan's *Art of Preaching*, which bases its discussion on an essentially common spoken language, texts in neither *Xunzhi* nor *Hanfeizhi* can thus be qualified as "rhetorical." No text on "public speech" was given and thus, one more observation calls for mention: "Neither Confucius nor other Chinese thinkers held a very high opinion of the intelligence of the general public; what they have to say about speech, persuasion, and other aspects of rhetoric is addressed to rulers or to their own philosophical students and does not consider techniques of addressing a mass audience." (Kennedy 1998, p. 143) This specific feature of "ancient Chinese rhetoric" is so discrepant from that of the West that no citation or mention of other texts than *Hanfeizi*

---

[14] Luk's translation with proper additions made by me. See Luk 1977, pp. 70–71. For Aleni's text, see Ai 1964, 1:28–30.

[15] D'Elia 1942, 1:37. For the English translation, I quote from Gallagher 1942, p. 28.

[16] As I will suggest in what follows, it has been a mistake to take *xiuqi xue* 修辭學 as an equivalent to "rhetoric;" I prefer *yantan zhishu* 言談之術 to it, though it is still different from Western idea of rhetoric.

[17] See *Xunzi* 1979, "Feixiang 非相," pp. 73–91; *Hanfeizi* 1964, "The Difficulties of Persuasion" ("Shuonan 說難"), pp. 73–79; and Liu Xie 劉勰, "Lunshuo 論說" and "Yidui 議對," in Liu 1985, pp. 126–33, 169–75. For a historical survey in this respect, see Song and Huang 1991, and Yuan and Zong 1990, pp. 9ff; Oliver 1971, pp. 84–257; and Garrett 1993, pp. 105–15.

and *Xunzhi* need be made hereupon. Actually, the respect for oral delivery become even worse since the civil service examination system (*kejia*科甲) had dominated the academia of the Han dynasty; writing rather than speaking was the only way to academic fame and political as well as social success, as I have intimated earlier in this paper. It therefore made no sense at all for Ricci and his Jesuit brothers to accord the same weight to rhetoric in China as they did in the West. Furthermore, Ricci was quite conscious that not even the written colloquial Chinese was highly respected in Ming society (Ricci 1942, vol. 1, p. 37).

The idea of rhetoric as *"wen,"* or "essay," embodies to the ultimate degree in the *Notitia linguæ sinicæ* by the Qing Jesuit Joseph de Prémare (1666–1736). The second part of this book discusses the Chinese literary language by using rhetorical terminologies from both Cicero and Aristotle. In the book, Prémare enlists rhetorical devices such as *antithesi, reptione, gradatione, confutatione (interogrationisbus), descriptione, comparationis, metaphora, fabula (yu-yen* 寓言), and *exemplum (pi-yu* 譬喻) to illustrate characteristics of Chinese literature. He might be motivated by the Chinese literatus Liu Ning 劉凝 (1620–c. 1715) to compose this part (Li 2015, pp. 123–28; Mungello 1979, pp. 8–9, 77–79; Lundbæk 1991, pp. 141–47), but his *"figuris orationis,"* interestingly, place more emphasis on the particulars of Chinese written language than on its spoken counterpart. (Prémare 1831, pp. 204–48) For *Notitia linguæ sinicæ*, rhetoric is thus not an *ars* of effective speaking but, instead, it is that of beautiful writing. In this Qing work of Prémare's, the echoes of Vagnone and Aeni's idea is clearly and strongly heard.

Given the Ming "rhetorical" circumstances, all the Jesuits could do to put the Alanian art of preaching into practice, besides verbal stories told occasionally, would have to depend greatly on written *exempla* or on *exempla* re-contextualized in, oxymoronically, written preaching, as Ricci has done in his *Jiren shipian* 畸人十篇 (Ten Chapters from a Strange Person, 1608; Li 2005). Trigault and Vagnone provided the first collections of classical, written *exempla* in Chinese in this period,[18] while Ricci and Aleni verbalized their tales in their written texts in different forms. They were Renaissance raconteurs fairly versed in the medieval art of story-telling, certainly in literary Chinese.

5. Exemplum and the Thematic Sermon

One may, of course, ask at this stage of my paper: Regardless of its Christian type, why does the medieval art of preaching also place stress on the classical, pagan type of *exemplum*? I have indicated previously that the Middle Ages were the climax of Christianizing brief stories from Greco-Roman lore. Most of the works at this period were done by the Dominicans and the Franciscans (Hinnebusch 1951, pp. 279–31; Bataillon 1985, pp. 191–205; Crane 1983, pp. 49–78), and their stories turned out to be direct or indirect sources of the short narratives found in the Ming Jesuits. This notwithstanding, one still has to return to Alan for a theoretical account for medieval interest in classical *exempla*. In his *Art of Preaching*, Alan gives the first definition of preaching in the history of the church; in it, the idea of authority is greatly accentuated. According to Alan, an "authority" is a quotation that authorizes an assertion a speaker or a writer makes, functioning almost as a proof text (Alan of Lille 1981, pp. 16–22). One finds that two types of preaching in the medieval pulpit were inspired specifically by Alan's emphasis on authorities as the fountainhead of preaching: the monastic sermon and the thematic one. Alan was himself a Cistercian, and his Cistercian peers such as St. Bernard of Clairvaux (c. 1090–1153) and Odo of Cheriton (c. 1185–c. 1247) were most enthusiastic practitioners of this or a similar theory by developing their sermons from biblical texts, the most authoritative "authorities" (McGuire 1983, pp. 211–67; Matarasso 1993, pp. 295–304). Side by side with this idea of authority arose the monastic form of preaching that was no more than a shapeless verse-by-verse comment on a passage from the Bible (Matarasso 1993, pp. 65–82). The Franciscans and the Dominicans were traveling mendicants preaching in and around the cities. Before they became prominent in the 1220s, they had prepared themselves for their preaching by studying at the new universities then being founded (Lesnick

---

[18]   See Kaufmann 1995, 4: 305–343; Gao 2009, vol. 4, pp. 3393–3401; cf. Li and Meynard 2014, pp. 182–341.

1989, pp. 94–95). With their scholastic background, they developed the first real homiletical form, known mostly as the thematic sermon; this form, I would argue, must have contributed greatly to the morphological formation of such Jesuit texts as Pantoja's *Qike* 七克 (The Conquest of the Seven Deadly Sins, 1614), Ricci's *Jiren shipian*, and Martino Martini's (衛匡國, 1614–1661) *Qiouyou pian* 逑友篇 (A Treatise on Friendship) (Li 1964, vol. 2, pp. 689–1126; vol. 1, pp. 93–282; Wei 1984, in Wu, 1:1–88).

Compared with the monastic sermon, the thematic one has more to do with the formal use of classical and Christian *exempla*. It was constructed on the basis of a theme, an authority in pulpit actuality. The theme would then be divided into a number of parts, and these were, in turn, subdivided into a number of sub-points. Alan's idea of authority became involved generally at this juncture of shaping the subdivision, for the affirmations made in each part of it were expected to be supported, or even "dilated," by the quotation of authorities, including illustrations by *exempla* (D'Avray 1995, pp. 263–73). Here, the idea of the authority had undergone a transmutation from the theme of a sermon to its illustration. What, then, constituted the medieval corpus of "authorities as illustrations"? In the words of Alan, first and foremost, "books of Holy Writ," then patristic writings, and finally "sayings of the pagan writers" (Alan of Lille 1981, pp. 20–22). In the mouth of the Dominicans and the Franciscans, Alan's specification for the last category would be generalized as "classical *exempla*," and the others would be the Christian type of exemplum.

To facilitate the composition of a sermon, the thematic one in particular, there appeared in the high and late Middle Ages several types of preaching aids or pastoral manuals, mostly in Latin.[19] Among them, two call for special attention: the collections of model sermons on virtues and vices and the collections of *exempla* arranged in alphabetical order by topics.[20] The former provided the Ming Jesuits with a base to be mined for form and material from which to construct their "written preaching" in literary Chinese on the same subjects. The latter, having been medieval "cyclopedias of illustration," supplied them with an inexhaustible treasury of Christian and classical tales to be enlisted in support of their themes, or the points they wished to make, in their "written preaching," or simply, "books on Christian *topoi*." To these two collections, one must add the collections of chreiai reworked on classical biographies or textbooks of basic rhetoric, when one considers the Jesuit use of anecdote.[21] I, together with Thierry Meynard, have written a book in English to illustrate what a chreia is, especially those in Chinese. In addition, I have also devoted one book to pinpointing part of my major concerns in this paper (Li 2005). To make it short, my arguments have been drawn partially from a linguistic comparison between the Jesuit tales in Chinese and their European counterparts found in the two types of preaching aids mentioned above.

6. Coda

Since both the classical and the Christian species of medieval *exemplum* is a form of sermon illustration, they certainly owe their genesis to classical rhetorical theory concerning examples; this fact accounts for my earlier reference to Aristotle's *On Rhetoric*. But a few more remarks in relation to the Jesuit use of a medieval preaching style discussed above need to be made before I move to the close of this paper. It is true that Aristotle's work on rhetoric had failed to exercise a direct influence on medieval rhetoric until the thirteenth century, but one can hardly disavow its role in the formation of the Alanian art of preaching. As is well known, the medieval art of pulpit oratory was greatly indebted to Book Four of St Augustine's (354–430) *Doctrina christiana* (Mountford 1991, pp. 27–53). St. Augustine's meticulous study on this subject, however, bases itself on Ciceronian rhetoric. Despite Cicero's theoretical renovations in rhetorical specifics such as speech stylistics and the five tasks of the rhetor, the major portion of his rhetorical thinking was derived from Aristotle (Cicero 1996, I. xxxII.

---

[19] There were, of course, exceptions in the vernacular. For examples in this regard, see Crane 1983, pp. cii–cxvi.

[20] For a discussion of the collections of model sermons, see Bataillon 1980, pp. 19ff. For discussions of the collections of "alphabet of tales," see Pfander 1934, pp. 19–29. Cf. Nolcken 1981, pp. 271–84.

[21] For an introduction to such collections and anthologies, see Kindstrand 1986, pp. 226–42; and Kloppenborg 1987, pp. 306–15.

144–145; Kennedy 1994, pp. 141ff.). For this reason, although the Greek rhetorician was absent from most of the medieval scene, he remained clearly felt through the Ciceronian school of rhetoric, which was then authoritative (Caplan 1933, pp. 73–96). Also for this reason, it takes little imagination to see that the Jesuits of the Ming and the Qing dynasty may have owed their employment of *exempla* to Aristotle's theory of logical proof as implied in the medieval art of preaching, not to mention their overt familiarity with it through Soarez's *De arte rhetorica*.

I have indicated at the outset of this paper that traditional scholars in the field of Christianity in China generally held that the Chinese converts in the Ming could be persuaded only by the Jesuit presentation of European material culture. What led to such a conclusion, to the best of my knowledge, might have been an ingrained sense of cultural superiority on the part of the Chinese. Before the middle of the Qing dynasty, Chinese official-scholars in the mainstream could hardly subscribe to the view that beyond China one could find a country of equal cultural excellence, especially in regard to literary achievement. However, the evangelical truth may have been the other way around, in that, as I have also pointed out earlier, religion is spiritual in essence and its proselytism can scarcely be dominated by material contributions alone. Sallie McFague forcefully indicates in her study of Jesus's parables that "Christian belief must always be a process of coming to belief–like a story" (McFague 1975, p. 3). She implies, in this observation, that sermon stories like the parables of Jesus, more often than not, may be the primary mover of one's spiritual formation. If McFague's theory is plausible, even if only in part, then the importance of the classical and Christian types of Jesuit *exemplum*, a religious sub-genre appropriated due to the Jesuit restoration of the medieval art of preaching, should not be underestimated. In this light, if what I have said in my books concerned is able to break down the long-standing, traditional prejudices concerning Chinese conversion in the late Ming and the early Qing dynasty and concerning the Jesuit contributions to Chinese culture at this period, that success may be credited to Aristotle and Cicero, the fountainhead, though indirect, of the medieval *ars praedicandi*.

Funding: This research received no external funding.

Conflicts of Interest: The author declares no conflict of interest.

References

Ahn, Jaewon. 2017. On *Xiguo Jifa* (『西國記法』) of Matteo Ricci (1552–1610). *Journal of Greco-Roman Studies* 56: 99–121.

Ai, Rulue, (Julius Aleni). 1964. *Xixue Fan*. Edited by Zhizhao Li. *Tienxue chuhan*. Taipei: Ricci Institute.

Ai, Yueshe, (Joseph Edkins). 2006. Xila wei Xiguo wenxue zhi zhu. In *Liuhe Congtan, Fu Jieti, Suoyin*. Edited by Shen Guowei. Shanghai: Shanghai cishu chupanshe.

Alan of Lille. 1981. *The Art of Preaching*. Translated by Gillian R. Evans. Kalamazoo: Cistercian Publication.

Anonymous. 2002. *Xingmi pian*. In *Yeshuhui Luoma Dan'anguan Ming Qing Tianzhujiao Wenxian*. Edited by Mingdan Zhong (Nicolas Standaert) and Dingke Du. Taipei: Ricci Institute, vol. 12, pp. 239–388.

Anonymous. 2009. *Shanyi Shengxue*. In *Faguo Guojia Tushuguan Ming Qing Tianzhujiao Wenxian*. Edited by Mingdan Zhong, Dingke Du and Xi Mon. Taipei: Ricci Institute, vol. 26, pp. 401–628.

Anonymous. 2013. *Lun fuli xiushi*. In *Xuejiahui Chanshulou Ming Qing Tianzhujiao Wenxian Xuibian*. Edited by Mingdan Zhong, Dingke Du and Renfang Wang. Taipei: Ricci Institute, vol. 23, pp. 469–582.

Anonymous. 2013. *Tianzhu shenjiao koduo*. In *Xuejiahui Chanshulou Ming Qing Tianzhujiao Wenxian Xuibian*. Edited by Mingdan Zhong, Dingke Du and Renfang Wang. Taipei: Ricci Institute, vol. 34, pp. 1–325.

Bataillon, Louis-Jacques. 1980. Approaches to the Study of Medieval Sermons. *Leeds Studies in English* 11: 19–30.

Bataillon, Louis-Jacques. 1985. Simitudines et exempla dans les sermons du XIIIe siècle. In *The Bible in the Medieval World: Essays in Memory of Beryl Smalley*. Edited by Katherine Walsh and Diana Wood. Oxford: Published for the Ecclesiastical History Society by Basil Blackwell, pp. 191–205.

Timothy Billings, trans. 2009, *[Matteo Ricci] On Friendship: One Hundred Maxims for a Chinese Prince*. New York: Columbia University Press.

Boyle, Marjorie O'Rourke. 1997. *Loyola's Acts: The Rhetoric of the Self*. Berkeley and Los Angeles: University of California Press.

Caplan, Harry. 1933. Classical Rhetoric and the Medieval Theory of Preaching. *Classical Philology* 28: 73–96. [CrossRef]

Carter, Minnie Luella. 1928. Studies in the *Scala celi* of Johannes Gobii Junior. Ph.D. dissertation, University of Chicago, Chicago, IL, USA.

Chen, Ding, comp. 1991. *Tonglin liezhuan*. In *Mingdai zhuanji congkan*. Edited by Junfu Zhou. Taipei: Mingwen, vol. 24.

Chu, Ping-yi. 1996. Shenti, linghuan yu Tianzhu: Mingmo Qingchu Xixue zhong de renti shengli zhishi. *Xinshixue* 7: 47–97.

Cicero. 1989. *Ad Herennium*. In *Cicero I*. Cambridge: Harvard University Press.

Cicero. 1996. *De Oratore*. In *Cicero III*. Translated by Edwad Wlliam Sutton, and Harris Rackham. Cambridge: Harvard University Press.

Crane, Thomas Frederick. 1983. Medieval Sermon-Books and Stories. *Proceedings of the America Philosophical Society* 21: 49–78.

D'Avray, D. L. 1995. Philosophy in Preaching: The Case of a Franciscan Based in Thirteenth-Century Florence (Servasanto da Faenza). In *Literature and Religion in the Late Middle Ages: Philological Studies in Honor of Siegfried Wenzel*. Edited by Richard G. Newhauser and John A. Alford. Binghamton: Center for Medieval and Renaissance Texts and Studies, State University of New York at Binghamton, pp. 263–73.

D'Elia, Pasquale. 1942. *Fonti Ricciane*. 3 vols. Rome: La Libreria dello Stato.

D'Elia, Pasquale. 1950. Le Generalita sulle *Scienze Occidentali* di Giulio Aleni. *Rivista degli Studi Orientali* 25: 58–76.

Engelfriet, Peter M. 1998. *Euclid in China: The Genesis of the First Chinese Translation of Euclid's Elements, Books I-VI (Jihe yuanben, Beijing, 1607) and Its Reception up to 1723*. Leiden: Brill.

Fan, Hongye. 1992. *Yesuhuishi yu Zhongguo kexue*. Beijing: Zhongguo renming daxue chubanshe.

Fitzpatrick, Edward A., ed. 1993. *St. Ignatius and the Ratio Studiorum*. New York: McGraw-Hill.

Front, Philos. 2019. The *Tianzhu Shilu*. Revisited: China's First Window into Western Scholasticism. *China* 14: 201–25.

Louis Joel. S.J. Gallagher, trans. 1942, *China in the Sixteenth Century: The Journals of Matthew Ricci: 1583–1610*. New York: Random House.

George E. Ganss, trans. 1996, *Constitutions of the Society of Jesus*. Saint Louis: The Institute of Jesuit Sources.

Gao, Yizhi, (Alfonso Vagnone). 1995. *Tongyou jaioyu*. In *Xujiahui changshulou Ming Qing Tianzhujiao wenxian*. Edited by Mingda Zhong, Dingke Du and Xi Mon. Taipei: Fangji Chupanshe, vol. 5.

Gao, Yizhi. 2009. *Lixue guyan*. Edited by Mingda Zhong, Dingke Du and Xi Mon. Taipei: Ricci Institute, vol. 26, pp. 1–66.

Garrett, Mary M. 1993. Classical Chinese Conceptions of Argumentations and Persuasion. *Argument and Advocacy* 29: 105–15. [CrossRef]

Gernet, Jacques. 1986. *China and the Christian Impact*. Translated by Janet Lloyd. Cambridge: Cambridge University Press.

Gregg, Joan Young. 1997. *Devils, Women, and Jews: Reflections of the Other in Medieval Sermon Stories*. Albany: State University of New York Press.

Grendler, Paul F. 1989. *Schooling in Renaissance Italy: Literacy and Learning, 1300–1600*. Baltimore: Johns Hopkins University Press.

Han, Qi. 2019. *Kangxi huangdi, Yeshuhuisi, Kexue Chuanbo*. Beijing: Zhongguo da baikequanshu chubanshe.

Hanfeizi. 1964. The Difficulties of Persuasion (Shuonan). In *Basic Writings of Mo Tzu, Hsun Tzu, and Han Fei Tzu*. Translated by Burton Watson. New York: Columbia University Press, pp. 73–79.

Hinnebusch, William A. 1951. *The Early English Friars Preachers*. Rome: Institutum Historicum FF. Praedicatorum.

Jin, Nige. 2009. *Kuangyi*. In *Faguo guojia tushuguan Ming Qing Tianzhujiao wenxian*. Edited by Mingdan Zhong, Dingke Du and Xi Mon. Taipei: Ricci Institute, vol. 4, pp. 305–43.

Kaufmann, Hanna Wanda. 1995. The Exemplum: Its Morphology, Function, Evolution and Transmission. Ph.D. dissertation, University of Texas, Austin, TX, USA.

George Kennedy, trans. 1991, Aristotle. In *On Rhetoric*. Oxford: Oxford University Press.

Kennedy, George A. 1994. *A New History of Classical Rhetoric*. Princeton: Princeton University Press.

Kennedy, George A. 1998. *Comparative Rhetoric: An Historical and Cross-Cultural Introduction*. Oxford: Oxford University Press.

Kindstrand, Jan Fredrik. 1986. Diogenes Laertius and the Chreia Tradition. *Elenchos* 71–72: 226–42.

Kloppenborg, John S. 1987. *The Formation of Q: Trajectories in Ancient Wisdom Collections*. Philadelphia: Fortress Press.

Lang, Robert T. 1952. The Teaching of Rhetoric in French Jesuit Colleges, 1556–1762. *Speech Monographs* 19: 286–98. [CrossRef]

Lesnick, Daniel R. 1989. *Preaching in Medieval Florence: The Social World of Franciscan and Dominican Spirituality.* Athens: University of Georgia Press.

Li, Madou. 1964. Xiguo jifa. In *Tianzhujiao Dongchuan Wenxian.* Edited by Xiangxiang Wu. Taipei: Xuesheng, pp. 1–70.

Li, Madou. 1965. *Tianzhu shiyi.* In *Tianxue Chuhan.* Edited by Zhizao Li. Taipei: Xuesheng, vol. 1, pp. 351–636.

Li, Sher-shiueh. 2005. *Zhongguo wan-Ming yu Ouzhou wenxue—Mingmo Yeshuhui zhengdao gushi kaoquan.* Taipei: Liangjing.

Li, Jiugong. 2009. *Lixiu Yijian. Faguo Guojia Tushuguan Ming Qing Tianzhujiao wenxian.* Edited by Mingdan Zhong, Dinke Du and Xi Mon. Taipei: Ricci Institute, vol. 7, pp. 67–179.

Li, Zhen. 2015. Shilun Ming Qing zhi ji lai Hua Yesuhuishi yu Rujia Jidutu zhi xueshu jiaowang: yi Ma Ruoshe yu Liu Ning wei zhongxin. *Beijing xingzhen xueyuan xuebao* 2: 123–28.

Li, Sher-Shiueh. 2017. The Multiple Beginnings of Modern Chinese 'Literature. In *A New Literary History of Modern China.* Edited by David Der-wei Wang. Cambridge: Harvard University Press, pp. 29–34.

Li, Sher-shiueh, and Kid Lam, eds. 2014. *Wan-Ming Tianzhujiao fanyi wenxue jianzhu.* Taipei: Institute of Chinese Literature and Philosophy, Academia Sinica, vol. 4.

Li, Sher-shiueh, and Thierry Meynard. 2014. *Jesuit Chreia in Late Ming China: Two Studies with an Annotated Translation of Alfonso Vagnone's "Illustrations of the Grand Dao".* Bern: Peter Lang.

Liu, Xie. 1985. Lunshuo and Yidui. In Liu Xie. *Wenxin diaolong [jiaozheng]* 文心雕龍[校證]. Annotated by Liqi Wang. Taipei: Mingwen.

Liu, Dachun, ed. 2018. *Xixue Dongjian.* Beijing: Zhongguo Remin Daxue Chubanshe.

Lu, Xing. 1998. *Rhetoric in Ancient China, Fifth to Third Century B.C.E: A Comparison with Classical Greek Rhetoric.* Columbia: University of Southern Carolina Press.

Luk, Bernard Hung-kay. 1977. Thus the Twain Did Meet? The Two Worlds of Giulio Aleni. Ph.D. dissertation, Indiana University, Bloomington, IN, USA.

Lundbæk, Knud. 1991. *Joseph De Prémare, 1666–1736, S.J.: Chinese Philology and Figurism.* Aarhus: Aarhus University Press.

Luo, Mingjian. 1966. Tianzhu Shengjiao Shilu. In *Tianzhujia Dongchuan Wenxien Xubian.* Edited by Xiangxiang Wu. Taipei: Xuesheng, vol. 3, pp. 755–838.

Luo, Mingjian. 2002. Tianzhu Shengjiao Shilu. In *Yesuhui Luoma Dang'an Guan Ming Qing Tianhujiao wenxian.* Edited by Mingdan Zhong and Dinke Du. Taipei: Ricci Institute, vol. 12, pp. 1–85.

Matarasso, Pauline, ed. 1993. *The Cistercian World: Monastic Writings of the Twelfth Century.* Harmondsworth: Penguin.

McFague, Sallie. 1975. *Speaking in Parables: A Study in Metaphor and Theology.* Philadelphia: Fortress Press.

McGinness, Frederick J. 1995. *Right Thinking and Sacred Oratory in Counter-Reformation Rome.* Princeton: Princeton University Press.

McGuire, Brian Patrick. 1983. The Cistercians and the Rise of the *Exemplum* in Early Thirteenth Century France: A Reevaluation of Paris BN Ms lat. 1592. *Classica et Mediaevalia* 34: 211–67.

Mei, Qianli, (Thierry Meynard). 2017. *Tongyuo jiaoyu jinzhu.* Beijing: Commercial Press.

Miller, Joseph M., Michael W. Prossel, and Thomas W. Benson, eds. 1974. *Readings in Medieval Rhetoric.* Bloomington: Indiana University Press.

Mountford, Roxanne Denise. 1991. The Feminization of the *Ars Praedicandi.* Ph.D. dissertation, Ohio State University, Columbus, OH, USA.

Mungello, David Emil. 1979. *Silencing of Jesuit Figurist Prémare.* Lanham: Lexington Books.

Murphy, James J. 1974. *Rhetoric in the Middle Ages: A History of Rhetorical Theory from Saint Augustine to the Renaissance.* Berkeley and Los Angeles: University of California Press.

Nolcken, Christina von. 1981. Some Alphabetical Compendia and How Preachers Used Them in Fourteenth-Century England. *Viator Medieval and Renaissance Studies* 12: 271–84. [CrossRef]

O'Malley, John W. 1993. *The First Jesuits.* Cambridge: Harvard University Press.

Oliver, Robert T. 1971. *Communication and Culture in Ancient India and China.* Syracuse: Syracuse University Press.

Pfander, Homer G. 1934. The Medieval Friars and Some Alphabetical Reference-Books for Sermons. *Medium Ævum* 3: 10–19. [CrossRef]

Prémare, Joseph Henri. 1831. *Notitia Linguæ Sinicæ.* Malaccæ: Collegii Anglo-Sinici.

Quintilian. 1993. *Insttutio oratoria*. Translated by Harold Edgeworth Butter. Cambridge: Harvard University Press, III. iii. 1-iv. 15.

Redaelli, Margherita. 2007. *Il mappamondo con la Cina al Centro: Fonti Antiche e Mediazione Culturale Nell'poera di Matteo Ricci S.J.*. Pisa: Edizioni ETS.

Ricci, Matteo, S.I. 1942. *Storia dell'Introduzione del Cristianesimo in Cina*. In *Fonti Ricciane*. Edited by Pasquale M. D'Elia S.I. Rome: La Libreria dello Stato, vol. 3.

Rosweyd, Herbert. 1864. *Vitae patrum sive historiæ eremiticæ libri decem*. In *Patrologiæ Lainæ*. Edited by J.-P. Migne. Paris: Excudebat Migne 1844–1855, 1862–1864, vol. 73.

Sánchez, Clemente. 1992. *The Book of Tales by A.B.C. (Libro de los exienplos por a.b.c)*. Translated by John Esten Keller, Louis Clark Keating, and Eric M. Furr. New York: Peter Lang.

Soarez, Cypriano. 1955. *De Arte Rhetorica*. In Lawrence J. Flynn, S.J. The *De Arte Rhetorica* (1568) by Cyprian Soarez, S.J.: A Translation with Introduction and Notes. Ph.D. dissertation, University of Florida, Gainesville, FL, USA.

Song, Silian, and Yuwen Huang. 1991. *Zhongguo Gudai Yanshuoshi*. Jilin: Dongbei Shifan Daxue.

Standaert, ed. 2001. *The Handbook of Christianity in China. Volume One: 635–1800*. Leiden: Brill.

Joseph N. Tylenda, trans. 1985, *A Pilgrim's Journey: The Autobiography of Ignatius of Loyola*. Collegeville: Liturgical Press.

Voragine, Jacobus. 1993. *The Golden Legend: Readings on the Saints*. Translated by William Granger Ryan. 2 vols. Princeton: Princeton University Press.

Waddell, Helen. 1987. *The Desert Fathers*. London: Constable.

Walsh, Patrick Gerald. 1977. Alan of Lille as a Renaissance Figure. In *Renaissance and Renewal in Christian History*. Edited by Derek Baker. Cambridge: Cambridge University Press, pp. 117–36.

Wei, Kuanguo, (Martino Martini). 1984. *Qiouyou pian*. In *Tianzhujiao Dongchuan Wenxian Sanbian*. Edited by Xiangxiang Wu. Taipei: Xuesheng, vol. 1, pp. 1–88.

Wilks, Michael. 1977. Alan of Lille and the New Man. In *Renaissance and Renewal in Christian History*. Edited by Derek Baker. Cambridge: Cambridge University Press, pp. 137–57.

Xie, Zaozhe. 1959. *Wu Zazhu, Juan 4*. Beijing: Zhonghua.

Xunzi. 1979. "Feixiang". In Xunzi, *Xunzi [jijie]*. Annotated by Disheng Li. Taipei: Xuesheng, pp. 73–91.

Yuan, Huan, and Tinghu Zong, eds. 1990. *Hanyu xiucixueshi*. Hefei: Anhui Jiaoyu.

Zhong, Mimgdan, Dingke Du, and Xi Mon, eds. 2002. *Jesuhui Luoma dan'angun Ming-Qing Tianzhujiao wenxian*. vol. 12.

Zhong, Mingdan, Dingke Du, and Xi Mon, eds. 2009. *Faguuo guojia toshuguan Ming-Qing Tianzhujiao wen xian*. Taipei: Ricci Institute, vol. 26.

Zhong, Mingdan, Dingke Du, and Renhuang Wang, eds. 2013. *Xujihui changshu lou Ming—Qing Tianzhujiao wenxian xubian*. Taipei: Ricci Institute, vol. 34.

Zhou, Zhi. 2013. *Shengjaio ge zhanli duoyin*. Vol 1. In *Xujihui changshulou Ming Qing Tianzhujiao wenxian xubian*. Edited by Mingdan Zhong, Dingke Du and Renhuang Wang. Taipei: Ricci Institute, vol. 27, pp. 1–210.

Zhu, Xi, anno. 1997. Confucius, *Lunyu*. In *Shishu Jizhu*. Taipei: Shijie.

Zou, Weilian. 2001. Pixie guanjian lu. In *Mingmo Qinchu Tianzhujiao Shi wenxian congbian*. Edited by Mifang Zhou. Beijing: Beijing Tushuguan Chubanshe, vol. 3.

Zürcher, Erik, ed. 1991. *Bibliography of the Jesuit Mission in China (ca. 1580–ca. 1680)*. Leiden: Center of Non-Western Studies, Leiden University, pp. 101–24.

Zürcher, Erik. 1996. Renaissance rhetoric in Late Ming China: Alfonso Vagnoni's Introduction to His *Science of Comparison*. In *Western Humanistic Culture Presented to China by Jesuit Missionaries (XVII–XVIII Centuries)*. Edited by Federico Masini. Rome: Institum Historicum S.I, pp. 331–60.

Article

Sheng Ren in the Figurists' Reinterpretation of the Yijing

Sophie Ling-chia Wei

Department of Translation, the Chinese University of Hong Kong, Hong Kong, China; sophielcwei@cuhk.edu.hk

Received: 13 July 2019; Accepted: 20 September 2019; Published: 26 September 2019

Abstract: Christian missions to China have sought to make their message more acceptable to their Chinese audience by expressing, in translations of Christian texts, Christian terms and concepts in language borrowed from China's indigenous Buddhist, Confucian, and Daoist traditions. The Jesuits were especially renowned for their accommodation policy. Interestingly, when the Jesuit Figurists arrived in China in the early Qing dynasty, they conducted exhaustive studies on the Chinese classics, studies in which they identified *Tian* and *Di* of Chinese culture with God or Deus in Latin; their descriptions of Jesus and Adam were decorated with "chinoiserie" through their association with the *Yijing* and Chinese mystical legends. Each Figurist, in investigating Figurism and interpreting the *Yijing*, had his own identity, focus, and trajectory. The Figurist use of *sheng ren* was employed in this paper to distinguish each signature approach and how they explained the image of Jesus and prelapsarian Adam using the ethical emotions and virtues of a *sheng ren* 聖人 in their reinterpretation of the *Yijing* and the *Dao*. This also led to the European people aspiring for a more in-depth understanding and more discussion of the *Yijing* and the *Dao*.

Keywords: Jesuit Figurists; *Yijing*; *sheng ren*; sage; Christianity; Confucianism; *Dao*

---

1. Introduction

Christian missions to China have sought to make their message more acceptable to their Chinese audience by expressing, in translations of Christian texts, Christian terms and concepts in language borrowed from China's indigenous Buddhist, Confucian, and Daoist traditions. The Jesuits were especially renowned for their accommodation policy. Interestingly, when the Jesuit Figurists arrived in China in the early Qing dynasty, they conducted exhaustive studies on the Chinese classics, studies in which they identified *Tian* and *Di* of Chinese culture with God or *Deus* in Latin; their descriptions of Jesus and Adam were decorated with "chinoiserie" through their association with the *Yijing* and Chinese mystical legends. The Figurists explained the image of Jesus and prelapsarian Adam using the ethical emotions and virtues of a *sheng ren* 聖人 in their reinterpretation of the *Yijing* and the *Dao*.

The image of the *sheng ren* 聖人 (sage) depicted in the *Yijing* is that of a sage with high virtues who embodies the ideals of a sage king from Chinese history. The *sheng ren* enjoys a supreme status due to his virtues and flawlessness, as described in Confucianism and Daoism; Joachim Bouvet (1656–1730) thus describes Jesus as a Confucian sage for the purpose of proselytization and Joseph Henri-Marie de Prémare (1666–1736) and Jean François Foucquet (1665–1741) also applied this term to their description of Jesus in their Chinese writings and in their dissemination of the *Dao* to Europe. While staying in the imperial court, Foucquet, under pressure from the Kangxi Emperor (1654–1722), employed his expertise of astronomical knowledge and deciphered the images of hexagrams in the *Yijing*, using them to draw parallels between the fall of Adam and the hexagram *Yi* 頤 (Corners of the Mouth/Nourishment) and redefined Jesus as a *sheng ren*.

On the other hand, Prémare, after being deemed unfit for the imperial court, lived in the coastal areas of China. As one of the most knowledgeable missionaries who had a great command of both

Classical and vernacular Chinese, he analyzed the compositions of Chinese characters; it was he who used the two hexagrams *Tai* 泰 (Peace) and *Pi* 否 (Stalemate) to indicate the image of the *sheng ren*.

In this paper, the concept of *sheng ren* are explored through the Chinese, Latin and French manuscripts of those Figurists; a close comparison and examination of their Chinese writings and manuscripts in European languages is made to identify the similarities and differences in their approaches in identifying Jesus and Adam as a type of Jesus,[1] with *sheng ren*. In these rarely examined Chinese, Latin, and French manuscripts, Jesus, as a *sheng ren*, has plural and dialogic identities, which not only mitigated the differences between Christianity and the *Yijing* and reflected a new facet of the *sheng ren* to Chinese readers but also helped communicate the *Dao* to Europe.

2. Saint or Sage?

A saint is a person who is recognized as having an exceptional degree of holiness or likeness or closeness to God. However, the use of the term "saint" depends on the context and denomination. In the Roman Catholic, Eastern Orthodox, Anglican, Oriental Orthodox, and Lutheran doctrines, all the faithful deceased in Heaven are considered saints, but some are considered worthy of greater honor or emulation (Woodward 1996, p. 16). According to Lawrence Cunningham, there are four general categories of saints: (1) godly people, (2) the blessed ones who are in heaven, (3) the persons publicly recognized for their holiness by the process of canonization in the Catholic Church, and (4) the justified, as that distinction is understood in the scriptures of the New Testament (Cunningham 1980, p. 62). When Christianity was brought by the first batch of Jesuit missionaries and they found they needed to translate the word "saint" into Chinese, the holiness of a saint was transferred and carried into the Chinese term they chose for translation, *sheng ren* 聖人 (literal translation: the holy man; semantic translation: the sage). In Latin, *sanctus* was usually used to refer to a saint or a holy man; in Chinese, it was translated into *sheng ren* 聖人 in the first Catholic catechism in Chinese, *Tianzhu Shengjiao Shilu* 天主聖教實錄[2] (The True Records of the Lord of Heaven), which was written in Latin by Michael Ruggieri and translated into Chinese by Matteo Ricci and published in 1630. In that text, for example, when paradise was discussed in the format of catechism, "as the merits and virtues of a *holy man* are discussed, (the holy man) could immediately ascend to heaven after death." In Chinese, it was written as "夫論聖人功德，死後即可升天" (Ruggieri 1584, p. 29). Another figure from the Bible, Moses (每瑟), was also referred to as a *sheng ren* in the *Tianzhu Shengjiao Shilu* (ibid., p. 32). Jesus, however, was still described as a godly figure, separate from the saints of Christianity. In this catechism, when there is a question about what the believers should believe in, the answer from a Western scholar concluded that the believers should believe in the resurrection of Jesus Christ (ibid., p. 35)[3] and explained that after the crucifixion, Jesus went to limbo and saved the spirits of the condemned and the saints. In this Chinese work, *sheng ren* was mentioned more than 100 times, mostly as a descriptor of saints or men of virtue.

However, when it came to the early Qing dynasty, this group of Jesuit Figurists, Joachim Bouvet, Joseph Henri-Marie de Prémare, and Jean François Foucquet, took a bold step by describing Jesus as a *sheng ren* in their reinterpretations of the *Yijing*. The Figurists were first led by their most representative forerunner, Joachim Bouvet. Bouvet had been sent by one of the first French Jesuit missions sponsored by the French King Louis XIV to China in 1687. Possessing expertise in mathematics and astronomy, Bouvet also carried on the hermetic tradition and a passion for hieroglyph characters from Athanasius Kircher. Bouvet was devoted to deciphering Chinese characters and finding esoteric messages in one of the ancient Chinese classics, the *Yijing* 易經 (the Book of Changes). Just as Kircher had seen

---

[1] Types are prophetic in nature. They always point forward to messianic times. Events, persons, or statements in the Old Testament are seen as types pre-figuring events or aspects of Christ or his revelation described in the New Testament. In Romans 5:14, the apostle refers to Adam as a type of Jesus Christ.

[2] Ruggieri, Michael. S.J. 1584. *Tianzhu Shengjiao Shilu* 天主聖教實錄 (*The True Records of the Lord of Heaven*). Manuscripts stored in the Biblioteca Apostolica Vaticana. Shelf Mark Borg. Cin. 324. No. 1.

[3] In Chinese, it is 當信耶穌身死，魂進於古聖寄所，名曰令薄。救出人類原祖亞當，及往古諸聖人之靈魂，引而升之於天堂受福。耶穌至於死後之第三日，以魂湊合其身，而復活於世。.

the hieroglyphs as containing secret, divine significance, Bouvet saw the diagrams of the *Yijing* as containing the keys to reducing all phenomena of the world into quantitative elements of number, weight, and measure (Mungello 1985, p. 31). In addition to the exhaustive studies of Chinese classics, Bouvet's main focus lay in the *Yijing*, which contained, in his eyes, the most mystic of figures and elements embedded in text by God. As a Figurist, Bouvet endeavored to prove that the mystic figures, numbers and elements in the *Yijing* were from the same God or the representations of the same God in Christianity. In his Chinese manuscripts, he was also preoccupied with paralleling the timeline of the Bible with the one beginning with the Chinese ancient legends. He also saw more symbols and mystic creatures in the Chinese classics as types of Jesus or used to describe the birth of Jesus.

It may sound far-fetched to the modern readers, but this group of Jesuit Figurists truly believed in what they expounded. During his early stay in China, Bouvet first witnessed the prevailing influence of the *Yijing* on the literati and even the royal class, such as the crown prince (Collani 1985, p. 29). He realized that, rather than building rapport with the Chinese literati, persuading the Kangxi Emperor by the associations between the Bible and the *Yijing* may have been the ticket to Christianize the emperor and, from there, the whole Chinese empire. The *Yijing* was the primary medium bridging the gap between Christianity and Chinese culture.

Bouvet's two protégés, Joseph Henri-Marie de Prémare, and Jean François Foucquet, espoused Bouvet's ideas while also diverging onto different paths, and each had a deeper understanding of Chinese culture and history. In 1693, Bouvet was sent back to Europe as legate of the emperor. He was also advised by the emperor to bring new Jesuits back to China. Prémare was one of those new Jesuits. He was summoned to Peking in 1714 but he did not win favor from the Kangxi Emperor. Foucquet instead received an imperial decree in 1711 to work with Bouvet on the *Yijing* and stayed in the imperial court until November 1720. As it turned out, Prémare became a master of the Chinese language and Chinese characters through his interactions with the local literati and his own hard work, while Foucquet exercised his astronomical knowledge during presentations on Figurism delivered to the Kangxi Emperor. The Figurists attempted to ease pressures from the Holy See and solve the Rites Controversies by means of such presentations, though their efforts failed. However, their bold attempts were not out of mere vain curiosity; thus, their serious intellectual studies of the *Yijing* demand further examination. In the following sections of this paper, I will identify each Figurist's approach of paralleling Jesus with *sheng ren* in their reinterpretations of the *Yijing*.

3. Bouvet's Confucian Sage

In the *Yijing*, *sheng ren* 聖人 is mentioned 38 times; the lines of hexagrams explained *sheng ren* as a model actor who waited for the right timing of nature and who practiced the virtues between Heaven and Earth. Its optimal image also coincides with the Confucian image of the *sheng ren* as a sage king possessing the virtues of *zhong* 忠 (loyalty; treating people right), *xiao* 孝 (filial piety), *ren* 仁 (benevolence) and *yi* 義 (righteousness).

A *sheng ren* depicted by Confucius in his works is modeled after the ancient sage kings, such as Fuxi 伏羲, Yao 堯, Shun 舜, Yu 禹, King Wen 文王, and King Wu 武王. While these ancient sage kings of Chinese myth were often treated as mystical, not historical, figures, it fit the needs and interests of Bouvet as he paralleled the timeline of these figures with the timeline of figures from the Bible. In addition, the image of *sheng ren* being a sage inside and assuming the outside identity of a king/ruler 內聖外王 coincides with the Jesuit Figurists' portrayal of Jesus Christ. Therefore, the image of a *sheng ren* in Confucianism was transposed onto the image of Jesus in Bouvet's manuscripts, to depict his filial piety and loyalty toward God as well as other Confucian virtues. With the transposed Confucian virtues, Jesus became true to life—the lives of the Chinese people.

Among Bouvet's hundreds of folios of manuscripts, it is most noted that two manuscripts stored in the Biblioteca Apostolica Vaticana, *Da Yi Yuan Yi Nei Pian* 大易原義內篇[4] (Inner Chapter of the Original Meaning of the Great *Yi*) and *Yi Gao* 易稿[5] (The Draft of the *Yijing*), are his interpretations of the first twelve hexagrams of the *Yijing*, with the first two hexagrams, *Qian* 乾 (the Creative) and *Kun* 坤 (the Receptive) in *Da Yi Yuan Yi Nei Pian* 大易原義內篇 and the remaining ten in the *Yi Gao* 易稿. The reason he only chose the first twelve hexagrams was unknown, but each hexagram was linked with the stories from the Bible, especially how Jesus Christ rose as a sage and how Adam forsook the Confucian virtues, resulting in his fall. While more details about Bouvet's interpretation of the *Yijing* may be found in another of the present author's books, *Chinese Theology and Translation: the Christianity of the Jesuit Figurists and their Christianized Yijing*, this paper is an extension from that book and further examines the Confucian virtues of *zhong* 忠 (loyalty; treating people right), *xiao* 孝 (filial piety), *ren* 仁 (benevolence) and *yi* 義 (righteousness) were transposed onto Jesus and Adam before the fall.

Among these twelve hexagrams reinterpreted by Bouvet, there are a few innovative parallels between Jesus and the Confucian *sheng ren*. For example, *Bi* 比 (Holding Together), composed of *Kan* 坎 (the Abysmal) as the upper trigram and *Kun* 坤 (the Receptive) as the lower, originally meant that the ruler was close to his marquises and conferred property and land to each of them to win their trust and loyalty. Bouvet, in his interpretation, turned *Bi* 比 into a hexagram describing Jesus as a sage king with benevolence and care for his people.

> The great sage (Jesus) with no errors and with original goodness and permanent perseverance took the throne to follow Pre-Heaven and to establish the kingdom of Latter Heaven. He was born following the order (of God). He has the virtues of benevolence and tenderness to nourish the people below and pardon the crimes of all quarters. . . . Therefore, his loving of benevolence reached all four quarters, and people in the world felt that they were fortunate to be pardoned with no errors. This is the Savior who had a close bond with mankind and exhausted the ways to develop a close rapport between (God) above and (man) below in Latter Heaven.
>
> (毫過貳元善永貞之大聖，繼先天立後天國之極，順命降生臨下，仁柔之德潤下，盡贖萬方之罪，... 由是仁恩四洽，世人幸沾赦罪咎之恩，... 比人捄世之主，而窮後天上下互比之道。) (Bouvet Borg. Cin 317. No. 7, p. 18. Author's translation.)

From the above description, Jesus was depicted as a sage with benevolence who pardoned the crimes of mankind. *Da sheng* 大聖 (great sage) was employed very frequently as a name for the flawless Jesus. *Ren* 仁 (benevolence) may be a common virtue across Christianity and Confucianism; it is quite obvious that Bouvet can easily borrow *ren* 仁 from Confucianism to depict Jesus's character. In addition to the common use of *ren* 仁 in these two manuscripts, there are more parallels between Jesus and a Confucian sage with virtues such as *zhong* 忠 (loyalty; treating people right), *xiao* 孝 (filial piety), and *yi* 義 (righteousness). For example, the *yang* line of the beginning place 初九 of *Qian* 乾 (the Creative) originally meant that the superior man or sage should maintain a low profile while it is not the right time to optimally utilize his potential (潛龍勿用). However, in Bouvet's interpretation, the *yang* line of the beginning place 初九 of *Qian* 乾 (the Creative) was transformed to portray Jesus as a filial son who followed the Holy Father's order to be born to the world; the timing not being ideal, Jesus could not yet accomplish his merits (Bouvet Borg. Cin. 317. No. 9, p. 8). Jesus in Bouvet's Chinese writing was usually depicted as the Heavenly Son born with no beginning of the Lord of Heaven, the Heavenly Father 天主聖父始所生之天子. Filial piety applied here was intended to evoke the same filial emotions

---

[4] Bouvet, Joachim. *Da Yi Yuan Yi Ne Pian* 大易原義內篇 (*Inner Chapter of the Original Meaning of the Great Yi*), Manuscripts stored in the Biblioteca Apostolica Vaticana. Shelf Mark Borg. Cin. 317. No. 9.

[5] Bouvet, Joachim. *Yi Gao* 易稿 (*The Drafts of Yi*). Manuscripts stored in the Biblioteca Apostolica Vaticana. Shelf Mark Borg. Cin. 317. No. 7.

and filial values the Chinese people already held but redirect them towards God. Jesus was thus depicted as a sage with filial piety.

Furthermore, in *Kun* 坤 (the Receptive), a comparison between Adam and Jesus was made, Adam being a type of Jesus. According to Bouvet, Adam was modeled on the Holy Father, but he was lured by Satan, the arrogant dragon 亢龍, and disobeyed the orders of the Lord of Heaven (ibid., pp. 17–18). In this hexagram, contrasting with Adam's betrayal, Jesus was illustrated by Bouvet as a full sage with three suitable virtues, *zhong* 忠, *xiao* 孝, and *xin* 信 (respect) (忠孝信三順全聖) (ibid.). With these three virtues, Bouvet then explained that Jesus travelled across *Da Qin* 大秦 (the Roman Empire) and spread the Christian teachings to the people. Jesus' twelve apostles and 72 disciples were compared to Confucius' 72 disciples (ibid., p. 17). Then, Bouvet also treated Confucius as a type of Jesus born hundreds of years before the birth of Jesus. Both wanted to spread the *Dao*, the way of God and the Christian teachings, to all people under Heaven.

Aside from these two manuscripts of twelve hexagrams, Bouvet also expounded in another of his Chinese works, the *Yi Yao* 易鑰[6] (The *Yijing* as the Keys to Christianity), about how ultimate a sage Jesus was.

> The Holy Son was ultimately submissive (to God) and was willing to shoulder the heavy responsibility. He sacrificed his body to pardon the crimes of all quarters. His sacrifice was for tens of thousands of people. His precious life was given on the cross to repair the faults of human beings, to correct their sins, and to rescue men from the ring of crimes. ... He was born as a god with infinite power. He was born to inherit the throne from God. He was ultimately divine, ultimately wise, ultimately righteous, ultimately benevolent, ultimately respectful, ultimately humble, and his true virtues may be paired with those of Heaven and Earth. He re-uplifted the heart of mankind and opened a new way (for mankind) in the period of Latter Heaven (after the birth of Jesus). He was an omnipotent, great sage.
>
> 聖子至順受命甘承重任，一躬付萬方之罪，自當犧牲代萬民，致其實命，以十字權衡之平補之，而出大過，其罪之鍰，... 以為永不絕之神配誕於世，而為繼天立極、至神至明、至義至仁，至尊至謙，真德配天地，再造人心。開後天之道，全能一大聖。 (Bouvet Borg. Cin. 317. No. 2, p. 19. Author's translation.)[7]

The seven mentions of the adjective "ultimate" 至 in the *Yi Yao* complements how Bouvet portrayed Jesus Christ as a Confucian sage with *zhong* 忠, *xiao* 孝, *xin* 信, *ren* 仁 and *yi* 義. The reinterpretation of these hexagrams in the *Yijing* amazed the Kangxi Emperor and he demanded more Chinese writings from Bouvet. However, the true agenda harbored by the Kangxi Emperor was that he wished to know more about Western mathematics and astronomy, which also prompted Foucquet, who stayed in the imperial court, to incorporate more astronomical studies.

4. The *Sheng Ren* in Foucquet's Astronomical Descriptions

Although these three main Figurists basically followed a consistent approach, identifying mystic symbols in the Chinese classics and treating them as messages left by God, each still had his own signature approach, based on his own expertise, and with the support and resources of the location he stayed in. Compared to Bouvet's eccentric association between the hexagrams and the Bible stories, Foucquet associated the irregularities of the constellations with his interpretation of the *Yijing*.

The French Jesuit Jean-François Foucquet had been in China since 1699, working as a missionary first in Fujian and then in Jiangxi. In 1711, he was summoned to the capital where he became involved in astronomy for several years. In the imperial court, he also needed to serve and satisfy the emperor

---

[6] Bouvet, Joachim. *Yi Yao* 易鑰 (The *Yijing* as the Keys to Christianity). Manuscripts stored in the Biblioteca Apostolica Vaticana. Shelf Mark Borg. Cin. 317. No. 2.

[7] This translation was also employed by the author in the third chapter of her book, *Chinese Theology and Translation: the Christianity of the Jesuit Figurists and their Christianized Yijing*, for a different purpose and explanation.

and his desire for astronomical knowledge and his enthusiasm for the *Yijing*. However, Foucquet, the Jesuit missionary with astronomical knowledge, was not the only source for the emperor's Western education. In addition to frequent debate with the Astronomical Bureau and the Office of Mathematics dominated by Chinese ministers, Foucquet also needed to bear the brunt of questioning from both his own confreres of the French mission and from the Jesuits of the Portuguese mission. The interpretation of the Chinese classics as well as views on how to put the sciences in the best interests of the mission divided the missionaries.

Surrounded by controversies, Foucquet's focus on astronomical studies worked as a means to protect the mission in China, while the optimistic attitude they had originally conveyed to their European audience turned into one of defense. *Ju Gu Jingzhuan Kao Tianxiang Bu Jun Qi* 據古經傳攷天象不均齊[8] (The Examination of the Irregularities in the Sky Based on the Ancient Classics) was written by Foucquet within this historical context. According to Witek, this book was completed sometime between 1712 and 1715 while Foucquet was serving in the Kangxi Emperor's court (Witek 1982, p. 454). As a loyal protégé of Bouvet, Foucquet also made parallels between figures in the Bible with the *Yijing*.

What was in common between Bouvet and Foucquet was that both employed hexagrams to symbolize the characters of the fallen Adam and the Savior, Jesus. What is different about Foucquet's interpretation is that he linked more closely with the *Dao*. Foucquet also delved into the true meaning of the hexagrams to demonstrate the virtues of a *sheng ren*, in this case, Jesus.

Via questions and answers in the catechism in the Chinese work *Ju Gu Jingzhuan Kao Tianxiang Bu Jun Qi* 據古經傳攷天象不均齊, Foucquet first explained that the regularities and irregularities in the movements of constellations are just like the changes and non-changes in the *Yijing*, and that there must be a reason behind the irregularities. He further quoted from several ancient classics, such as *Huainanzi* 淮南子 (Master(s) from Huainan) and *Liezi* 列子 (Master Lie), to illustrate major changes from Pre-Heaven 先天 to Latter Heaven 後天. He indicated that Pre-Heaven does not refer to the stage before the creation of Heaven and Earth, but to the stage immediately after the creation of Heaven and Earth. Everything was in order and formed a dynamic and harmonious schema by mutual generation (*xiangsheng* 相生). It could be seen from the arrangement of the eight trigrams in Pre-Heaven. However, when it came to the Latter Heaven, Fire and Water are against each other, symbolizing the confrontation between man and Heaven. Summer turned into winter and everything was withering. The changes and the irregularities were caused by the errors of the ancestors. Who were the ancestors? Foucquet examined and refuted Yan Junping's theory 嚴君平, who examined the identity of human ancestors, and Foucquet especially pinpointed that the ancestors 先祖 in Yan Jungping's *Laozi Zhigui* 老子指歸 (The Essential Meaning of the Laozi) were not the ancestors of the Han dynasty. Instead, the ancestors were the ancestors of the human beings in the Bible, Adam and Eve.

In addition, unlike Bouvet's detailed explanations for the first twelve hexagrams, Foucquet picked several hexagrams which were related to his interpretation of the Bible stories and fit these hexagrams in his explanations about why there were irregularities in the sky. For example, Foucquet applied *Gen* 艮 (Standing Still, Mountain) to depict the original virtue of Adam, whose character is pure and simple (有易簡之德. Author's translation). If Adam had been submissive to the order of God, his merits would have been great and lasting (Foucquet Borg. Cin. 317. No. 13, p. 8). However, Adam had alienated himself from the heart of *Meng* 蒙 (Youthful Folly) and now man suffers from desire, deceit, sadness from loss and from being an orphan or a widow (ibid., p. 10). Thirdly, the grace and pureness in *Pi* 賁 (Grace) were also added to the original virtues of Adam.

> The ancestor was a loyal minister with sagacious benevolence. He is as white and pure as *Pi* 賁, without losing his virtues.

---

[8]   Foucquet, Jean François. *Ju Gujing Zhuan Kao Tianxiang Bu Junqi* 據古經傳攷天象不均齊 (*The Examination of the Irregularities in the Sky based on the Ancient Classics*). Manuscripts stored in the Biblioteca Apostolica Vaticana. Shelf Mark Borg. Cin. 317. No. 13.

先祖為善之忠臣，則賁白素朴不失其德。

(Foucquet Borg. Cin. 317. No. 13, p. 12. Author's translation)

Next, Foucquet further employed the symbol of *qiu* 丘 (a hill) in *Pi* 賁 (Grace) and *Yi* 頤 (the Corners of the Mouth) to compare the situations before and after Adam and Eve had committed their sins. The archaic character of *qiu* 丘 is 𠀌 or 𠀉, both of which symbolize two people standing on the ground (ibid.). In Foucquet's interpretation, they were similar to Adam and Eve in Eden. Originally, the *yin* line of the fifth place of *Pi* 賁 (賁之六五) meant: Grace in hills and gardens. The roll of silk is meager and small. Humiliation, but in the end good fortune[9]. This line was then transformed by Foucquet to depict Adam's prelapsarian purity. Interesting, another hexagram using the metaphor of *qiu* 丘, *Yi* 頤 (the Corners of the Mouth) was applied to indicate the dangers after Adam and Eve betrayed God.

Turning to the summit for nourishment,

Deviating from the path

To seek nourishment from the hill.

Continuing to do this brings misfortune.

(六二，，拂于丘，征凶。)

(ibid., pp. 12–13. Richard Wilhelm's translation. Wilhelm 1977, p. 109.)

Adam, being lured by Satan, caused the irregularities of the five planets五緯 (*Chenxing* [辰星], *Taibai* [太白], *Yinghuo* [熒惑], *Suixing* [歲星] and *Zhenxing* [鎮星]). *Qiu Yuan*丘園 (The Garden, Eden) was turned into *qiu shu* 丘墟 (the ruins of the garden).

With the fall of Adam from being the ancestor with pure virtue to one tainted with sin, the sage, Jesus Christ, rises. Here, I compare his *Ju Gu Jingzhuan Kao Tianxiang Bu Jun Qi* 據古經傳攷天象不均齊[10] (The Examination of the Irregularities in the Sky Based on the Ancient Classics) in Chinese and Latin. It was assumed to be written in Chinese first and followed by the Latin translation in manuscript Borg. Cin. 380. No. 6.

故垂瞽命。必有大聖降。而道濟天下焉。此大聖非他。即古經籍所載。參天地。致中和。之大聖也。為人類之首，人倫之至。萬夫之望。百代真儒之所需待者 … … 凡古經稱為聖。為神。為后。為君。為師。為大人。為至誠至聖者。

… futurum aliquando ut magnus sanctus ad terras descenderet, et mundo succurrens, in integrum omnia restitueret. magnus ille sanctus non alius est ab aevo(?), quem Libri Canonici et caetera vetustissima monumenta (other most ancient monuments) celebrant; quem aiunt operari cum caelo et terrâ revocaturum res mundanas producentibus, quem asserunt adducturum concordiam, qua olim in medio | in Paradiso viguit: quem praedicant ut Caput humani generis, ut humanorum officiorum* apicem, ut spem bonorum omnium, ut eum quem ab aveo(?) veri sapientes expectant …

quicumque in antiquis Libris vocatur sanctus aut summe sanctus item vocatur Spiritus et Praeclaris aut Principis et Regis aut Pastor, aut doctoris aut viri magni, aut summe veri, aut supremae veritatis ipsius, nominibus κατ'ἐξοχὴν insignitur, non alius ab ipso est.

---

9   In Chinese, it is 賁之六五，賁于丘園，束帛戔戔。吝，終吉。 The English is from Richard Wilhelm's translation (Wilhelm 1977, p. 93).

10 Foucquet, Jean François. *Ju Gujing Zhuan Kao Tianxiang Bu Junqi* 據古經傳攷天象不均齊 (*The Examination of the Irregularities in the Sky based on the Ancient Classics*). Manuscripts stored in the Biblioteca Apostolica Vaticana. Shelf Mark Borg. Cin. 380. No. 6.

English translation from Latin: Sometime in the future the great holy man would descend to the earth, and while saving the world, would rebuild all things into a whole. That great holy man is no other than [unrecognizable?] whom the Canonic Book (經) and other most ancient monuments commemorate; whom they say to work with the Heaven and Earth, for recalling the worldly affairs to come forward; whom they claim for bringing harmony, which was once flourishing in the middle, in paradise: whom they praised as the Head of mankind (Caput humani generis), the climax of the offices* of humans (人倫), as the hope of all goodness, as the one whom the eternal true wise men (真儒) expect.

(Foucquet Borg. Cin. 380. No. 6, p. 28. Author's translation.)

In both versions, Foucquet depicts Jesus as a holy man, the bright one, the Lord and King, the pastor, the teacher, the great gentleman, the highest true one, or himself the supreme virtue. In this way, not only did Foucquet resonate with Bouvet's idea of Jesus harboring the virtues of a loyal minister, he also dug further into the true meaning of these hexagrams and decorated Jesus with terms with holiness: *sheng* 聖 (saint), *shen* 神 (spirit), *hou* 后 (empress), *jun* 君 (lord) and *shi* 師 (master) are names referring to Jesus Christ; in the end he quotes from Chapter 18 of the *Daodejing* to explain why the *da sheng* 大聖 (the great sage) was born (Foucquet Borg. Cin. 317. No. 13, p. 25). In manuscript No. Borg. Cin. 371, *Problèmes théologiques*[11], Foucquet elaborates for more than 330 pages on his interpretation of the *Dao* and his equation of the *Dao* with Deus. The term *sheng ren* 聖人 in Chapters 34, 47, 49, 58, 70 and 78 of the *Daodejing* was identified with the Holy Son of the Bible (Wei 2018, p. 10).

Remaining in the imperial court and working with Bouvet, Foucquet was still dedicated to locating God's traces and messages in the *Yijing*. In order to cater to the interests of the Kangxi Emperor, Foucquet spiced up his presentation of Figurism with his astronomical expertise. Going further than Bouvet, he further delved into the studies of the *Dao* and the *Daodejing* and linked Jesus with the *sheng ren* in the *Dao*, which may have aroused the interests of the European readers after the manuscripts were brought back to Europe. His correspondence with Voltaire and Montesquieu helped later French scholars to develop Sinology in France (Witek 1998, p. 220).

5. The *Sheng Ren* in Prémare's Anatomy of Chinese Characters and Hexagrams

Prémare, also a Figurist, had a different fate and path than those of Foucquet. After Foucquet rejected a confrere who had been appointed to be his superior, he then returned to France and became a bishop at the Propaganda Fide ([Sacred Congregation for the] Propagation of the Faith) in Rome. On the other hand, Prémare worked as a missionary mainly in Guangxi. When the Christian faith was prohibited by the Yongzheng Emperor (1678–1735) in January 1724, Prémare was confined with his colleagues to Canton. Later, a still more rigorous edict banished him to Macao. Without imperial support, Prémare could only look to the local mission and the local literati for assistance. Among these literati, Prémare learned the most from Liu Ning 劉凝, who he is thought to have met around 1702. In several of Prémare's Chinese works, such as the *Taiji Lüe Shuo* 太極略説[12] (The Rough Explanation of *Taiji*) and *Jingzhuan Yi Lun* 經傳議論 (Discussions on Classics and Commentaries), Liu Ning was praised and quoted to support Prémare's own analysis of Chinese words and characters. Prémare himself was dedicated to studying Chinese languages and philology, and he commented several times about the influence he received from Liu Ning (Li 2014, p. 46; Wei 2018, p. 11).

Being away from the imperial court and dissenting from his mentor Bouvet's eccentric interpretations, Prémare had more freedom to concentrate on his own analysis of Chinese characters. The *sheng ren* 聖人 may be the most frequent term used in the *Yijing*, and Prémare also employed this term *sheng ren* in his Chinese works, such as *Jingzhuan Yi Lun* 經傳議論 as well as *Liu Shu Shi Yi* 六書實

---

[11] Foucquet, Jean François. *Problèmes théologiques*. Manuscripts stored in the Biblioteca Apostolica Vaticana. Shelf Mark Borg. Cin. 371.

[12] Prémare, Joseph Henri-Marie de. *Taiji Lüe Shuo* 太極略説 (*The Rough Explanation of Taiji*). Manuscripts stored in the Biblioteca Apostolica Vaticana. Shelf Mark Borg. Cin. 317. No. 5.

義[13] (The True Meaning of the Six Methods). This paper will further examine his interpretation of the *sheng ren*, which sets his Figurist approach apart from those of the other Figurists.

As the Jesuit missionary with the best command of Classical and vernacular Chinese, Prémare analyzed the composition of Chinese characters and treated each part as a symbol or message from God. One example given here is from compound ideographs (會意; hui yi; "joined meaning"), which are also called "associative compounds" or "logical aggregates". These are compounds of two or more pictographic or ideographic characters to suggest the meaning of the word to be represented. *Yang* 羊 (lamb) was borrowed to indicate the image of a *sheng ren*. The correlation between the image of *yang* 羊and Jesus as a *sheng ren* could easily be seen since the Bible refers to Jesus Christ as the "Lamb of God" (John 1:29; Peter 1:19). In the *Liu Shu Shi Yi* 六書實義 (Prémare Manuscript no. Chinois 906, stored in Bibliothèque nationale de France, p. 20), Prémare described *yang* 羊 as an auspicious sign that meant fortune and benevolence. Therefore, the characters formed with *yang* 羊 as a constituent radical, such as *yi* 義 (righteousness), *mei* 美 (beauty) and *xiang* 祥 (auspiciousness) are all good characteristics of a *sheng ren*. In addition, the character, shan (goodness; an archaic character for 善) is composed by a lamb flanked by *yan* 言 (words; to speak) on both sides. According to Prémare's anatomy, it must be an auspicious sign, while the right and the left of *Yang* 羊, the *sheng ren*, both *say* 言 something good and righteous (ibid.) about the *sheng ren*.

In addition, *Tai*泰 (Peace) and *Pi* 否 (Stalemate) also are applied to explain that ▬ ▬ both follow the principle of *zhishi* 指事 (self-indicative) to represent *Tian* 天 (Heaven) and *Di* 地 (Earth) (ibid., p. 14). In the next part, he further explains that *sheng ren* should stop *Pi* 否 (Stalemate) and open *Tai*泰 (Peace).

> *Yi* (易) is the sage of no shape, while the sage is the *Yi* in a tangible shape. *Qian* and *Kun* integrate and then the way of *Yi* facilitates. Because Heaven and Earth are positioned, a sage is then born. He towers high above the multitude of creatures, and all kingdoms are united in peace. Heaven above and man below are mutually communicating with one another. ... However, the one who could build the link between Heaven and man is the only sage. His position is central and correct, right and appropriate. Therefore, (he should) stop *Pi* and open *Tai* to solicit more blessings and original fortune.
>
> (易者其無形之聖乎,而聖人者有形之易乎。乾坤合焉而易道行,天地位焉而聖人生。首出庶物,萬國咸寧。上天下人,互為相通。... 然天人締結而成一位,惟至聖一人而已。惟其位中而正,正而當,故休否而開泰,以祉元吉。) (ibid., p. 15. Author's translation.)

In addition to employing *Tai*泰 (Peace) and *Pi* 否 (Stalemate) to indicate the harmonious relationship of the *sheng ren* between Heaven and Earth, Prémare also further utilized ▬ ▬ to indicate the image of the *sheng ren*. According to Prémare, "what the Great *Yi* may indicate is (the appearance) of the ultimate sage only" (ibid., p. 16. Author's translation). Therefore, ▬ ▬ was employed, which refers to the sage's being able to be shaped. He further expounded that the *Hetu* 河圖 (Yellow River Chart), the *Luoshu* 洛書 (Inscription of the River Luo) and the Great *Yi* are all the representations and images of the *sheng ren* (ibid., p. 16. Author's translation).

In the *Liu Shu Shi Yi* 六書實義, Prémare expounded his definition of a *sheng ren* and how his analysis of Chinese characters and hexagrams was associated with the characters and virtues of a *sheng ren*. However, except for the implicit association of *yang* 羊 in archaic characters with Jesus as a *sheng ren*, the rest of the descriptions of the *sheng ren* only reflect Prémare's deep influence from the local literati's studies of Chinese literature and his lesser inclination to associate his interpretation with the stories in the Bible, as Bouvet and Foucquet had done. The location he was situated in and the support he received may have influenced his divergence from those two Figurists.

---

[13] Prémare, Joseph Henri-Marie de. *Liu Shu Shi Yi* 六書實義 (*The True Meaning of Six Methods*), Manuscript no. Chinois 906, stored in Bibliothèque nationale de France.

6. Concluding Remarks

Past scholarship grouped these three Jesuit Figurists together, attributing to all of them a focus on the hermetic messages left by God in the Chinese classics. However, as I have shown herein, each Figurist, in investigating Figurism and interpreting the *Yijing*, had his own identity, focus, and trajectory. The Figurist use of *sheng ren* was employed in this paper to distinguish each signature approach. Prémare inherited his passion for Chinese characters from Bouvet; Foucquet possessed astronomical expertise, as did Bouvet. Although, unlike Bouvet's association of the lines in hexagrams with the image of Jesus or Adam, Prémare and Foucquet started from their own expertise, one from Chinese characters and the other from astronomical knowledge, to further investigate the meaning of hexagrams. This also led to the European people aspiring for a more in-depth understanding and more discussion of the *Yijing* and the *Dao*.

Funding: This paper was supported by Direct Grant offered by the Faculty of Arts, The Chinese University of Hong Kong, Hong Kong [grant project code: 4051105], and 2018–2019 Early Career Scheme Grant: Genealogies of the *Dao*—the Jesuits' *Dao* Journey (Project Number: 24601818), sponsored by RGC during the period 1 January 2019 to 31 December 2020.

Conflicts of Interest: The author declares no conflict of interest.

References

Collani, Claudia von. 1985. *P. Joachim Bouvet S.J. Sein Leben und sein Werk*. Nettetal: Steyler.

Cunningham, Lawrence S. 1980. *The Meaning of Saints*. San Francisco: Harper & Row Publishers.

Li, Zhen. 2014. *Maruose hanyu zhaji yanjiu* 馬若瑟漢語札記研究 *(The Studies on Prémare's Notitia Linguae Sinicae)*. Beijing: The Commercial Press.

Mungello, David E. 1985. *Curious Land: Jesuit Accommodation and the Origins of Sinology*. Honolulu: University of Hawai'i Press.

Wei, Ling-chia Sophie. 2018. In the Light and Shadow of the *Dao*—Two Figurists, Two Intellectual Webs. *Journal of Translation Studies, New Series* 2: 1–22.

Wilhelm, Richard. 1977. *The I Ching or Book of Changes: The Richard Wilhelm Translation*. Translated by Cary F. Baynes. Princeton: Princeton University Press.

Witek, John W., S.J. 1982. *Controversial Ideas in China and in Europe: A Biography of Jean-François Foucquet, S.J. 1665–1741*. Rome: Institutum Historicum S.I., vol. XLIII.

Witek, John W., S.J. 1998. Foucquet, Jean-François. In *Biographical Dictionary of Christian Missions*. Edited by Gerald H. Anderson. New York: Macmillan Reference USA, p. 220.

Woodward, Kenneth L. 1996. *Making Saints*. New York: Simon & Schuster.

Article

The Catholic *Yijing*: Lü Liben's Passion Narratives in the Context of the Qing Prohibition of Christianity

John T. P. Lai * and Jochebed Hin Ming Wu *

Department of Cultural and Religious Studies, The Chinese University of Hong Kong, Hong Kong, China
* Correspondence: johntpl@cuhk.edu.hk (J.T.P.L.); jochebed321@gmail.com (J.H.M.W.)

Received: 17 June 2019; Accepted: 28 June 2019; Published: 2 July 2019

Abstract: *Yijing benzhi* 易經本旨 (original meaning of the *Yijing*, 1774) constitutes a unique piece of Christian literature produced by the Chinese Catholic believer Lü Liben 呂立本 in the Qing period. Following in the footsteps of Jesuit missionaries such as Joachim Bouvet (1656–1730), Lü represents a rare Chinese voice of the Figurist interpretation of the *Yijing* by claiming that ancient Chinese sages had received and recorded God's divine revelation in this venerated Chinese classic. Focusing on his narratives of Christ's Passion, this paper examines the ways in which Lü interprets the symbolic meanings of the trigrams/hexagrams and deduces their theological connotations in light of Catholic thought. The interweaving of religious devotion, tradition and experience underpinned a creative re-interpretation of the Passion narratives, which strives to sustain the faith of Chinese Catholic communities in the context of the Qing prohibition and persecution of Christianity.

Keywords: The *Yijing* (The Book of Changes); Lü Liben; Figurism; Passion narratives; Prohibition of Christianity; Qing dynasty

1. Introduction: The *Yijing*-Figurism

In her latest monograph, Chen Xinyu 陳欣雨 examines the influence of the rising intellectual phenomenon during the Qing period known as Jesuit Figurism, with a focus on the *Yijing* (The Book of Changes) thoughts of the French Jesuit Joachim Bouvet (1656–1741). In concluding, she remarked that "The *Yijing*-Figurism being largely suppressed by the missionary headquarters in Europe, the Figurists were unable to publish their works in Europe and their thoughts were merely known by a few. In the meantime, their works had neither been issued in China, and hence we have hitherto yet found any assessment or studies on the subject matter by ancient Chinese literati."[1] However, the recent discovery of the *Yijing benzhi* 易經本旨 (original meaning of the *Yijing*) by the Qing Catholic believer Lü Liben 呂立本 may suggest otherwise.

Like Chen, most scholars in the field agree that the Chinese Figurist movement was short-lived and far from influential. It commenced with the sinological studies of Joachim Bouvet, followed by those of Jean-François Foucquet (1665–1741) and Joseph Henri Marie de Prémare (1666–1736). These French Jesuits were convinced that the *Yijing*, one of the oldest Chinese classics, was not in the ownership of the Chinese, but a prophetic work belonging to the Judeo-Christian tradition, speaking not only of the true God, but also about the Messiah. To validate this provocative claim, they applied to the *Yijing* the *Figurisme*, a typological exegesis which has always been applied to the Old Testament in the Catholic tradition.[2] The biblical typology aims to find, in certain persons or events in the Old Testament, some prefiguration of the New Testament and thus convince the Jews of the Christian

---

[1]   易學索隱思想因在歐洲總體上受到教廷傳教總部的壓制，著作無法在歐洲出版發行，其思想也只能為少數人知曉，且在中國關於索隱派的易學著作亦從未刊行發表，故尚未發現有古代中國文人對其進行評價和研究。(Chen 2017, p. 333).

[2]   (Mangenot 1924, pp. 1912–13)

message. By the same token, the Jesuit Figurists believed that if the most profound mysteries of Christianity could be revealed by the *Yijing*, they might convince the Chinese people that Catholicism was deeply rooted in their own culture, which would facilitate the Catholic missionary movement in China.[3] This is considered an evolution of the cultural accommodation approach established by their predecessor Matteo Ricci (1552–1610).[4]

Having the privilege to reside in the Forbidden City, these elitist Jesuit missionaries cultivated contacts with the Qing Emperor and scholar-officials in Peking (Beijing) and attempted to find receptive minds for their Figurist interpretation of the *Yijing*. The Kangxi Emperor (1654–1722), in particular, showed his interest in Bouvet's *Yijing* study. Not only did he monitor Bouvet's learning progress, the emperor also discussed Bouvet's work in depth with some of his ministers.[5] Unfortunately, the Figurists' views soon became entangled with the controversy over the Chinese rites in 1700.[6] While restrictions were imposed on their discussions about the *Yijing* with the Kangxi Emperor,[7] these missionaries were hereafter forbidden to write on Figurism in Chinese[8] and to get their treatises published during their lifetime. Taking these contexts into account, it is justifiable to extrapolate that *Yijing*-Figurism had blossomed but failed to bear fruit in the Qing society.[9]

The discovery of the *Yijing benzhi*, however, may point to the "afterlife" of Jesuit *Yijing*-Figurism. Deposited in Zikawei Library (Xujiahui Library, Shanghai), the manuscript was composed in the eighteenth century by Chinese Catholic believer Lü Liben, who took a similar hermeneutic approach as the Jesuit Figurists. Making a pioneering analysis of Lü's manuscript, this paper attempts to locate the missing piece in the puzzle of the Chinese Figurist movement. On the basis of a succinct introduction of the manuscript, the paper will focus on Lü's narratives of Christ's Passion by elucidating the theological connotations hidden in the symbolic trigrams/hexagrams, and by examining the dynamic interplay between Christian faith and Chinese identity against the backdrop of the prohibition of Catholicism in early Qing China.

2. The Figurist Remnant: Lü Liben and the *Yijing benzhji*

Yijing benzhji (also named as *Yijing lüzhu* 易經呂註) was originally written in the thirty-ninth year (1774) of the reign of Qianlong Emperor by Lü Liben, a Chinese Catholic from Hedong Jinyi 河東晉邑, Shanxi province.[10] With no proof that the text got published, at least eight copies of the manuscript are found in the Zikawei Library (see Appendix A). Unfortunately, most of the copies are fragments and have been deposited in the Library for centuries without attracting much scholarly attention. Thanks to the efforts of Nicolas Standaert, Adrian Dudink, and Wang Renfang, one of the most complete copies of the forgotten text has recently been documented and reprinted in *Xujiahui cangshulou Ming Qing Tianzhujiao wenxian xubian* 徐家匯藏書樓明清天主教文獻續編 (The Sequel to the Chinese Christian Texts from the Zikawei Library).[11] Bound in four volumes, the manuscript consists of a substantial prologue and commentaries on forty hexagrams. It is also the only copy in which the transcribers' names, the places and years of transcription are stipulated. According to the epilogues of each volume,[12] the text was subsequently copied around the tenth to eleventh year (1871–1872) of the

---

3   Previous studies have examined such issues as the intellectual background of Figurism, the life and works of Figurists. See (von Collani 1985; Witek 1982; Rule 1986; Lundbæk 1991; Zhang 1978, pp. 514–98).
4   (Mungello [1985] 1989, pp. 300–7)
5   For the relationship between the Kangxi Emperor and Bouvet's study of the *Yijing*, see (Fang 1943; Luo 1997; Zhang 2005).
6   (Mungello [1985] 1989, p. 311)
7   (Witek 1982, p. 176)
8   Ibid., 237.
9   (von Collani 1985, p. 207; Lundbæk 1991, p. 15; Witek 1982, p. 331)
10 (Lü 2013, vol. 1, p. 5)
11 (Lü 2013, vol. 1, pp. 3–198; vol. 1, pp. 199–396; vol. 1, pp. 397–586; vol. 2, pp. 3–206).
12 (Lü 2013, vol. 1, pp. 3–198; vol. 1, p. 396; vol. 1, p. 586; vol. 2, p. 206).

reign of the Tongzhi Emperor by three Catholic believers, namely Francis方濟各, Cheng Xiaolou程小樓 and Borgia 玻爾日亞 in Yunjian 雲間 (Shanghai).

With limited biographical information about Lü Liben, the prologue sheds light on his interpretative approach of the *Yijing*. Lü proclaims that the *Yijing* "is an ancient scripture with hidden mysteries, and the very first holy scripture since the beginning of history."[13] In the subsequent section of *Xici zhuan* 繫辭傳 (The Great Treaties), which states that "Thus the *Yijing* consists of the images; the images are reproductions (是故易者象也，象也者像也),"[14] Lü maintains that the *Yi* images originated from divine inspiration to reveal the mysteries of Christian salvation. Unfortunately, owing to later generations' misinterpretations, the truth has been concealed. Lü did not hesitate to make his severe critique:

> The original meaning of the *Yijing* consists of images, depicting the Logos, the true Lord coming down to Earth to save humankind. But because of Wang Bi's approach of "sweeping away the images," the truth has been lost. [...] Furthermore, there are fools who only bluff about false images without entity, deceiving people through divination to make money. Alas, they are so deluded! They have been committing cardinal sins, all because of their failure to understand the original meaning of the *Yijing*, and hence their descent into heresy and evil.[15]

This suggests that Lü may likely be walking in the footsteps of Jesuit Figurists. Producing a Catholic commentary to the *Yijing*, the "Figurist remnant" Lü attempts to interpret the symbols of all the sixty-four hexagrams and expounds their connotations in light of the salvation story and Catholic thought. Despite the fact that some portions of his commentaries are missing in the four-volume manuscript,[16] Lü's work is still more complete and systematic than the Jesuit missionaries' fragmented Chinese writings.[17]

Taking advantage of the multifarious symbolic dimensions of the trigrams and hexagrams, Lü strives to unearth the "original meaning" of the *Yijing*. According to Lü, each trigram, the basic *Yijing* sign consisting of three lines, is associated with a specific image from different figures of Christianity and stages of the salvation history (see Figure A1). *Qian* 乾 (1) ☰, *Dui* 兌 (2) ☱, and *Li* 離 (3) ☲ denote the three divine persons—respectively, the Holy Father, the Holy Spirit, and the Holy Son. *Zhen* 震 (4) ☳ indicates God's indignation upon sin, pouring water down on earth for forty days to destroy human civilization as an act of retribution. *Xun* 巽 (5) ☴, the Eldest Daughter, represents Virgin Mary, who turns over a new leaf by giving birth to Jesus Christ, the savior of all humankind. *Kan* 坎 (6) ☵ then denotes the toil and sufferings of Christ and the subsequent *Gen* 艮 (7) ☶ the Seven Last Words of Christ on the cross on Mount Calvary. Last but not least, *Kun* 坤 (8), the Earth ☷, signifies the redemption of *bafang zhi ren* 八方之人 (People from the eight directions).[18] On the basis of these images of the component trigrams, Lü offers further theological interpretation on individual hexagrams. In this fashion, the trigrams and hexagrams are regarded as the archetypal keys to unlock biblical revelations.

While the Crucifixion occupies a pivotal position in Catholic theology, the Passion narratives naturally captivate the attention of Lü Liben in his *Yijing* commentary. Theological reasons aside,

---

[13] 《易》乃古經隱義而為開闢以來第一聖經也。 (Lü 2013, vol. 1, p. 3). The English translations of the *Yijing Benzhi* 易經本旨 (original meaning of the *Yijing*) are by the authors.

[14] Unless otherwise specified, all English translations of the *Yijing* are from the Richard Wilhelm and Cary F. Baynes's version. See (Wilhelm 1967).

[15] 《易經》本旨有像，乃真道真主降世救人之像也，乃因王弼掃象而失其本來之像也[...]且有一種愚者只論其無實形之虛像，而以卜算命為事，以騙愚民錢財，迷甚哀哉！乃犯罪之大者也，皆因不明《易經》之本旨，而歸入異端邪妄之中矣。 (Lü 2013, vol. 1, p. 34–5).

[16] In the discovered copies of *Yijing benzhi*, a total of 44 hexagrams are reinterpreted. See Appendix A.

[17] Several Jesuit Figurists' Chinese manuscripts of the *Yijing* have been discovered, including *Gu jin jing tian jian* 古今敬天鑒 [The Mirror of Paying Homage to God in the Ancient Times and at Present], *Yi yin* 易引 [Introduction of Yi], *Zhouyi yuan zhi tan* 周易原旨探 [The Exploration of the Original Essence of *Zhouyi*], *Yi yao* 易鑰 [The Keys to the Yijing], *Yi jing zong shuo gao* 易經總說稿 [The Collection of All the Talks on Yijing], *Da yi yuan yi nei pian* 大易原義內篇 [Inner Chapter of the Original Meaning of the Great Yi], and *Yi Gao* 易稿 [Drafts of Yi]. In total, only 12 hexagrams, from *Qian* 乾 (The Creative) to *Pi* 否 (Standstill), were interpreted and elaborated.

[18] (Lü 2013, vol. 1, p. 23).

there might be another vital factor underlying his emphasis on the Passion narratives. The *Yijing benzhi* was written in 1774, when Catholicism was strictly prohibited by the Qing court. In 1724, the Yongzheng Emperor (reigned 1722–1735) issued a formal prohibition against the propagation of the Catholic faith in the provinces.[19] All churches were closed and followers were ordered to renounce their faith.[20] Adopting a policy similar to that of his predecessor, the Qianlong Emperor (reigned 1735–1796) continued to ban the missionaries from entering China. In 1746, foreign missionaries were found ministering to Chinese Catholics in Fuan, Fujian province. The emperor went so far as to order all local officials to expel or execute anyone preaching or embracing Catholicism.[21] This was followed by the persecution of the Chinese Catholics, the population of which was steadily increasing during his entire reign.[22] In 1757, the Qianlong Emperor confined all foreign maritime trade to Canton (Guangzhou) and required each and every arriving Western vessel to be supervised by a Chinese mercantile house.[23] Under these circumstances, it became more difficult for foreign missionaries to preach or perform priesthood duties in local communities. Many church activities were forced to cease or be driven underground. In *Yijing benzhi*, there are signs indicating that Lü composes his work during this time of religious persecution. Notably, in his exegesis of hexagram *Feng* 豐 ䷶ (Abundance [Fullness]), where he interprets it as a symbol for the golden age of Chinese Catholicism, Lü heaves a deep sigh that "unfortunately I was not born in those golden years."[24] He even makes his accusation rhetorically: "For those who turn to encumber our holy religion, is it the proper way of people aspiring benevolence?"[25] Against this historical milieu, the themes of suffering and martyrdom embodied in the Passion narratives become particularly pertinent and significant.

Among the eight trigrams, the images of *Kan*, *Gen*, *Li*, and *Xun* are intimately connected with Christ and his Passion in Lü's commentary. These four trigrams, in conjunction with several related hexagrams, will be critically examined with a view to analyzing the ways in which Lü takes advantage of the trigrams' symbolic potentials to construct his unique Passion narratives. The sections of *Kan* and *Gen* will focus on how Lü integrates and transforms Chinese and Catholic textual traditions in his own narratives, while the sections of *Li* and *Xun* will highlight his representation of Christ and Virgin Mary in response to the Qing contexts of Christian prohibition and persecution.

3. ☵ *Kan*: The Toiling Savior of Modesty and Merit

In Lü's exegesis, the trigram *Kan* ☵ (The Abysmal, Water) functions as one of the key symbols of the Passion. From the perspective of *Yijing* symbolism, Jesus Christ endured great sufferings in the Passion, just like the one yang (unbroken) line being trapped between the two yin (broken) lines in *Kan*. Lü expounds this idea by quoting "*lao hu Kan* 勞乎坎 (He toils in the sign of the Abysmal)" from the *Shuogua zhuan* 說卦傳 (Discussion of the Trigrams) where *Kan* is illustrated as "the trigram of toil, to which all creatures are subject (勞卦也，萬物之所歸也)." He argues that this statement refers to the Holy Son who "was trapped in the midst of human transgressions, and suffered death for all peoples of all times, paying the debts for their sins."[26] From his reading, the yang line represents a Christ with incomparable power and virtue while the yin lines signify the void attributable to human sin and persecution.

Seemingly irrelevant and far-fetched, Lü's interpretation is not without support from *Yijing*'s commentarial tradition. Kong Yingda 孔穎達 (574–648) regards *Kan* as signifying *xianxian* 陷陷

---

[19] (Standaert 2001, p. 520).
[20] (Gu 2000, pp. 87–9).
[21] (Clark 2011, p. 78).
[22] (Zhang and Liu 1987, pp. 180–6; Xiao 2015).
[23] (Schottenhammer 2007, pp. 33–4).
[24] 惜吾不遇其盛時也。(Lü 2013, vol. 2, p. 46).
[25] 今反閉塞聖教之人，仁人之位當如此乎？(Lü 2013, vol. 2, p. 54).
[26] 乃一聖子在于上下眾惡之中，乃替普世前古後今為世萬民受難受死，以補贖萬代世人之辜債。(Lü 2013, vol. 1, p. 44).

(trap and danger), in accordance with its image of water in the depths of an abyss.[27] Zhang Huang 章潢 (1527–1608) further refers *Kan* to man's heart of nature.[28] As Wu Shen 吳慎 remarks, the yang line denotes one's divine nature, being locked within the natural inclinations and tendencies, and thus in danger of being engulfed by carnal desires and passions.[29] This echoes with the Bible in which trap and danger are often used to symbolize temptations and lusts. For instance, 1 Timothy 6:9 states that those who desire wealth will fall into "temptation and a snare, and into many foolish and hurtful lusts, which drown men in destruction and perdition."[30] Another example is 1 Peter 5:8, where the Devil, the great tempter, is depicted as a dangerous roaring lion prowling around, seeking someone to devour.

While water's destructive power represents danger, trap, and death, its unceasing flow and nourishing nature denote truthfulness, fertility, and life. This results in the double, and apparently contradictory, meanings of the symbol *Kan*. According to Cheng Yi (1033–1193), "the centre of *Kan* is solid and strong, like water flows on without piling up anywhere, and even in dangerous places it does not lose its dependable character."[31] In *Tao Te Ching* (*Daode jing* 道德經), the placid and contented nature of water is taken as the embodiment of the most lofty virtue, and the magnanimity of a superior man. As Laozi 老子 extols, "Lofty nobility is like water. Water's nobility is to enrich the ten thousand things and yet never strive: it just settles through places people everywhere loathe. Therefore, it's nearly Way."[32] In this connection, the idea of *lao* as encapsulated in the trigram *Kan* (water) is a polysemy, with the coexistence of two possible meanings: *laoku* 勞苦 (toil) and *gonglao* 功勞 (merit). By capturing both meanings, Lü views Jesus as the true superior man, symbolized by the only yang line in *Kan* to suffer all the toils and to achieve the merit of benefiting all things.[33] Lü's highlight of the toils of the Savior also echoes with the description in Isaiah 53:11 concerning the Messiah, the "righteous servant," who "shall see of the travail of his soul," "justify many," and "bear their iniquities." 1 John 3:5 also makes it clear that in Jesus there is no sin, while Hebrews 4:15 refers Jesus as the only "high priest" who can overcome the temptation of sin throughout human history.

Lü's viewpoint of the symbol *Kan* and its attribute *lao* forms a solid basis for his further interpretation of the hexagram *Qian* 謙 ䷎ (Modesty), where he acclaims Jesus Christ as the "superior man of modesty and merit" (*laoqian junzi* 勞謙君子). Known as *jiusan* 九三 (Nine in the third place), line 3 of *Qian* is the ruler of the hexagram, it being the only yang line trapped by five yin lines. Its statement reads, "A superior man of modesty and merit. Carries things to conclusion. Good fortune (勞謙，君子有終，吉)." In Lü's reading, line 3 constitutes the middle line of *Kan*, the "toiling trigram" (*laogua* 勞卦), and thus denotes Christ's Passion. His interpretation bears a strong resemblance to Lai Zhide 來知德 (1525–1604)'s commentary to the same line where the Ming-dynasty *Yijing* scholar adopts the principle of interlocking trigram (*hugua* 互卦)—that is, using three of the central lines of *Qian* ䷎ (lines 2, 3 and 4) to form the nuclear trigram *Kan* ☵, allowing line 3 to share the trigram's implied meanings. *Lao*, as mentioned above, indicates both the toil and merits of the central line of *Kan*. In Lai's view, the yang line illustrates one who "flees from the dangers and brings forth achievements (出險而有功)."[34] Henceforth, according to Lü, line 3 of the hexagram *Qian* hints not only at the trials and tribulations of Christ's Passion, but also at His resurrection and ascension, which are indicated in the

---

27 (Li 2000, p. 152).
28 (Li 2002, p. 242).
29 Ibid., pp. 242–3.
30 All English translations of the biblical quotations in the book are taken from the King James Version unless otherwise specified. See (*King James Bible* 1996).
31 陽剛中實，居險之中，行險而不失其信者也。(Cheng 2011, p. 163).
32 上善若水。水善利萬物而不爭，處人之所惡，故幾於道。The English translation of the *Daode jing* is based on David Hinton's version. See (Hinton 2015, p. 40).
33 本旨一陽者，乃吾主也。因謙而降，受苦難而救人，是故曰〈勞謙〉。(Lü 2013, vol. 1, p. 375).
34 (Lai 2013, p. 138).

line statement by the phrase "*youzhong* 有終 (success at the end)." Lü further remarks that whoever submits to Christ and follows His path shall ultimately receive the fortune of *yongzhong* 永終 (eternity).

When interpreting "all the people obey him (萬民服)," from the *Xiaoxiang zhuan* 小象傳 (Commentary on the Line's Image) attached to line 3, Lü highlights Christ's humility in the Passion on the grounds that line 3 lies under the upper trigram *Kun* ☷ (lines 4, 5 and 6), which denotes all peoples on Earth. According to Xun Shuang 荀爽 (128–190), line 3, the only yang line in the hexagram, should have occupied the honorable fifth place, typically reserved for the governing rulers and monarchs, just like the "Flying dragon in the heavens (飛龍在天)" for the Nine in the fifth place for the *Qian* 乾 hexagram; but instead it voluntarily humbles itself to descend to the third place and goes right underneath the upper trigram *Kun*. For the *Yijing* scholar Xun, this is a sign of a governing ruler who intends to mingle himself among his people. According to the *Yijing* principle of the yin obeying the yang, the image of one yang surrounded by five yins also denotes the obedience of the masses to their ruler.[35] Lü shares this view and further expounds its profound Catholic implication—the transposition of line 3 from the fifth place signifying Christ leaving his heavenly kingdom to descend on Earth to accomplish the work of atonement for sinners. Along this line of thought, he identifies Jesus Christ as the "Real Ruler of All Peoples (*wanmin zhezhu* 萬民真主)" to whom all peoples should submit (*wanmin fu* 萬民服). On the other hand, those who lose their heart and reject Jesus as the savior shall bear eternal punishment for their own sins. Most intriguingly, the multiple inferences of the symbol *Kan* allow Lü to encapsulate the life-in-death paradox of the Passion. In Catholic theology, salvation is inextricably intertwined with suffering, in which the crucified Christ is the archetypal example. In order to save the human soul, the Son of God had to suffer agonizing torture and humiliating death. Crucifixion, on the one hand, is an instrument of death and penalty for sin, but on the other, it is the only path to eternal life and the only solution for sin.[36] Taking full advantage of the symbolic potentials of *Kan*, Lü is able to illustrate both the pain and hope in Christ's suffering on the cross: that *Kan* as trap and danger denotes Christ's physical, emotional, and spiritual sufferings; while *Kan* as the source of life indicates the power of His resurrection and final victory over sin. And Lü's Figurist interpretation does not come to a stop there. He proceeds to portray Christ's path to crucifixion by drawing on the symbolic meanings of the trigram *Gen*.

4. ☶ *Gen*: The Gradual Progress to Mount Calvary

Known as the site of Christ's crucifixion, Mount Calvary (also called Golgotha) has been revered as one of the holiest places in Christianity. It represents the culmination of Christ's life journal on earth. Among the eight trigrams, *Gen* ☶ (Keeping Still), consisting of one yang line above two yin lines, denotes the image of a mountain. For the Figurist Lü, there is no better symbol than *Gen* ☶ to represent Jesus's final site in his earthly pilgrimage. Lü adopts this analogy in his interpretation of the image of the hexagram *Jian* 漸 ䷴ (Gradual Progress), composed of the upper trigram *Xun* (wood) and the lower trigram *Gen* (mountain). Evoking an image of trees growing with the seasons and making the landscape of the mountain rise gradually, the hexagram hence signifies the concept of gradually progressing. In Lü's view, hexagram *Jian* denotes how Jesus slowly embarks on his arduous path to Calvary.

Correspondingly, in his exegesis of line 6 of the hexagram *Sui* 隨 ䷐ (Following), Lü focuses on the hexagrammatic image to recount Jesus' final steps. The line statement attached to line 6 reads, "firmly held and clung to, yea, and bound fast. [We see] the king with it presenting his offerings on the Western Mountain (上六，拘係之，乃從維之，王用亨于西山)."[37] According to Zhu Xi 朱熹 (1130–1200), this particular imagery originates in a ritualistic practice of Zhou dynasty. *Xishan* 西山 (Western Mountain)

---

[35] (Li 2016, p. 118).
[36] For the paradox of crucifixion, see (Behr 2006; Pius-Raymond 1954).
[37] James Legge's English translation is adopted in this particular paragraph in order to highlight the notion of "presenting offerings". See (Legge 1963, p. 94).

refs to *Qishan* 岐山 (Mount Qi), where sacrifice to the Mountains and Rivers would be performed.[38] In Lai Zhide's understanding, the image is suggested by the nuclear trigram *Gen* ☶ (mountain) (lines 2, 3 and 4 of *Sui* ䷐), and the upper trigram *Dui* ☱, which lies in the west.[39] Lü weaves together some traditional *Yijing* commentaries to formulate his unique interpretation in the light of biblical accounts and Catholic theology. He connects the Zhou sacrificial practice to Christ's priesthood and sacrifice, and argues that the sacrifice performed on *xishan* refers to Christ the King "offering his body and blood to God the Father on Mount Calvary."[40] In his reading, Christ in Passion appears as both the priest and sacrifice. This is in perfect harmony with the Epistle to the Hebrews, where Christ is described as the only real, eternal and perfect High Priest whose self-sacrifice brings about redemption (Hebrews 5:5; 7:26; 9:14; 10:10).[41] On top of that, Lü's interpretation coincides with Yu Fan 虞翻 (164–233)'s idea of the lower interlocking trigram *Gen* ☶ (hand) and upper interlocking trigram *Xun* ☴ (rope),[42] signifying that one is "firmly held and clung to, yea and bound fast."[43] Lü explicitly takes this image to refer to Jesus being arrested and bound by the ruffians in Gethsemane.

Drawing upon the allusive potentialities of the image of *Gen*, Lü evokes a series of images of the Passion and even illustrates its theological implication. As he states, "It is said: 'He brings them to perfection in the sign of Keeping Still.' This refers to the Seven Last Words of our Lord on the cross on *Gen* the Mount, where the work of salvation was accomplished."[44] *Chengyan hu Gen* 成言乎艮 literally means "statements made in *Gen*." With *Gen* being traditionally numbered seventh among the eight trigrams, Lü refers the statements to the Seven Last Words of Christ.[45] His interpretation is based on the discussion of *Gen* in *Shuogua zhuan*, reading: "Keeping Still is the trigram of the northeast, where beginning and end of all creatures are completed. Therefore it is said: 'He brings them to perfection in the sign of Keeping Still' (艮，東北之卦也，萬物之所成終而所成始也，故曰成言乎艮)." Kong Yingda uses Terrestrial Branches (*Dizhi* 地支), the cyclical counting system, to elucidate that "Gen is the trigram of the northeast, which is positioned in between *yin* 寅 and *chou* 丑. *Yin* indicates the end of old year while *chou* the beginning of the new year. Thus the trigram denotes that the beginning and end of all creatures are completed."[46] Cheng Yi takes another approach by remarking that only in the deep-hidden stillness can the end of everything be joined to a new beginning, and thus *Gen* the trigram of stillness represents the transition from the old to the new.[47] Meanwhile, Lü analogically regards this as Jesus's crucifixion and death, the turning point of the human history. Lü's reading complies with the Catholic doctrine in that the cross is the barrier breaker which fulfils all the moral, ceremonial and juridical precepts of the Old Testament worship and creates a new alliance for the reconciled people of God.[48]

Along this line of Figurist interpretation, Lü retells salvation history by his unique reading of another hexagram *Gu* 蠱 ䷑ (Work on What Has Been Spoiled [Decay]) from the Catholic lens. The name of the hexagram is derived from its structure and the attributes of its trigrams. The upper trigram *Gen* ☶ refers to the strong, upward-striving force, while the weak, sinking force of *Xun* ☴ takes the lower position. This results first in stagnation and ultimately in decay. Lü goes a step further to refer

---

38 (Zhu [2009] 2018, p. 92).
39 (Lai 2013, p. 91).
40 在噶瓦山上，用聖體聖血功勞，于天主聖父也。(Lü 2013, vol. 1, p. 411).
41 For the scriptural proof and theological significance for the priesthood of Christ, see (Cullmann 1963, pp. 83–9; Richardson 1958, pp. 225–9; Durrwell 1969, pp. 136–48).
42 According to the interlocking trigram principle, the lower interlocking trigram is formed by lines 2, 3 and 4 and the upper interlocking trigram by lines 3, 4 and 5.
43 Li Dingzuo 李鼎祚, *Zhouyi jijie* 周易集解, 130.
44 成言乎艮，乃吾主成七言，而救世之功在于艮山之上。(Lü 2013, vol. 1, p. 44).
45 His interpretation exhibits some characteristics of numerical mysticism which will be discussed in more details in the following section.
46 艮是東北方之卦也，東北在寅丑之間，丑為前歲之末，寅為後歲之初，則是萬物之所成終而所成始也。(Li 2000, p. 386).
47 (Cheng and Cheng 2006, p. 87).
48 For the sacramental significance of the cross, see Richardson 1958, pp. 229–32; Durrwell 1969, pp. 186–201.

the hexagram to the fall and decay of mankind. According to him, the upper trigram *Gen* ☶ and the upper interlocking trigram *Zhen* ☳ form the new hexagram *Yi* 頤 ䷚ (The Corners of the Mouth), which represents the consumption of food and thus denotes the first man Adam and the first woman Eve eating the forbidden fruit in the Garden of Eden. The world was thus spoiled and needed to be reset. In Lü's view, the nuclear trigram *Xun* ☴ (Eldest Daughter) represents Virgin Mary who gave birth to Christ. Like "crossing the great water (*li she da chuan* 利涉大川)," stated in the *Tuan zhuan*彖傳 (Commentary on the Decision), Christ entered the spoiled world and exposed himself to the multitudinous dangers. His pilgrimage came to the end as the yang line of *Gen* reaches the top—to the cross on Calvary where he made his seven last statements. Lü proceeds to elucidate that *Gen* denotes the turning point of the ages: it ends the Age of Commandment (*shujiao*書教) and begins the Age of Grace (*chongjiao* 寵教). In this manner, Lü highlights the unique significance of the Passion of Christ in the whole salvation history. Strikingly, his narrative echoes with Giulio Aleni (艾儒略, 1582–1649)'s *Kouduo richao* 口鐸日抄 (Diary of Oral Admonitions, 1630–1640), where the Italian Jesuit missionary has mapped God's salvation work into three different stages: the Age of Nature Law (*xingjiao*性教), the Age of Commandment (*shujiao*書教), and the Age of Grace (*chongjiao*寵教). According to Alenio, the announcement of the Ten Commandments signals the end of the Age of Nature Law while the birth of Jesus Christ inaugurates the Age of Grace.[49] The use of identical theological terms suggests that Lü's work is consistent with, and probably makes direct reference to, the Jesuit narrative and interpretation of the salvation history, as expounded in some contemporary Chinese Catholic texts.

5. ☲ *Li*: The Yin-yang King on the Cross

Concerning the protagonist of the Passion, the trigram *Li* ☲ was taken by Lü to represent Jesus Christ himself. In Lü's view, *Li,* traditionally numbered third among the eight trigrams, implies the three attributes of Christ—*zhuti yi*主體一 (one subject [one God]), *lingti er*靈體二 (two natures [divinity and humanity]), and *xingti san*形體三 (three forms [the Father, the Son and the Holy Spirit]).[50] On the dual nature of Christ, Lü acclaims Him as the "Yin-yang King" (*yin yang wang* 陰陽王) who masters the "yin-yang opposites" (*yin yang*陰陽), "spirits and gods" (*gui shen* 鬼神), "dark and light" (*you ming* 幽明), "life and afterlife" (*shengqian sihou* 生前死後), and "judgement and punishment" (*shangshan fa'e* 賞善罰惡).[51] In most instances in his *Yijing benzhi*, Lü makes reference to *Li* as the sign of Christ, the *Li* King (*Li wang* 離王), and develops his theological interpretations on the basis of such an analogy.

A case in point is his reading of *Lü* 旅 ䷷ (The Wanderer). Utilizing his own system of symbolism, Lü explicates the hexagrammatic image as follows: *Li* King is above *Gen* the Mountain, where the trigrams visualize the image of Jesus on the Calvary. To substantiate his line of thought, Lü adopts several interpreting strategies to reconstruct the imagery of Jesus's crucifixion. One of them is using the trigram numbers to produce symbolic images. According to Lü, the sum of the nuclear trigram *Gen* (7) and the upper trigram *Li* ☲ (3) is ten (*shi* 十), which implies the cross; the sum of the upper trigram *Li* ☲ (3) and the upper interlocking trigram *Dui* ☱ (2) is five, which represents the Five Holy Wounds; and, the sum of the lower interlocking trigram *Xun* ☴ (5) and the upper interlocking trigram *Dui* ☱ (2) is seven, which denotes the Seven Last Words. Then Lü attempts to supply more details of the crucifixion by examining the trigrammatic images. As he proclaims, the upper trigram *Li* ☲ (burning sun) implies that the crucifixion began at noon; that the upper interlocking trigram *Dui* ☱ (rain) illustrates the darkening sky; and that the nuclear trigram *Gen* ☶ (death of Christ), which is reversed to become *Zhen* ☳ (quake), denotes the earthquake at the moment of Jesus's death. Last but not least, he creatively remarks that the sum of the nuclear trigram *Gen* ☶ (7) and the lower interlocking trigram *Xun* ☴ (5) is twelve, which indicates the crucifixion event lasts for a total of twelve quarters of an hour (*ke* 刻),

---

49 (Aleni 2002, vol. 7, 108–9).
50 (Lü 2013, vol. 1, p. 22).
51 Ibid., p. 42.

the equivalent of three hours.[52] He proceeds to elucidate the implication of the imagery. The *Daxiang zhuan* 大象傳 (Commentary on the Image) attached to the hexagram reads, "Fire on the mountain: the image of the Wanderer. Thus the superior man is clear-minded and cautious in imposing penalties, and protracts no lawsuit (山上有火，旅。君子以明慎用刑而不留獄)." Not surprisingly, Lü refers Jesus as the superior man who "paid the penalty of sin for humankind, freeing souls from Hell."[53]

At first glance, Lü's numerical interpretative approach may seem unorthodox, if not heretical. The underlying assumption behind the development of his ideas, however, echoes largely with Shao Yong 邵雍 (1011–1077)'s Image-Number study. The famed *Yijing* scholar believed that numbers in the *Yijing* were far from meaningless. Thus, to discover some possible hidden meaning of the text, we must take into account the numerical representations. As he stated in *Huangji jingshi shu* 皇極經世 書 (Supreme Principles for Governing the World):

> If there are ideas, there must be words. If there are words, there must be images. If there are images, there must be numbers. After the numbers were established, then the images were produced. After the images were produced, then the words were clear. After the words were clear, then the ideas were manifest.[54]

Lü first utilizes numbers as a unique starting point for an imaginary reconstruction of the entire scene of Christ's Passion. Then, step by step, he reproduces the biblical accounts with the use of trigrammatic images, and further expounds the text in the light of Catholic doctrine. Here in his exegesis of *Li*, Christ in the Passion is featured as the Savior who brings justice to the world. Instead of underscoring His suffering, Lü highlights the divine power Christ, who came to liberate man from the shackles of sin and death.[55] It is worth mentioning that his interpretation resembles the distinctive symbol of the Jesuit Order: a flaming sun with the monogram IHS—the first three letters of Jesus's name in Greek (ΙΗΣΟΥΣ)—which is surmounted by a cross and subtended by three nails. In both cases, Christ in the Passion is symbolized as the sun that brings light to the world.

Lü's interpretation of *Shi He* 噬嗑 ䷔ (Biting through), on the other hand, narrates the Passion story from a different perspective. The name of the hexagram is explained in the light of its structure. The top and bottom yang lines symbolize the upper and lower jaws. The yang line 4 standing between the two yin lines signifies some hard foodstuff (signifying an obstacle) to be tackled by biting through it. In the social context, line 4 refers to some criminals who constitute an obstacle to the harmonious social life. As Kong Yingda remarks, the image of biting denotes judgement and punishment.[56] Lü infers that line 4 symbolizes Jesus who accepts and undergoes punishment voluntarily in lieu of all human beings to remove sin from the world. Lü notes that the line is positioned in between the upper interlocking trigram *Kan* (water, danger) and the upper trigram *Li* (fire, glory). Like fire being put out by water, Lü perceives, the glory of Christ the *Li* King was extinguished in the Passion when He was insulted and executed as a criminal. Along this line of interpretation, the phrase *shi ganzi* 噬乾胏 (Bites on dried gristly meat) attached to line 4, is interpreted as Christ having shed all His blood in the excruciating Passion till all his flesh had dried. Lü goes on to explain the statement of line 5, which reads "Bites on dried lean meat. Receives yellow gold. Perseveringly aware of danger. No blame (噬乾肉，得黃金，貞厲，無咎)." To Lü, the phrase *de huangjin* 得黃金 (Receives yellow gold) constitutes an analogy of the divine judicial authority being bestowed upon Christ as a reward of his Passion, while *zhen li* 貞厲 (Perseveringly aware of danger) refers to *zhen lie* 貞烈 (virtues of integrity) as manifest by his selfless

52 (Lü 2013, vol. 2, p. 61)
53 代世人受補罪之刑，而不留人靈于地獄也。 (Lü 2013, vol. 2, p. 64)
54 有意必有言，有言必有象，有象必有數。數立則象生，象生則言彰，言彰則意顯。The English translation of the text is based on Birdwhistell version. (Birdwhistell 1989, p. 76).
55 For Christ's victory over death, see (Richardson 1958, pp. 190–214).
56 (Li 2000, p. 118).

sacrifice. In this way, Lü constructs an exemplary model out of a suffering Christ, who has endured internal and external agonizing pain for his faith.[57]

Lü Liben strives to guide his readers to view Jesus as the archetypal martyr and the perfect example for all Catholic believers. He elaborates this point by explicating "His loud cries are as dissolving as sweat. Dissolution! A king abides without blame (渙汗其大號，渙王居，無咎)" and "'A king abides without blame.' He is in his proper place (王居無咎，正位也)," the statement and *Xiaoxiang zhuan* attached to line 5 of *Huan* 渙 ䷻ (Dispersion):

> 'Dissolving [his] sweat' originally indicates our Lord shedding His sweat and blood on behalf of sinners. This sets an example for all missionaries that one shall shed its sweat and blood as our Lord did. [...] Our Lord's body is the holy temple for the Trinity; yet he reconciled to give it up for us. I shall die in His name as if I was in my proper place. Jesus is my teacher while I am His disciple. How could I call myself His disciple if I did not follow His example?[58]

It is important to inquire the reason behind Lü's strong declaration. Viewing the text through the lens of its context may offer some insight into Lü's intentions. After the 1724 decree, only a few foreign missionaries had managed to stay or enter the Shanxi province.[59] Since their distinctive appearance made them easy to be tracked down by local officials, they usually hid in the houses of their native converts in daytime and went out to perform their ministerial duties until very late at night. As a result, many of the pastoral responsibilities were shifted to the local Chinese Catholics.[60] Putting their own lives at risk, they protected the foreign missionaries and found ways to preserve and preach on the doctrines. Some of them were arrested or even banished to die in exile.[61] Evidently, it is not an exaggeration to claim that one shall shed his sweat and blood for the sake of Christ. Under the imminent threat of religious persecution, Lü utilizes the *Yijing*—the most practical and disguising instrument for Chinese Catholic communities to remember the sacred event of crucifixion that lays the Catholic foundation—to reaffirm their religious identity by bearing witness to the wounds of Christ who reveals his vulnerability, his inner being, and his incarnation.[62] More importantly, in Lü's exegesis, Christ in the Passion serves as a powerful symbol of unflinching faith and steadfast hope. By means of the example of Christ, Lü may inspire the faith communities that the affliction they were experiencing is merely transient, that the honor and glory would be eternal.

6. ☴ *Xun*: The Tree of Life and the Queen of Martyrs

As the mother of Jesus Christ, Virgin Mary played a prominent role in Lü Liben's Passion narratives. Notably, in the *Jian* hexagram, Lü positions Mary at the very center of the crucifixion event and narrates the story from her point of view. As discussed earlier, Lü interprets that the hexagram evokes an image of Jesus on his way to Mount Calvary. In Lü's depiction of the scene, Mary was single-heartedly accompanying her son along the Via Dolorosa, manifesting the depths of her sorrow and suffering:

> Our Lord encountered His Mother on his way, and in His will he said, "Why do you follow me to this squalid place to deepen my pain? You shall return home." [...] Ascending the Mount Calvary, all the bitter sufferings were at hand, her heart torn as if a knife had plunged

---

[57] For Christ's bodily suffering, see (Guardini 1964, pp. 37–41; Chardon 1957).

[58] 本旨渙汗者，乃吾主為罪人，而出流血汗也。以示傳教者，當效吾主需出其血汗也 [...] 吾主之聖身乃為聖三之居，而忍為吾輩捨之。吾當以死還死，乃正位也。耶穌為師，我為其徒，不效耶穌，何以為之徒也？(Lü 2013, vol. 2, p. 115).

[59] (Ricci 1929, p. 10).

[60] Ibid., p. 32.

[61] (Liu 2017, p. 75).

[62] For the symbolic significance of Christ's wounds, see (Glotin 1979; Sava 1954).

and wrenched in it. Had it not been for the Lord's grace, her life would not have been preserved. Our Lady was in great distress—all because of mankind's sin.[63]

The imagery, in Lü's view, is encapsulated by the upper trigram *Xun* ☴, with the judgement to the hexagram *Jian* saying, "Development. The maiden is given in marriage. Good fortune. Perseverance further (漸，女歸吉，利貞)." In Lü's own symbolism, *Xun*, the Eldest Daughter, is used to signify Virgin Mary in her relations with the trigram *Li* ☲. According to Lü, when line 1 of *Xun* exchanges its position with line 2, the trigram *Li* (signifying Christ) is formed. Lü claims that line 1 (yin) and line 2 (yang) of *Xun* represent respectively the human nature and the divinity of the Holy Son; and therefore, the transposition of these two lines symbolizes the unity of Christ's humanity and divinity in the womb of the Virgin. Furthermore, Lü literally interprets *gui* 歸 as *guijia* 歸家 (return home), which captures two meanings: "the return of Mary" and "the repentance of sinners." For the former, Lü argues that Mary could have chosen to return home and not to witness her son's suffering; but instead, she opted to endure the pain for the sake of all humankind. Mary has further been portrayed not as a spectator, but as an indispensable participant in Christ's Passion.

More remarkably, the Figurist Lü goes further to put Mary on the Cross. Discussing the hexagrammatic image, he applies the image of "tree on the mountain (山上有木)" to the Cross and the Virgin. In his reading, the Cross is denoted as the tree on Calvary while the Virgin is portrayed as the "Tree of Life (常生之樹)," which bears the "Fruit of Life (常生之)," Jesus Christ. The multi-layered symbolic meanings of *Xun* allow Lü to reiterate the obedience of the Cross (necessary for Christ's death) in an attempt to recall the obedience of the Virgin (necessary for Christ's birth). It is noteworthy that Lü's portrayal of Mary bears a strong resemblance to Sirach 24:22–25, part of the Hebrew wisdom text that is applied to the Virgin in the traditional Roman Breviary.[64] In the scripture the personified wisdom says:

> I have stretched out my branches as the turpentine tree, and my branches are of honour and grace. As the vine I have brought forth a pleasant odour: and my flowers are the fruit of honour and riches. I am the mother of fair love, and of fear, and of knowledge, and of holy hope. In me is all grace of the way and of the truth, in me is all hope of life and of virtue.[65]
>
> (我如得肋賓多樹展枝，我枝是榮寵的。我如葡萄樹開奇香花，此花使人得榮富。我是正愛、敬畏、大通、誠望之母。惟我能賞人行正路，明正道，盼加神力得常生。)[66]

Here in the biblical metaphor, Mary has been depicted as a tree of honor and grace, and as a mother given to all believers to bring forth virtue in them, and to lead them in the path to truth and life. Lü presents similar Marian images in his commentary. In his exegesis of *Kun* 坤 ☷, Mary is titled as "the Queen Mother of Heaven and Earth" (*Tiandi zhi Muhuang* 天地之母皇) and "the Patron of the whole World" (*Pushi zhi zhubao* 普世之主保), who "takes charge of everything important on Earth and was taken up into Heaven by grace."[67] The honorific titles are almost identical as those found in the early-Qing Daoist text *Lidai shenxian tongjian* 歷代神仙通鑑 (Comprehensive Accounts on the Immortals through the Dynasties, 1700), in which Mary (*Maliya* 瑪利亞) is presented as "Queen Mother of Heaven and Earth" (*Tiandi zhi Muhuang* 天地之母皇) and "Patron of All Peoples in the World" (*Shiren zhi zhubao* 世人之主保). While *Lidai shenxian tongjian* positions Mary as one of the Daoist immortals in the supernatural world,[68] Lü reinterprets Mary as an ideal model of Confucian morality from the

---

63 吾主路遇聖母，乃吾主聖意曰:「何為躓此污穢之，以甚吾之苦乎？惟有旋歸而已。」 […] 進上瓦略山，重苦在眼前，五內如刀攪崩裂母心肝。若非主恩佑，其命不保全。皆因世人罪，主母多眼。(Lü 2013, vol. 2, p. 5).

64 A note omitted in the New American Bible Revised Edition (NABRE) recalls this tradition: "In the liturgy this chapter is applied to the Blessed Virgin because of her constant and intimate association with Christ, the incarnate Wisdom." For the Marian interpretation of Sirach 24 in Catholic tradition, see (Catta 1961, vol. 6, pp. 828–31, 860–1; Ratzinger 1983, pp. 25–7).

65 The English translation is based on Douay-Rheims' version.

66 The Chinese translation is based on Poirot's Guxin version. See (de Poirot 2014, vol. 6, p. 2150).

67 主保人世間欽事貴，放效蒙恩引升天。(Lü 2013, vol. 1, p. 125).

68 (Song 2018).

perspective of the *Yijing* discourse. Illustrating "Thus the superior man who has breadth of character carries the outer world (君子以厚德載物)," the commentary of the image attached to the hexagram *Kun*, Lü characterizes the Virgin as the "superior woman" (*nüzhong junzi* 女中君子) who takes up a heavy responsibility of the guardian of morality for all humankind. Furthermore, he foregrounds modesty as the exemplary virtue of Mary. In the section of line 3, Lü, by adopting the principle of changing lines (*bianyao* 變爻), points out that *Kun* would become *Qian* ䷫ when line 3 changes from yin to yang. In that event, the solid line 3 conveys the meaning of *laoqian* 勞謙. Lü acclaims Mary as the "*laoqian junzi* 勞謙君子" who gave virgin birth to Christ while retaining her modesty and humility. As discussed in the previous section regarding Lü's exegesis of the Qian hexagram, Jesus Christ has similarly been venerated as the *laoqian junzi* for his toil and merit in completing the salvation work through the Passion. Apparently the Figurist intends to demonstrate the extent to which Mary may parallel Christ in her contribution to the accomplishment of the salvation.

Mary's unparalleled merit has further been augmented by Lü's subsequent interpretation of hexagram *Da Guo* 大過 ䷛ (Preponderance of the Great), where he depicts Mary as the "Queen of Martyrs (*wei yi zhiming zhi mu* 為義致命之母)". The commentary on the hexagram image reads, "The lake rises above the trees: The image of Preponderance of the Great. Thus, the superior man, when he stands alone, is unconcerned; And if he has to renounce the world, he is undaunted (澤滅木，大過。君子以獨立不懼，遯世無悶)." According to Lü, *Dui* represents the Holy Spirit. This association is based on "He gives them joy in the sign of *Dui* (說言乎悅)" from the *Shuogua zhuan*, which he literally interprets as speaking in joy. Therefore, to him *Dui* is "the Holy spirit, the Holy love, whose words I [he] love to share."[69] Since *Dui* ☱ is above *Xun* ☴, the hexagrammatic image depicts symbolically the Holy Spirit impregnating Mary. Making this analogy, Lü once again refers the "superior man" to Mary whose own passion has set an example for all martyrs. The unwed mother was not concerned about her unique and unexpected pregnancy even when rumors of a scandal emerged. On top of that, she was undaunted when having to hide in Egypt to flee from the persecution of King Herod. In Lü's words, Mary "seeks not to be known by man, but by God. Though she may be all unknown, unregarded by the world, she feels no regret (不求人知而求神知，與世不見知而不悔)." Lü's phrase "*yushi bujianzhi er buhui* (與世不見知而不悔)" in praise of Mary's noble virtues is slightly modified from the *Zhongyong* 中庸 (The Doctrine of the Mean), where it is further stated that "only the sage who is able for this (唯聖者能之)."[70] In this connection, Mary has vividly been portrayed not only as an obedient and modest handmaid but as a venerable sage able to overcome the religious persecution with unwavering courage and perseverance. By means of manifesting Mary's exemplary deeds, martyrdom is perceived not only as an act of Catholic faith but also as an expression of the Confucian ideals.

Lü's narratives could be viewed as a direct response to the Qing contexts. Since the Chinese Rites Controversy, Shanxi Catholics had often been estranged from their fellow Chinese because they refused any adaptation to local customs they deemed to go against their faith.[71] One of the most common disputes was the paying of village or communal taxes for the purpose of celebrations or festivals considered idolatrous by church authorities. This causes conflicts between the Catholics and non-Catholics. In some local communities, the practice of Catholicism was ridiculed or even berated as a betrayal of Chinese traditions.[72] Catholics were forced to leave and form their own communities in some deserted regions. This kind of isolated faith communities became even more common during the time of religious persecution. In a bid to avoid being taken captive by the officials, many Catholics

---

[69] 兌為聖神，為聖愛，是吾喜言聖神之語。(Lü 2013, vol. 1, p. 43).

[70] The original line from *Zhongyong* reads, 君子依乎中庸，遯世不見知而不悔，唯聖者能之。[The superior man accords with the course of the Mean. Though he may be all unknown, unregarded by the world, he feels no regret. It is only the sage who is able for this.] The English translation of *The Doctrine of the Mean* is based on James Legge's version. See (Legge 1861, vol. 1, pp. 56–128).

[71] (Zhao et al. 1993, p. 283).

[72] (Xiao 2015, p. 65).

escaped into mountainous areas to conceal themselves.[73] Against this background, the story of the holy family fleeing to Egypt to escape from King Herod's persecution becomes particularly relevant and encouraging. Mary's example encourages the fleeing Catholics to take a firm stance regardless of the social stigma and secular values. Moreover, by positioning Mary as a Confucian sage, Lü demonstrates that the practice of Christianity is not a betrayal, but a return to their own cultural tradition.

7. Concluding Remarks

Viewed as a whole, *Yijing benzhi* demonstrates Lü Liben's mastery of exegesis, figura, and typology. Weaving together some traditional *Yijing* commentaries, he captures the multi-layered embodiments of *Kan* to encapsulate the life-in-death paradox of the Passion, and of the image of *Gen* to evoke the picture of Christ's Passion and illustrate its theological implication. In the exegesis of *Li*, he makes good use of the trigrammatic number and image to produce his Christology. In conjunction with several related hexagrams, he proceeds to feature Christ in the Passion as not only the powerful Savior but also a devoted, persevering martyr. By transposing the trigram lines with those of *Li*, he associates *Xun* with the Virgin Mary. More remarkably, he takes advantage of *Xun*'s multifarious symbolic potentials to demonstrate Mary's indispensable role in Christ's Passion. By commenting on several related hexagrams, he further represents Mary as a noble sage and the Queen of Martyrs. The image of Christ and the Virgin, in accord with both Christian spirituality and Confucian morality, provides a firm basis for consolidating the faith of Chinese Catholic believers before the persecution in the context of the Qing prohibition of Christianity. Lü's *Yijing* commentary manifests a unique and remarkable blend of the Chinese and Catholic traditions. The trigrammatic number and image and their symbolic implications have been enriched with a new Christian reading. Lü's creative contribution to both the *Yijing* studies and Christian theology has also facilitated the formulation of an inculturated Chinese theology.

In comparison with the Jesuit Figurists' scholarly treatises, Lü's *Yijing* exegesis demonstrates higher practicality and simplicity. Their distinctive interpretative approaches may be attributed to the difference of historical contexts. The Jesuit missionaries' *Yijing* study in the imperial court was officially assigned by the Kangxi Emperor.[74] And they had regular interactions with the renowned literati at the imperial court, such as Li Guangdi 李光地 (1642–1718), the Scholar of Wenyuange 文淵閣大學士 who compiled the official commentary *Zhouyi zhezong* 周易折中 (Balanced Annotations on the *Zhouyi*). Undoubtedly, the emperor and imperial scholars had great impacts on the Figurist's hermeneutical approach and strategy of the *Yijing*.[75] Lü's *Yijing benzhi*, on the other hand, is apparently a self-initiated project without the presence and supervision of the missionaries. His commentary is structured as a teaching manual for the common masses, rather than the intellectual elites. This allows him to enjoy greater flexibility in interpreting the classic. Compared with the Jesuit missionaries, Lü is more at home with the Chinese commentarial traditions of the *Yijing*. Hence, he is able to utilize traditional reading strategies and develop his own distinctive interpretation. Strikingly, *Yijing* as the *youhuan zhi shu* 憂患之書 (Book of Anxiety and Fear) has satisfied the need for giving prominence to the theme of suffering in response to the imminent religious persecution of his time. The notion of "anxiety and fear" becomes the common ground between the *Yijing* and the struggle of Chinese Catholics and plight under the Qing government. Taking the Figurist approach to the *Yijing*, Lü connects its system of thought with Christian doctrine and constructs a Catholic *Yijing*—a new *shengjing* 聖經 (holy scripture) that enables Chinese Catholic communities to integrate their religious identity with their cultural heritage. As this pioneering study has demonstrated, the analysis of this unique manuscript will open up avenues for further research on the influence of *Yijing*-Figurism in Chinese communities and on the intersections of Christianity with religious and cultural frontiers in the late imperial period.

---

[73] (Liu 2017, p. 86).
[74] (von Collani 1985, p. 62).
[75] For the influence of Li Guangdi on Bouvet's *Yijing*-Figurism, see (von Collani 2007).

Author Contributions: John Lai was in charge of conceptualizing, supervising, and polishing the paper, while Jochebed Wu did the preliminary research and wrote the first drafts.

Funding: This research received no external funding.

Conflicts of Interest: The authors declare no conflict of interest.

Appendix A

Table A1. Copies of *Yijing benzhi* Found in Zikawei Library.

No.	Title	Contents	Transcribers	Reference No.
1	*Yijing benzhi*易經本旨	Prologue Volume 1 (*Qian* 乾 ䷀–*Meng* 蒙 ䷃) Volume 2 (*Xu*需 ䷄–*Yu* 豫 ䷏) Volume 3 (*Sui*隨 ䷐–*Da Guo* 大過 ䷛) Volume 4 (*Jian* 漸 ䷴–*Wei Ji*未濟 ䷿)	Francis 方濟各 Cheng Xiaolou 程小樓 Borgia 玻爾日亞	213000 94441-94445B (Reprinted in *CCT Zikawei Sequel*)
2	*Yijing benzhi (huitang shishi cangben)* 易經本旨(堂石室藏本)	Prologue Volume 1 (*Qian* 乾 ䷀–*Meng* 蒙 ䷃)	Unknown	213000 94440B
3	*Yijing benzhi*易經本旨	Prologue Volume 1 (*Qian* 乾 ䷀–*Meng* 蒙 ䷃)	Unknown	213000 94931-94935B
4	*Yijing benzhi*易經本旨	Prologue Volume 1 (*Qian* 乾 ䷀–*Meng* 蒙 ䷃)	Unknown	213000 95644B
5	*Yijing benzhi*易經本旨	Prologue Volume 1 (*Qian* 乾 ䷀–*Meng* 蒙 ䷃)	Unknown	213000 94945B
6	*Yijing benzhi*易經本旨/ *Yijing lüzhu* 易經呂註	Volume 2 (*Xu*需 ䷄–*Yu* 豫 ䷏) Volume 3 (*Sui*隨 ䷐–*Da Guo* 大過 ䷛)	Unknown	213000 95679-95680B
		Volume 5 (*Sun*損 ䷨–*Cui*萃 ䷬)	Unknown	213000 95678B
7	*Yijing benzhi*易經本旨/ *Yijing lüzhu* 易經呂註	Volume 6 (*Jian* 漸 ䷴–*Wei Ji*未濟 ䷿)	Unknown	213000 95681B
8	*Yijing benzhi*易經本旨/ *Yijing lüzhu* 易經呂註	Volume 6 (*Jian* 漸 ䷴–*Wei Ji*未濟 ䷿)	Unknown	213000 95677B

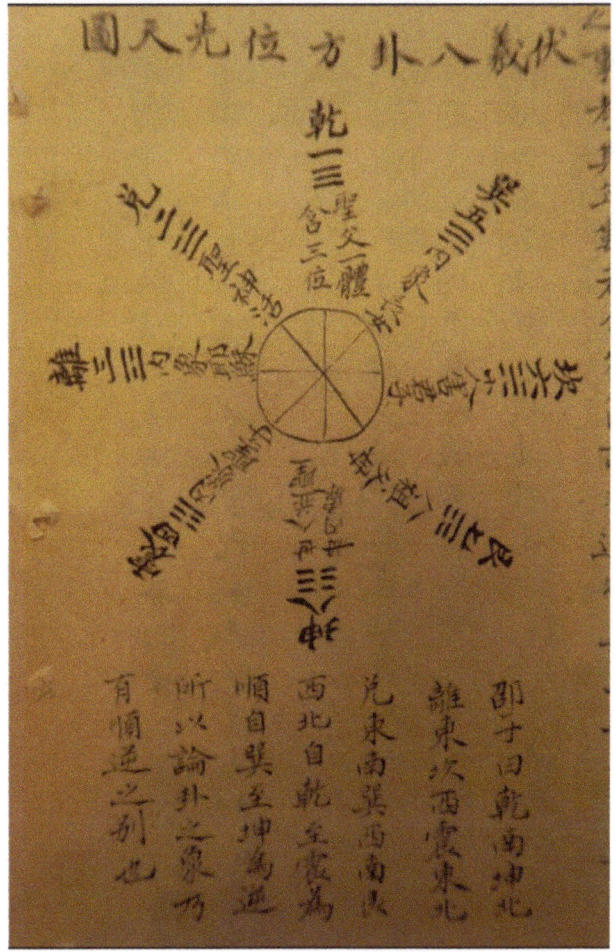

Figure A1. "Fuxi bagua fangwei xiantian tu伏羲八卦方位先天圖," from the prologue of *Yijing benzhi*.

References

Aleni, Giulio. 2002. Kouduo richao 口鐸日抄 [Diary of Oral Admonitions]. In *Yesuhui Luoma Dang'anguan Ming-Qing Tianzhujiao wenxian* 耶穌會羅馬檔案館明清天主教文獻 [Chinese Christian Texts from the Roman Archives of the Society of Jesus]. Edited by Nicolas Standaert and Adrian Dudink. Taipei: Taipei Ricci Institute.

Behr, John. 2006. *The Mystery of Christ: Life in Death*. Crestwood: St. Vladimir's Seminary Press.

Birdwhistell, Anne D. 1989. *Transition to Neo-Confucianism: Shao Yung on Knowledge and Symbols of Reality*. Stanford: Stanford University Press.

Catta, Etienne. 1961. Sedes Sapientiae. In *Maria: études sur la Sainte Vierge*. Edited by Hubert Du Manoir de Juaye. Paris: Beauchesne.

Chardon, Louis. 1957. *The Cross of Jesus*. Translated by Richard Murphy and Josefa Thornton. St. Louis: Herder.

Chen, Xinyu 陳欣雨. 2017. *Baijin Yixue sixiang yanjiu: Yi Fandigang tushuguan jiancun zhongwen Yixue shuju wei jichu* 白晉易學思想研究—以梵蒂岡圖書館見存中文易學數據為基礎 [A Study of Bouvet's Thought on the Yijing on the Basis of Relevant Materials in Chinese Collected in the Bibliotheca Apostolica Vaticana]. Beijing: Renmin chubanshe.

Cheng, Yi 程頤. 2011. *Zhouyi Cheng shi zhuan* 周易程氏傳 [Cheng's Commentary on the Zhouyi]. Collated by Wang Xiaoyu 王孝魚. Beijing: Zhonghua Book Company.

Cheng, Hao 程顥, and Yi Cheng 程頤. 2006. *Er Cheng ji* 二程集 [Collected Writings of the Two Chengs]. Beijing: Zhonghua Book Company.

Clark, Anthony E. 2011. *China's Saints: Catholic Martyrdom during the Qing (1644–1911)*. Bethlehem: Lehigh University Press.

Cullmann, Oscar. 1963. *The Christology of the New Testament*. Translated by Shirley C. Guthrie and Charles A. M. Hall. Philadelphia: The Westminster Press.

de Poirot, Louis 賀清泰. 2014. *Guxin shengjing cangao* 古新聖經殘稿 [An Incomplete Manuscript of Poirot's Chinese Bible]. Edited by Li Sher-shiueh 李奭學 and Zheng Haijuan 鄭海娟. Beijing: Zhonghua Book Company.

Durrwell, François-Xavier. 1969. *The Resurrection: A Biblical Study*. New York: Sheed and Ward.

Fang, Hao 方豪. 1943. Shiqiba shiji laihua xiren dui woguo jingji shi yanjiu 十七八世紀來華西人對我國經籍之研究 [The Foreigners' Study of Chinese Classics in the Seventeenth and Eighteenth Century]. *Shixiang yu shidai* 19: 185–202.

Glotin, Edouard. 1979. *Catechetical Value of a Symbolic Sign: The Wounded Heart of Jesus Christ*. Rome: International Institute of the Heart of Jesus.

Gu, Weimin 顧衛民. 2000. Zhongguo yu luoma jiaoting guanxi shi 中國與羅馬教廷關係史 [A History of the Relations between China and the See of Rome]. Beijing: Dongfang chubanshe.

Guardini, Romano. 1964. *The Humanity of Christ: Contributions to a Psychology of Jesus*. New York: Burns & Oates.

David Hinton, trans. 2015, *Tao Te Ching*. Berkeley: Counterpoint.

King James Bible. 1996. Cambridge: Chadwyck-Healey.

Lai, Zhide 來知德. 2013. *Zhouyi jizhu* 周易集註 [Collected Annotations on the Zhouyi]. Shanghai: Shanghai guji chubanshe.

Legge, James. 1861. The Doctrine of the Mean. In *The Chinese Classics*. Hong Kong: The Author.

James Legge, trans. 1963, *The I Ching, or Book of Changes*. New York: Dover Publications.

Li, Xueqin 李學勤, ed. 2000. Zhouyi zhengyi 周易正義 [The True Meaning of the Zhouyi]. In *Shisanjing zhushu zhengli ben* 十三經注疏 (整理本) [Commentaries and Subcommentaries on the Thirteen Confucian Classics (Collated Edition)]. Beijing: Peking University Press.

Li, Guangdi 李光地. 2002. *Zhouyi zhezhong* 周易折中 [Balanced Annotations on the Zhouyi]. Annotated by Li Yixin 李一忻. Beijing: Jiuzhou chubanshe.

Li, Dingzuo 李鼎祚. 2016. *Zhouyi jijie* 周易集解 [Collected Explanations on the Zhouyi]. Beijing: Zhonghua Book Company.

Liu, Anrong 劉安榮. 2017. Zhongguohua shiye xia Shanxi tianzhujiao shi yanjiu (1620–1949) 中國化視野下山西天主教史研究 (1620–1949) [The Study of the History of Shanxi Catholicism in the View of Sinolization (1620–1949)]. Beijing: Zongjiao wenhua chubanshe.

Lü, Liben 呂立本. 2013. Yijing benzhi 易經本旨 [Original Meaning of the Yijing]. In *Xujiahui cangshulou Ming Qing Tianzhujiao wenxian xubian* 徐家匯藏書樓明清天主教文獻續編 [The Sequel to the Chinese Christian Texts from the Zikawei Library]. Edited by Nicolas Standaert, Adrian Dudink and Wang Renfang. Taipei: Taipei Ricci Institute.

Lundbæk, Knud. 1991. *Joseph de Prémare (1666–1736), S. J.: Chinese Philology and Figurism*. Aarhus: Aarhus University Press.

Luo, Lida 羅麗達. 1997. Baijin yanjiu Yijing shishi jikao 白晉研究《易經》史事稽考 [Historical Examination of Bouvet's Yijing Studies]. *Sinology Research (Taiwan)* 15: 173–85.

Mangenot, Eugene. 1924. *Dictionnaire de théologie catholique*. Paris: Librairie Letouzey et Ané.

Mungello, David E. 1989. *Curious Land: Jesuit Accommodation and the Origins of Sinology*. Honolulu: University of Hawai'i Press. First published in 1985.

Pius-Raymond. 1954. *The Cross and the Christian*. Translated by Angeline Bouchard. St. Louis: Herder.

Ratzinger, Joseph. 1983. *Daughter Zion: Meditations on the Church's Marian Belief*. San Francisco: Ignatius Press.

Ricci, Giovanni. 1929. *Vicariatus Taiyuanfu: seu Brevis historia antiquae Franciscanae missionis Shansi a sua origine ad dies nostros (1700–1928)*. Pekini: Congregationis Missionis.

Richardson, Alan. 1958. *An Introduction to the Theology of the New Testament*. New York: Harper.

Rule, Paul A. 1986. *K'ung-tzu or Confucius? The Jesuit Interpretation of Confucianism*. Sydney, London, Boston: Allen & Unwin.

Sava, Anthony. F. 1954. The Wounds of Christ. *Catholic Biblical Quarterly* 16: 438–43.

Schottenhammer, Angela. 2007. *The East Asian Maritime World 1400–1800: Its Fabrics of Power and Dynamics of Exchanges*. Wiesbaden: Harrassowitz.

Song, Gang. 2018. The Many Faces of Our Lady: Chinese Encounters with the Virgin Mary between 7th and 17th century. *Monumenta Serica* 66: 341–4.

Standaert, Nicolas. 2001. *Handbook of Christianity in China, Volume One: 635-1800*. Leiden: E.J. Brill.

von Collani, Claudia. 1985. *P. Joachim Bouvet S. J. Sein Leben und sein Werk*. Nettetal: Steyler Verlag.

von Collani, Claudia. 2007. The First Encounter of the West with the *Yijing*: Introduction to and Edition of Letters and Latin Translations by French Jesuits from the 18th Century. *Monumenta Serica* 55: 227–387. [CrossRef]

Richard Wilhelm, trans. 1967, *The I Ching, or Book of Changes*. Translated from German by Cary Baynes. Princeton: Princeton University Press.

Witek, John W. 1982. *Controversial Ideas in China and in Europe: A Biography of Jean-François Foucquet, S.J., (1665–1741)*. Roma: Institutum Historicum S.I.

Xiao, Qinghe 肖清和. 2015. *Tianhiu yu wudang: Mingmo Qingchu Tianshujiaotu qunti yanjiu* 「天會」與「吾黨」：明末清初天主教徒群體研究 ["Tianhu" and "Wudang": A Study on Catholic Convert Groups in Late Ming and Early Qing]. Beijing: Zhonghua Book Company.

Zhang, Xiping 張西平. 1978. *Ouzhou zaoqi hanxueshi zhongxi wenhua jiaoliu yu xifang hanxue de xingqi* 歐洲早期漢學史—中西文化交流與西方漢學的興起 [A History of Early Sinology in Europe: Chinese-Western Cultural Exchange and the Rise of Western Sinology]. Beijing: Zhonghua Book Company.

Zhang, Xiping 張西平. 2005. *Yijing yanjiu: Kangxi he faguo chuanjiaoshi baijin de wenhua diuhua* 《易經》研究：康熙和法國傳教士白晉的文化對話 [The Study of Yijing: The Cultural Dialogue between the Kangxi Emperor and French Missionary Bouvet]. *Wenhua zazhi* 54: 83–93.

Zhang, Li 張力, and Jiantang Liu 劉鑒唐. 1987. *Zhongguo jiao'an shi* 中國教案史 [A History of China's Religious Court Cases]. Chengdu: Sichuan sheng shehui kexueyuan chubanshe.

Zhao, Peicheng 趙培成, Ruyang Wang 王如陽, and Yuanping Jin 晉原平. 1993. *Xinzhou diqu zongjiao zhi* 忻州地區宗教志 [Xinzhou District Religion Gazetteer]. Taiyuan: Shanxi renmin chubanshe.

Zhu, Xi 朱熹. 2018. *Zhouyi benyi* 周易本義 [Original Meaning of the Zhouyi]. Annotated by Su Yong. Beijing: Peking University Press, First published in 2009.

Article

Theology of Religions and Intertextuality: A Case Study of Christian–Confucian and Islamic–Confucian Dialogue in the Early 20th-Century China

Wai Luen Kwok

Department of Religion and Philosophy, Hong Kong Baptist University, Hong Kong; wlkwok@hkbu.edu.hk

Received: 29 May 2019; Accepted: 30 June 2019; Published: 3 July 2019

Abstract: In this paper, I will propose an intertextual theology of religions from a non-Western cultural perspective through the works in *The True Light* Review, an official magazine of Chinese Baptist churches, and *Yue Hua*, a prominent and long-lived Muslim magazine. My aim is to show that the religious discourses in these Chinese religious periodicals inform us of an alternative understanding of literary construction of religious plurality and challenge the current versions of theology of religions. With the concept of intertextuality, the differentiation and integration of religious identities indicates that language-constituted realities are multi-dimensional and multi-directional. In some respects, religious believers would like to differentiate themselves in the search for an authentic and meaningful life, but, they are nonetheless already interconnected and interrelated. In some other respects, they approach and embrace each other for integration to assert a common identity among religions in that area, but that could transform their religions with new meaning. Our case study will also further theological reflection of the nature of Christian life in predominantly non-Christian societies as an intertextual religious reality.

Keywords: theology of religions; intertextuality; postliberal theology; Chinese Christianity; Chinese Islam; Confucianism

---

1. Introduction

The aim of this paper is to show that the religious discourses in Chinese religious periodicals inform us of an understanding of the literary construction of religious plurality alternative to that of the missionaries. The analysis can help us to think afresh the relationship, interaction and blending between Christianity, Islam and Confucianism. Also, it will further theological reflection of the nature of Christian life in predominantly non-Christian societies as an intertextual religious reality. In the area of theology, I will focus primarily on the Christian discussion because an intensive Islamic theological discussion cannot be meaningfully undertaken within one article. However, this paper can show that both monotheistic religions in China share a similar construction which provides us with evidence for the assertion of an intertextual religious reality.

In the religious history of China, Confucianism has been the dominant ideology and religion of society (Yang 1961). In the imperial period, we can see many examples of religions attempting to show their affinity with Confucianism. Conversely, Confucian scholars, who were usually government officials, criticized religious teachings that did not converge with Confucianism as "evil doctrines" or "heterodoxies" (Liu and Shek 2004, pp. 6–7). One may wonder if the Sinicizing process of religions in China of that period was a product of power and coercion. The relationship between religions may have been likely to have been twisted by political authority.

However, in the Republican period (1911–1949), Confucianism lost its political dominance. Although there was a campaign to call for establishing Confucianism as the state religion between 1912 and 1916, it ultimately failed. Meanwhile, the advancement of modern Western science and technology in China made Confucianism an outmoded school of thought in the eyes of intellectuals (Gao 2007). However, Confucianism was still influential in the culture. Therefore, it is interesting to study how Christianity and Islam, which were considered to be "foreign" religions in China, approached Confucian teaching in this period. This will inform us how this important religion has been embraced, integrated and differentiated by monotheistic Christians and Muslims.

Religious periodicals will be the research materials of this study. Periodical literature reflects immediate responses of the contemporary religious sentiment of the groups. Also, articles are much shorter than monographs, which mean that the authors can only put the most important points and arguments in them. The spontaneity and brevity of the works has made them good subjects for observing the patterns of engagements of different religious norms and worldviews. I will use the works in *The True Light* Review, an official magazine of Chinese Baptist churches, and *Yue Hua*, a prominent and long-lived Muslim magazine to propose a theology of religions from a non-Western cultural perspective.

The True Light Review was a long-running Chinese-language Christian periodical in the early twentieth century. It was first published as *The True Light Monthly* in 1902 and edited by an American Baptist missionary, Robert E. Chambers. In 1911, the magazine had subscribers in China, the United States, Canada, South America, Europe, Australia, New Zealand, the Philippines, Hawaii, Japan, the East Indies, Burma, and South Africa (Mu Lu (Contents) 1911, p. 1). In 1917, its name was changed to *The True Light Review*. It has been considered as the 'ancestor' of Chinese Christian periodicals and one of the six most important Christian periodicals from 1914 to 1937 (Tang 1938a, p. 5; 1938b, p. 6). In 1926, the editorial office moved from Canton to Shanghai and in 1932, the magazine had enough financial resources to construct its own office building within the Shanghai International Settlement (Liao 1932). In 1936, the China Baptist Alliance passed a resolution to install *The True Light Review* as the official magazine of the China Baptist Church (Liu and Liang 1937, p. 66).

Yue Hua was founded by *ahongs* (from Persian *akoond*, equivalent to the Arabic *imam*), Hui literati, and local Hui leaders in October 1929 at Peiping. It served as a bulletin of the Chengda Normal School. The founders were Ma Fuxiang (a powerful Hui warlord and joined the Kuomintang in 1928), Tang Kesan (the principal of the Chengda Normal School), Sun Shengwu, Sun Youming, and Zhao Zhenwu (Ning Xia Shao Shu Min Zu Gu Ji Zheng Li Chu Ban Gui Hua Ling Dao Xiao Zu Ban Gong Shi 2010, p. 1). The Hui are an ethnic minority group in China with foreign ancestral origins that follows a form of Islam that is highly Sinicized in its language and cultural practice (Gladney 1991). In terms of Islamic theology, we can consider *Yue Hua* was influenced by the Islamic Modernism of Al-Azhar University in Egypt (Matsumoto 2006; Benite 2013). *Yue Hua* has been praised as a long-lasting Muslim periodical with a circulation of about 10,000 copies (Bai 1939; Wang 1939). Zhao Zhenwu wrote that the periodical had subscriptions from all over China, Southeast Asia, India, Middle East, Africa, Europe, and America (Zhao 1936, p. 25). The impact of *Yue Hua* was also noticed by overseas scholarship on Chinese Muslims (Matsumoto 2006, p. 118; Benite 2013, p. 253). The founding aims of the magazine were to: 1. Illustrate Islamic teachings that are relevant to modern trends; 2. Report the Muslim news around the world; 3. Promote the knowledge and status of Chinese Muslims; 4. Resolve the misunderstanding between the Old Sect and the New Sect; 5. Develop the national identity among Muslims in China; 6. Promote the education and livelihood of Muslims (Ben Kan Zong Zhi [The Aims of the Magazine] 1929). In this sense, the magazine bore a mission of building a national identity of the Republican China and promoting a religious revival among Chinese Muslims.

In Sections 2 and 3 of the paper, I will introduce the concept of intertextuality and how it can be related to the discussion of the theology of religions. From the Sections 4–7, I will unfold my analysis with the evidence of religious discourses in *Yue Hua* and *The True Light Review*. Finally, I will offer a theological remark on revising the theology of religions with a vision of intertextual reality.

2. Conceptualizing Intertextuality

As mentioned above, in this paper, I propose to understand our case study as an intertextual religious reality. It implies that we should understand text ontologically. According to John Frow, intertextuality means that,

> a culture is structured as a complex network of codes with heterogeneous and dispersed forms of textual realization ... In this sense the 'reality' both of the 'natural' and the social worlds is text-like in that it can be thought as a grid or a texture of significations, an intrication of heterogeneous materials. (Frow 1990, p. 47)

One can assert that the reality is a "grid of significations", because we find that, "Texts are made out of cultural and ideological norms; out of the conventions of genre; out of styles and idioms embedded in the language; out of connotations and collocative sets; out of clichés, formulae, or proverbs; and out of other texts" (Frow 1990, p. 45). In other words, applying the concept of intertextuality, I will study how the discourses in religious periodicals revealed the complexity of the structure of religious faith and the reality of Monotheistic Christians and Muslims in China.

One may be aware that understanding religion as a kind of textual or literary reality is walking along the path of postliberal theology. According to George Lindbeck, "A religion can be viewed as a kind of cultural and/or linguistic framework or medium that shapes the entirety of life and thought" (Lindbeck 1984, p. 33). "[R]eligions are thought of primarily as different idioms for constructing reality, expressing experience, and ordering life" (Lindbeck 1984, pp. 47–8). Through the case study, we will find that language does not only represent or express the beliefs of Chinese Christians and Muslims, but that the language, and its cultural/religious matrix, also regulates and formulates their reality. Although the postliberal theology can capture the main idea of a textual construction of reality, I have chosen to use intertextuality as the basis of my analysis and I will investigate whether postliberal theology should be revised to accommodate the fact of intertextual reality in the discussion of the theology of religions.

3. Theology of Religions: A Reflection on Current Thought

What is a Christian theology of religions? According to Veli-Metti Kärkkäinen,

> Theology of religions is that discipline of theological studies which attempts to account theologically for the meaning and value of other religions. Christian theology of religions attempts to think theologically about what it means for Christians to live with people of other faiths and about the relationship of Christianity to other religions. (Kärkkäinen 2003, p. 20)

He considers the "main question" of theology of religions to be "naturally, that of salvation: Is salvation to be found only in Christianity, and more specifically in the church" (Kärkkäinen 2003, p. 23)? In other words, theology of religions comes to the discussion because Christianity meets other religions and needs theological accounts to articulate the experience. In particular, its main discussion topic is whether other religions are salvific, an agenda which comes from a missionary concern. One can be aware that Kärkkäinen and his Catholic counterpart in the field of theology of religions, Paul Knitter, approaches the theology of religions in a similar way. Knitter suggests that a theology of religions is a discipline of "Christians trying to understand themselves and their faith in relation to their religious neighbors and their faiths" (Knitter 2002, p. 2).

Although he aims for a transformation in mainstream discussion, Gavin D'Costa still shares a similar missionary mindset. He states that the theology of religions comes to exist because,

> Christianity was born into a religiously pluralist world and has remained in one ever since. The mandate to go preach the gospel to the corners of the earth, as well as its own socioeconomic political position in society, has resulted in a complex range of relations and responses to other religions. (D'Costa 2005, p. 626)

In short, in the theology of religions of these theologians, Christians are considered as one group and other religious believers another. Thus, the theology of religions is mainly on inter-religious interaction, and the purpose of interaction is to discern whether other religions are salvific.

However, this approach shows that it is an outgrowth of missionary enterprise. It assumes that Christianity is fundamentally different from other religions and that when Christians interact with other religions, our main concern is whether their believers will be saved or converted. One may change the perspective from that of missionaries to that of native Christians in the missionary field. Native Christians need to engage with world religions theologically not because we want to have a mere dialogue or understanding of the other, but because the religions are already part of our *self*. For native people in the missionary field, they were living *in and as* other religion(s) before they became Christians or Christianized. The religions constitute their social and cultural life. More importantly, native Christians in the missionary fields *are still living* in cultures that are blended with religions of that part of the world. The task of theology of religions or an inter-religious dialogue is to make sense of this experience.

Even if we stick to a missionary approach to theology of religions, we will find that the religious reality of the native people presents a challenge. The challenge can be seen when one discusses the relationship between religion and culture. For example, though Harold Netland, an evangelical missiologist, emphasized that we should not reduce religion to culture; he admits that the line between religion and culture is complicated and "intertwined." Netland's words are worth quoting at length,

> Although religion and culture are closely interconnected, we must be careful not to reduce a religion to its particular cultural expression ... The connection between religion and culture has significant implications for missiology. A central concern of missiology is contextualization, which involves using forms or symbols that are sufficiently familiar to a particular culture and that adequately convey biblical meanings in an effort to maximize understanding and acceptance of the gospel within that culture. Since culture and religion are often so intertwined, serious consideration of contextualization inevitably leads to questions about the relation of Christian faith to indigenous religious beliefs and practices, affecting everything from translation of the Scriptures to how Christians should regard local customs. The line between cultural and religious issues can be imprecise. (Netland 2001, p. 329)

Lesslie Newbigin, a missionary and theologian active in the discussion of religious pluralism, straightforwardly pointed out the division of religion and life is artificial: "In most human cultures religion is not a separate activity set apart from the rest of life" (Newbigin 1989, kindle loc. 3226). He also frankly criticized the assumption that the only question of theology of religions is, "What happens to the non-Christian after death" (Newbigin 1989, kindle loc. 3315)? He wisely told us that, "Wherever the gospel is preached it is preached in a human language, which means the language of one particular culture; wherever a community tries to live out the gospel, it is also part of one particular human culture" (Newbigin 1989, kindle loc. 3546). However, it is very perplexing that although he recognized the cultural matrix that Christians in the missionary field are living in and with, his suggestion for Christians' dialogue and social life with other religious believers neglects this important reality and goes back to a mode of self-centered monologue. He proposed that an exchange, interaction and dialogues with other religious believers "will be initiated by our partners, not by ourselves" (Newbigin 1989, kindle loc. 3407), and that Christian dialog "will simply be the telling of the story, the story of Jesus, the story of the Bible. The story is itself, as Paul says, the power of God for salvation" (Newbigin 1989, p. 3417). He conceived that the first group of Christian converts in the missionary fields are those "radicals" that "question" their traditions (Newbigin 1989, p. 3551). From missionary history in China, we can find that Newbigin's assertion cannot be valid. For example, when Matteo Ricci (1552–1610) and other Jesuits came to China, they were evangelizing Confucian scholars that were dedicated members of Chinese society and culture. Theologizing the meaning of Confucianism for Christians in the late Ming dynasty was not a passive task. The effort of

Jesuit missionaries and native Christians of that time was certainly not merely "telling of the story of Jesus" (Hsia 2012).

Newbigin's analysis of religion and culture clearly showed that a contextual faith is one that is embedded within a cultural-religious matrix. However, one should recognize that theology of religions is not a theological discussion of *others*. It should address and articulate the complexity of the construction of our *selfhood*. At this point, Raimon Panikkar has valuable insight for an ontological reflection:

> We are conscious of things (the "external" world), and at the same time conscious that this light of consciousness is within and without ourselves ... We have to obey not only the external things but also the structure of our own thinking, which has been given to us. Our very consciousness is a given, a gift. Nevertheless, the fact that we are the bearers of that consciousness makes all the difference with regard to everything else. Human life is not just what we detect with our experiments. It is the "we" which is alive, which makes the experiments and endures the experiences. (Panikkar 2013, kindle loc. 7391–7396)

From the complexity and interconnectedness of our conscious life, Panikkar further suggests that "the very constitution of the real" is a "solidarity of all beings" (Panikkar 2013, kindle loc. 7457). In this light, theology of religions from a native Christian perspective is a description of the wholeness of our reality. However, I should point out that Panikkar's assertation of "solidarity" neglects the complexity of the interconnectedness. In many examples, religions and our life experience are not in unity, but rather, in conflict though interconnected. Panikkar's position may be in danger of removing the complexity and becoming a self-harmonized projection. Our religious reality is an intertextuality rather than a unified text.

If Christian theology of religions should be an articulation of one's real experience of religious complexity, the usual categories of "exclusivism," "inclusivism," and "pluralism" are not very helpful for the task. These words can only refer to the discussion of salvation and divine reality in the relation between Christianity and other religions. Or, they may only account for the self-identity of Christians in a non-Christian society and cannot explicate how and why local Christians engage, embrace and integrate or reject particular aspects of other religious traditions in their Christian life theologically. I hope that my analysis can chart out how practices and articulations reflect a self-understanding of multi-religious embedded life of Chinese Christians and Muslims. Also, I hope that I can offer a tentative proposal of theology of religions for further reflection.

If religious reality is governed and operated by discourse, it seems that postliberal theology is the most suitable candidate for a renewed theology of religions. However, George Lindbeck suggested that different religions and philosophies are incommensurable (Lindbeck 1984, p. 49). He believed that if we attempt to use a given religious framework to introduce ideas from other religions or philosophies, the discourse is reduced to "simply babbling" (Lindbeck 1984, p. 49). Knitter read Lindbeck's notion of incommensurability as establishing a hard boundary between religions. According to Knitter,

> To describe just how Lindbeck and the Acceptance Model look at proper relations between religions, we can use the image of "a good neighbor policy." But to do that, each of them needs to recognize that, indeed, "good fences make good neighbors." Each religion has its own backyard. There is no "commons" that all of them share. (Knitter 2002, p. 183)

In our case study, we will find that the conception of religions as self-contained and incommensurable ghettoes is not accurate. If language constitutes our reality, and religions are textual reality, then the experience of Chinese Christians and Muslims indicates that they do not live in cultural-linguistic ghettoes. Rather, their linguistic realities embed and intersect with other religions and form a complex life-world. Our case study shows that Lindbeck's understanding of religion as cultural-linguistic reality is too neatly linear and one-dimensional. Likewise, using the theological concept of the Divine common grace to explain this phenomenon will also be too simplistic.

Our theological reflection will be much more fruitful if we can illustrate and explicate the patterns, rationales, and implications of such cultural-linguistic reality theologically and furthermore, the concept of intertextuality can help us to capture the logic of the phenomenon. In the following sections, I will attempt to show how inter-religious discourses of Chinese Muslims and Christians can operate in this logic.

4. The Tension between Foreign Religions and Confucianism and Self-Identity

When we talk about Christian–Confucian and Muslim–Confucian dialogue, we quickly become very aware that Islam and Christianity were experiencing tensions with Confucianism in the period of Republican China. From Christian and Muslim perspectives, Confucianism discriminates against other religions. Zhang Wenkai (alias Yijing), the editor of *The True Light Review* from 1905 to 1931, complained that "when the discussion of installing Confucianism as the national religion began in the last year [i.e., 1913], there were incidents of using Confucianism to persecute Christianity in different provinces" (Zhang 1921, p. 48).[1]

Jin Jitang (alias Qishu), a renowned Chinese Muslim scholar, cited Confucian *Shiji* (*The Book of Poetry*) and *Analects* to show that Confucianism has a long tradition of antiforeignism and self-centrism. He quoted that, "In *Shiji* (*The Book of Poetry*), [it stated], 'To deal with the tribes of the west and north, and to punish [those of] Jing and Shu.' Confucius said, 'The rude tribes of the east and north have their princes, and are not like the States of our great land which are without them.'" Even the Chinese words rendered for unreasonable and irritating speech and acts are "*Hu Shuo*" (words of northern barbarians) and "*Man Bu Jiang Li*" (unreasonable as southern barbarians) (Jin 1935, p. 10).

The tension arose from a fear of minority religious identities being entirely assimilated into Confucianism. Jin criticized Chinese Muslim attempts at "interpreting Islam through Confucianism" in the Qing Dynasty for having a very bad impact on the Chinese Muslim community. It made Islam "flattering" (*e fu*) to Confucianism so that Muslim and ordinary Chinese became nearly indistinguishable with one another (Jin 1935, p. 10). Another author asserted that because Confucianism was under the patronage of the emperors, no religion in conflict with it could exist in China. As a result of this, "our [Muslim] scholars always relate Confucianism and Islam with far-fetched analogies" (Wang 1931, p. 8). In *The True Light Review*, a Chinese pastor and later a leader of Chinese Baptist Church, Princeton S. Hsu, described the Chinese religious culture as a "Salt Sea" that can dissolve everything within it. Confucian scholars in the imperial period absorbed every other religion into Confucianism and became a religious syncretism (Hsu 1932, p. 22). He warned that Christianity should not change its nature in order to adapt to Chinese culture (Hsu 1932, p. 32).

Chinese Christians and Muslims rejected Confucianism also because they found it ethically, socially and spiritually incompetent. In the Republican period, Christianity enjoyed a privileged position for the presence of western scientific power in China. One author in *The True Light Review* simply called for replacing Confucianism with Christianity because Confucianism was backward and unscientific (Yu 1934). A second author rejected Confucianism because it allied itself with monarchical authoritarianism and a philosophy of social hierarchy. Confucianism was considered to be inappropriate for a modern society. Conversely, he argued, Christianity could meet the needs of modern society for it promoted a democratic society with values of equality, freedom, love, sacrifice and industriousness (Ji 1928, p. 57). Zhang Wenkai criticized the Chinese superstition veneration of idols as coming from Confucianism (Zhang 1921, p. 29). Islam in China by that time was in a weak social and political position, but nonetheless, from the Chinese Muslim point of view, Confucianism was "incomplete. It can only be a part of the philosophy of life. It cannot support the whole life" (Wang 1931, p. 11). Another author claimed that, "All crimes in the world are caused by individualism. Individualism is an idea of I ... Confucianism dunked too deep in the idea of I ... Confucianism is merely an individualism"

---

[1] The book is a collection of articles that Zhang Wenkai has published in *The True Light Review*.

(Ding 1931, p. 9). Arguments that Islam or Christianity are the only way of salvation usually follow. Zhang Wenkai advised that Confucius is only a lamp and Christ a sun. If we reject the light of the sun and remain under the lamp, our life will be as illusory and hopeless as opium addiction (Zhang 1921, p. 75). Ding Zhengxi commented that Confucianism is individualist and Moism is collectivist. Islam is superior to either for it addresses the dimensions of both the individual and the community, leading individuals and communities back to Allah (Ding 1931, p. 9).

I would call the tension described in this section as an action of language differentiation. We may find that the segregation and conflict between religious communities entails a differentiation in religious discourses. Interestingly, this differentiation exists exactly because the communities are living together, interacting with each other, and searching for a better life and society. Muslims and Christians continue to follow their religions because they believe that their faith gives them a better life, which excels among their Confucian fellow Chinese. Because they dwell within a common lifeworld, they search for the good but come to be aware of their differences. In this sense, a theology of religions begins with a desire for a common good life with an awareness of different claims about that life. Differentiation is a description of the resources of my religion and the limitations of other religions for achieving that goal. Theologically speaking, we can find that the exclusivist position in the theology of religions accounts for the inadequacy of good in other religions to the absence of sole salvation of God in them. For Christianity, it is the salvation of Jesus Christ as the Son of God. For Islam, it is *tawhid*, the acknowledgement that *Allah* alone is God and that all worship, service and obedience are due unto Him alone (Al-Faruqi 1998, p. 79). Both *The True Light Review* and *Yue Hua* are in this "exclusive" mode of thought, but one should note that the logic of exclusivism is a comparison of good and a claim to own the supreme and irreplaceable good.

5. Studying the 'Learning/Scholarship of the Nation' (*Guo Xue*) or the 'National Heritage' (*Guo Gu*) and Theology of Religions

However, in the midst of tension and "exclusivism", we can find that Chinese Christians and Muslims cannot merely treat Confucianism as the other. Confucianism is an inescapable reality within the life of Chinese Christians and Muslims. In *Yue Hua*, Jin Jitang argued that Chinese Muslims should learn *Guo Gu* (national heritage) for it is the essence of Chinese civilization, which "nationals have a duty to learn it" (Jin 1935, p. 9). Jin cited a Confucian idiom, "texts is supposed to carry the way [truth]" (*Wen Yi Zai Dao*),[2] and advised that Muslims need good classical knowledge and literary skills to articulate Islamic doctrines:

> If there are persons, who do not only understand the theory and teaching of the [Islamic] religion ... but are also deeply immersed in Chinese literature, can in the greatest extent publish and promote the teaching of the sacred texts in Chinese; one can anticipate the day that the doubts of outsiders will be relieved, the ignorance of fellow believers will be removed, and the true religion will be revived. (Jin 1935, p. 10)

Chinese traditions in the past, obviously including Confucianism, signified by text can embody Islamic messages—they can carry the *Dao*. Language, and thus the text, is a powerful tool for presenting Islam as a reality in China. Also, *Guo Gu* can inform the Chinese Muslim community about their historical development. The historical past is not only a piece of information, but also a reality directly related to Muslims. Jin wrote that, "In summary, our people were born here, were clothed here, live on the land and eat what it produces. The milieu here really has a direct relationship with our people ... The national heritage (*Gao Gu*) is the essence of all times and of above and below." Jin believed that the national heritage has formed the belief and practice of Hui Muslims. Muslims should perceive the changes in the modern Chinese society through understanding the lives of Muslims in the past. It helps

---

2   The idiom comes from Song Dynasty Neo-Confucian scholar Zhou Dunyi's (1017–1073) book, *Tong Shu* (*The Gist of Confucian Thought*).

to form a more effective Muslim life mode in the present time (Jin 1935, p. 10). Ma Songting, one of the founders of *Yue Hua*, explicitly used an analogy of a body's life to explicate the point. He stated that, "Our people have settled in China for a thousand and hundreds of years. We are mostly common in language and habits with others. Thus, our people should drink from this spring for behavioral principles that are appropriate for our people living in the present time" (Ma and Zhao 1934, p. 20).

For Christians, we can also find this embodiment of Confucianism. In the 25th anniversary issue of *The True Light Review*, Zhang Wenkai requested Fan Bihui, the editor of the *Association Progress* of the Young Men's Christian Association, to write "Scholarship of the nation in two thousand five hundred years" as the first article of the issue. Fan argued that Confucius was the master establishing the learning of the nation and had the most influence on thought throughout Chinese history. Confucius's main contribution was to establish the canon (*Jin*) of Chinese civilization. He asserted that "No scholarship of the later time can escape from the scope of the classical study" (Fan 1927, pp. 3–4).

In *The True Light Review*, T. C. Chao (Zhao Zichen), a famous Christian theologian at Yenching University, wrote that Chinese Christianity cannot secure a foothold in China unless it becomes indigenized. He clearly expressed that indigenized Christianity is an embodied representation of Chinese religion and culture. According to Chao, a Chinese "indigenous church" is a creation of Chinese Christians. He explained that,

> Our creating method is to digest and then write. [It] makes the Chinese and the Western cultures in our blood and consciousness become forms of expression of Chinese Christian life. Sophisticated doctrines, music, architecture, and rituals are signs of self-expression of religious life. Theory that can be understood by itself is science. Theory, that is immanent within theory and at the same time transcends theory, and that nearly becomes metaphor and conveys its elusive mystery, is religion. Religion does not make us radiant from without. It expresses from within. (Chao 1927, p. 9)

Although religious communities would like to differentiate themselves from others, relatively recently introduced religions cannot avoid inheriting qualities of their older counterparts. In this respect, language is not only a tool for differentiation and self-identity, but also constitutes a space for interaction and communal life. Under this light, theology of religions in its primary operational level is not inter-religious dialogue; instead it is the reality of the language-events of different religions taking place. We need to chart out how different religions occupy the common place, interpret human life and how the newer religions take on qualities of their context. In particular, this means what idioms, story, ideas, and religious beliefs are employed and shared by believers of different religions in the same region should be investigated.

6. Paralleling and Transposing Confucian Texts and Theology of Religions

In our case of *Yue Hua* and *The True Light Review*, we will find that at a deeper level, the reality of inheritance points to an integration between Confucianism and Islam/Christianity. The integration is accomplished by transposing Confucian words and concepts in religious discourses, or at least by placing them in parallel. The parallelization and transposition present an immediate interconnectedness between the religions.

In the front-page article of the first issue of *Yue Hua*, Imam Wang Meng Yang pointed out that Islam and Confucianism could "collaborate" with each other, for Confucianism teaches benevolence/love (*Ren*) and righteousness (*Yi*), and Islam the most mercifulness of Allah (Meng 1929). Imam Ding Zhanbin taught that Confucian 'five constant virtues'—benevolence/love (*Ren*), righteousness (*Yi*), propriety (*Li*), wisdom (*Zhi*), fidelity (*Xin*) can be understood as the five pillars of Islam. For example, *Ren* is the testimony of faith. Because Allah created human beings and shows his mercy to Muslims, the true love or *Ren* for Muslims is to bear the testimony of faith in every moment (Ding 1935).

In another piece of work, the author praised Confucianism for its very insightful teaching on love. He then put the Confucian and Islamic teachings in parallel and implied that they are in harmony with each other. He wrote that,

> The totality of human life is the venerate [ion of] (Jing) [heaven] and love (Ai). For example, we perform the eight great works [in The Book of Great Learning]: extend our knowledge, investigate things, [are] sincere [in] our thoughts, rectify our hearts, cultivate our persons, regulate our families, govern the state rightly, and make the whole kingdom tranquil and happy. Or, [we uphold] the five pillars: testimony, prayer, giving, fasting, and pilgrimage. [We uphold] the five cardinal virtues of relationships, which are kindness, filiality, friendship, humility, gentleness and faithfulness ... They are helping us to know how to live as a person, handle the things, and serve heaven for achieving veneration and love. Therefore, Allah teaches us veneration and love, and sowed the spirit of love within humanity. (Zhang 1934, p. 21)

We can find similar practice in *The True Light Review*. For example, in an article, "Only love can move people," the author used an idiom aligned to Confucius' saying in *Analects*, "sacrifice life for fulfilling benevolence/love" to describe Jesus Christ's salvation work (Deng 1912). We can also find the strategy of paralleling the texts in the magazine. Zhang Wenkai, wrote that,

> The problem of people is that they do not turn round upon themselves. Mencius said, "That whereby the gentleman (Jun Zi) is distinguished from other men is what he preserves in his heart—namely, benevolence/love and propriety. The benevolent man loves others. The man of propriety shows respect to others. He who loves others is constantly loved by them. He who respects others is constantly respected by them. Here is a man, who treats me in a perverse and unreasonable manner. The gentleman in such a case will turn round upon himself, 'I must have been wanting in benevolence/love; I must have been wanting in propriety—how should this have happened to me?' He examines himself, and is especially benevolent. He turns round upon himself, and is specially observant of propriety. The perversity and unreasonableness of the other, however, are still the same. The gentleman will again turn round on himself, 'I must have been failing to do my utmost.' He turns round upon himself, and proceeds to do his utmost, but still the perversity and unreasonableness of the other are repeated. On this the gentleman says, 'This is a man utterly lost indeed! Since he conducts himself so, what is there to choose between him and a brute? Why should I go to contend with a brute?'" ... "Do not hate the enemy". "Do not let the sun go down on your wrath". "Forgive people until seventy times seven". "Love others as yourself". "Whatever you desire for men to do to you, you shall also do to them". "First remove the beam out of your own eye, and then you can see clearly to remove the speck out of your brother's eye". All these are ultimate works of turning round upon oneself. (Zhang 1924, p. 90)

Zhang interpreted Christian doctrines of interpersonal relationship as "ultimate works" of the Confucian "turning round upon oneself." In other words, Christians live according to a Confucian concept, which is at the same time ultimately Christian. From Zhang's alignment of Confucian with Christian teaching, we can expect that Zhang holds Confucianism in high regard. He asserts that Christians should learn Confucianism and venerate Confucius in the manner of Confucians (Zhang 1925, p. 81).

One may think that what we have seen above is similar with Knitter's "fulfilment model": "They believe that other religions are of value, that God is to be found in them, that Christians need to dialogue with them and not just preach to them" (Knitter 2002, p. 63). However, the fulfilment model is different from my analysis on the point of the direction of dialogue. The fulfilment model's direction of dialogue is mainly towards the religious other. However, my analysis shows that it is also an exploration and a realization of the self. With the strategy of transposing and paralleling, Chinese Muslims and

Christians are creating new integration of Confucianism and their own religions. Language facilitate a practice of "mutual participation." Transposing and paralleling creates an interface that allows the meaning of the original cultural or religious languages to arrive at a new convergence.

7. Translating Western/Arabian Works into Chinese and Theology of Religions

Finally, the integration and mutual participation can reflex back to the original religious tradition. From *Yue Hua* and *The True Light Review*, one can find that the magazines published many articles that were originally written in Arabic or English. More importantly, these works are usually on doctrinal expositions. In this sense, one may argue that the language does not only function as a way to cross over traditions and create openness, it also acts as the connection between religious communities and their original religious tradition. For example, in *Yue Hua*, Li Tingbi translated an article on the interpretation of *Quran* from the Indian Muslim magazine, *The Light*.[3] The article recommended that Muslims should use a scientific mindset to study the *Quran* (Li 1931, p. 5). In the translation postscripts, Li encouraged Hui Muslims to gain education for themselves and criticized them for preventing girls and women from receiving education, asserting that the practice is un-Islamic but Chinese (Li 1931, p. 6). In *The True Light Review*, Chen Haosheng translated some sections of an English book titled, *Pungent Paragraphs*. Interestingly, he titled his column as "*Yu Dao Xiao Pin* (Homiletical Illustrations)". He believed that the translation can help preachers to acquire good public speech skills and use illustrations that are relevant to Chinese social life (Chen 1928, pp. 69–70).

Moreover, in translated language, a text is already something new to the original religious tradition. It creates a new experience between the religious communities and original religious tradition. Arabic is always considered to be irreplaceable and sacred in Islam, but *Yue Hua* translated passages of the *Quran* and gave detailed commentary on them. For example, in *Yue Hua*, Ma (1932) cited a poem of Li Bai (701–762, a famous Chinese poet in Tang Dynasty), *Chun Ye Yan Tao Li Yuan Xu* (*Preface to the Feast in Peach and Plum Garden on a Spring Night*) to comment on Surah *Al-Mulk* (67:2), "[He] who created death and life to test you [as to] which of you is best in deed—and He is the Exalted in Might, the Forgiving." Ma cited the following lines of the poem (Ma 1932, pp. 1–2):

> The universe is a temporary inn for all living things. Time is the transit visitors over the span of one hundred generations. This drifting life is like a dream. There is too little time to enjoy the pleasure of living. Thus, it was quite appropriate for ancient people to, with candlelight in hand, roam at night. (translated by Edward C. Chang)

Ma's application of a classical Chinese poem as a part of commentary of the *Quran* made his interpretation very different from Arabic commentaries available for Muslims. Although the Christian *Bible* has already been translated, *The True Light Review* frequently translated hymns and religious poems. In these translated works, we can find similar applications of Chinese classical idioms and literary phrases. An author with the *nom de plume*, Zhi Bai (direct and easy to understand), translated a poem "*Ni Le Ye Mo?* (Are you willing?)". In one of the verses, he used a Chinese idiom, "*Sui Yu Er An*" (be at ease with one's current situation) for his translation (Bai 1937, p. 51). The move also indicated that the translation added new sensibility to the original.

More strikingly, the translation process is able to have an impact on the original tradition and urge readers to be open to a wider understanding of other religious realities. Lian Xi's work, *The conversion of missionaries: liberalism in American Protestant missions in China, 1907–1932*, showed how this influence in turn changed the missionaries' understanding of Chinese culture and religions (Lian 1997). Also, in Islam, Ma Jin's (alias Muhammad Makin) Arabic translation of Confucius's *Analects* aroused a great deal of interest in Chinese culture among Egyptian Muslim scholars (Benite 2013). I would

---

[3] *The Light* is an English magazine of *Ahmadiyya*, an Indian Islamic revival movement in the early 20th century.

call it a language-event of bringing back and consider it to have created a new tension and possibility for openness.

8. Concluding Remarks and Tentative Theological Proposal

In the process of articulating a religious self-identity and relation with Confucianism, we can find that language constitutes reality for Chinese Christians and Muslims. More strikingly, Islam and Christianity are working in a similar manner. In this light, the theology of religions should not operate in the mode of missionary encounter. Rather, it should describe how our religious discourse formulates and negotiates our religious identity, how it enables our distinctiveness, creates new common experience, and creates possibilities for changes in the religious communities.

Yue Hua and *The True Light Review* showed that Chinese Muslims and Christians do not live within one religious-linguistic reality. Their life is constituted by multi-linguistic realities and this is where intertextuality happens. As Julia Kristeva put it, "any text is constructed as a mosaic of quotations; any text is the absorption and transformation of another" (Kristeva 1980, p. 66). The differentiation and integration of religious identities indicated that language constituted realities are multi-dimensional and multi-directional. In some respects, religious believers would like to differentiate themselves, because they searching for an authentically meaningful life according to their teaching. But, we find as a given that at the same time they are already interconnected and interrelated. In some other respects, they approach and embrace each other for integration, because they are asserting a common reality among religions in that area—but it will also transform religions with new meaning. It is the intertextuality that constitutes the religious believers' selfhood. Putting back this finding to a discussion of the Christian theology of religions, Robert Jenson wisely pointed out that language links us with the past, the present, and the future:

> What I mean is this: the language in which you say to me "Good morning" comes to us both from the past; the conventions that make words of these sounds were already set before you spoke, otherwise you could not have spoken. Yet the utterance of these words is the breaking into my life of someone other than me, and that means of something new and different from me. I am challenged to see what I was not seeing, to take up new tasks and expectations; utterance opens the future. (Jenson 1995, p. 2)

Here, a theology of religions is not a public relations nor a preaching task. It reminds us of the ontological nature of the church, Christians, and the whole world as beings called into existence by the Word of God. This leads us depart from the debate of exclusivism, inclusivism, and pluralism. Also, Lindbeck's postliberal theology is inadequate in describing the interconnectedness of the language. When Christians integrate words, concepts, and expressions of their own religious culture with their present Christian life, we should study carefully how, where and why the convergence happened. In the past, theologians used syncretism to describe the phenomenon, but as our case study shows, the native religious believers intentionally blended the religions in particular areas while at the same time maintaining their own religious identity. They did not consider themselves to be syncretizing their religion, but offering instead differentiated and faithful religious discourses. It is a general phenomenon across Islam and Christianity, two monotheistic religions, that they emphasize special revelation. Our case shows that a revised theology of religions should articulate a doctrine of creation and Christian life that can encompass the religious others. In Colossians 3:11, Paul reminded us that "Christ is all, and in all." Then, he taught that Christ can dwell in our teaching, psalms, hymns, and spiritual songs, which we can counsel one another (3:16). Paul Fiddes reminds us that if we realize the whole world is a complex system of signs and if text is always a kind of extension of our body; we should be convinced that "the whole world of a text . . . the space in which we find ourselves addressed, where we can hear the Word of God and see as God sees" (Fiddes 2013, p. 342). Christian belief thus does not "exclude the presence of God in the world through all bodies" (Fiddes 2013, p. 345). The task for theologians committed to theology of religions is that how we discern Christ in every moment of the Christian life and our life with others, which is already intertextual and multi-linguistic. In this sense, the theology of religions will go beyond a discussion of the salvific power of other religions and start to investigate "the same [trinitarian] pattern in all other bodily life" (Fiddes 2013, p. 345).

Funding: This research is funded by The General Research Fund of the Research Grant Council of Hong Kong Special Administrative Region Government, grant number 12403714.

Conflicts of Interest: The author declares no conflict of interest.

References

Al-Faruqi, Isma'il R. 1998. *Islam and Other Faiths*. Leicester: The Islamic Foundation and the International Institute for Islamic Thought.

Bai, Zhi. 1937. Ni Le Ye Mo (Are you willing)? *The True Light Review* 36: 51.

Bai, Zhongqi. 1939. Yue Hua Bao Shi Zhou Ji Nian Gan Yan (A Tribute to the 10 Anniversary of Yue Hua). *Yue Hua* 11: 17.

Ben Kan Zong Zhi [The Aims of the Magazine]. 1929. *Yue Hua* 1: 1.

Benite, Zvi Ben-Dor. 2013. Taking Abduh to China: Chinese-Egyptian Intellectual Contact in the Early Twentieth Century. In *Global Muslims in the Age of Steam and Print*. Edited by James L. Gelvin and Nile Green. Berkeley: University of California Press, pp. 249–68.

Chao, Tzu Chen. 1927. Wo Dui Yu Chuang Zao Zhong Guo Ji Du Jiao Hui De Ji Ge Yi Jian (My Suggestions for Creating Chinese Christian Church). *The True Light Review* 26: 1–13.

Chen, Haosheng. 1928. Yu Dao Xiao Pin (Homiletical Illustrations). *The True Light Review* 27: 69–70.

D'Costa, Gavin. 2005. Theology of Religions. In *The Modern Theologians: An Introduction to Christian Theology Since 1918*, 3rd ed. Edited by David Ford and Rachel Muers. Oxford: Blackwell Publishing, pp. 626–44.

Deng, Diesheng. 1912. Wei Ai Neng Gan Ren Lun (Only Love Can Move People). *The True Light Review* 10: 21–4.

Ding, Zhengxi. 1931. Hui Jiao Yu Zhong Guo Ru Mo Zhi Bi Jiao Guan (A Comparison of Islam, Confucianism and Moism). *Yue Hua* 3: 6–10.

Ding, Zhanbin. 1935. Zong Jiao Shang De San Gang Wu Chang (The Three Cardinal Guides and Five Constant Virtues in the Religion). *Yue Hua* 7: 590–92.

Fan, Bihui. 1927. Er Qian Wu Bai Nian Lai Zhi Guo Xue (Scholarship of the Nation in Two Thousand Five Hundred Years). *The True Light Review* 26: 1–29.

Fiddes, Paul S. 2013. *Seeing the World and Knowing God: Hebrew Wisdom and Christian Doctrine in a Late-Modern Context*. Oxford: Oxford University Press.

Frow, John. 1990. Intertextuality and Ontology. In *Intertexuality: Theories and Practice*. Edited by Judith Still and Michael Worton. Manchester: Manchester University Press, pp. 45–55.

Gao, Mingshi, ed. 2007. *Zhong Guo Wen Hua Shi (Chinese Cultural History)*. Taipei: Wu-Nan Book.

Gladney, Dru C. 1991. *Muslim Chinese: Ethnic Nationalism in the People's Republic*. Harvard East Asian Monographs 149. Cambridge: Harvard University Press.

Hsia, R. Po-chia. 2012. *A Jesuit in the Forbidden City: Matteo Ricci 1552–1610*. Oxford: Oxford University Press.

Hsu, Princeton S. 1932. Zhong Guo Zong Jian Zhi Mi (The Mystery of Chinese Religion). *The True Light Review* 31: 20–34.

Jenson, Robert W. 1995. *Essays in Theology of Culture*. Grand Rapids: Eerdmans.

Ji, Ping. 1928. Ye Ru Zhi Yan Jiu. In *A Quarter of a Century of True Light, Selected*. Edited by Yijing Zhang. Shanghai: China Baptist Publication Society.

Jin, Jitang. 1935. Zhong Guo Hui Jiao Li Shi Wen Ti (The Historical Question of Chinese Islam). *Yue Hua* 7: 9–12.

Jin, Qishu. 1935. Yan Jiu Guo Gu Yu Hui Jiao (Study National Heritage and Islam). *Yue Hua* 7: 9–10.

Kärkkäinen, Veli-Matti. 2003. *An Introduction to the Theology of Religions: Biblical, Historical, and Contemporary Perspectives*. Downers Grove: IVP Academic.

Knitter, Paul F. 2002. *Introducing Theologies of Religions*. Maryknoll: Orbis Books.

Kristeva, Julia. 1980. *Desire in Language: A Semiotic Approach to Literature and Art*. New York: Columbia University Press.

Li, Tingbi. 1931. Gu Lan Jing De Jie Shi (The Interpretation of *Quran*). *Yue Hua* 3: 3–6.

Lian, Xi. 1997. *The Conversion of Missionaries: Liberalism in American Protestant Missions in China, 1907–1932*. University Park: Pennsylvania State University Press.

Liao, Yunxiang. 1932. Juan Tou Yu (Forewords). *The True Light Review* 31. n.p.

Lindbeck, George A. 1984. *The Nature of Doctrine: Religion and Theology in a Postliberal Age*. Philadelphia: Westminster Press.

Liu, Zhanen, and Gen Liang. 1937. Zhong Hua Jin Hui Quan Guo Lian He Hui Qi Shi (A Notice of China Baptist Alliance). *The True Light Review* 36: 65–7.

Liu, Kwang-Ching, and Richard Shek. 2004. Introduction. In *Heterodoxy in Late Imperial China*. Edited by Kwang-Ching Liu and Richard Shek. Honolulu: University of Hawai'i Press, pp. 1–28.

Ma, Yugui. 1932. Qu Lan Yi Jie (Translation and Interpretation of *Quran*). *Yue Hua* 4: 1–5.

Ma, Songting, and Zhenwu Zhao. 1934. Wu Nian Lai De Yue Hua Bao (Five Years of Yue Hua Journal). *Yue Hua* 6: 15–25.

Matsumoto, Masumi. 2006. Rationalizing Patriotism among Muslim Chinese: The Impact of the Middle East on the Yuehua Journal. In *Intellectuals in the Modern Islamic World: Transmission, Transformation, Communication*. Edited by Stéphane A. Dudoignon, Hisao Komatsu and Yasushi Kosugi. New Horizons in Islamic Studies. London and New York: Routledge, pp. 117–42.

Mu Lu (Contents). 1911. *The True Light Monthly* 10: 1.

Netland, Harold A. 2001. *Encountering Religious Pluralism: The Challenge to Christian Faith & Mission*. Downers Grove: InterVarsity Press.

Newbigin, Lesslie. 1989. *The Gospel in a Pluralist Society*. Kindle Version. Grand Rapids: Eerdmans.

Ning Xia Shao Shu Min Zu Gu Ji Zheng Li Chu Ban Gui Hua Ling Dao Xiao Zu Ban Gong Shi. 2010. Yue Hua Bian Yin Shuo Ming [An Explanation of the Editing and Publishing Policy of Yue Hua]. *Yue Hua* 1: 1–4.

Panikkar, Raimon. 2013. *Rhythm of Being: The Gifford Lectures*. Kindle Version. Maryknoll: Orbis Books.

Tang, Yan. 1938a. Zhong Wen Ji Du Jiao Za Zhi Jian Tao (An Overall Review of Chinese Christian Periodicals). *The True Light Review* 37: 1–6.

Tang, Yan. 1938b. Zhong Wen Ji Du Jiao Za Zhi Jian Tao, Xu Wan (An Overall Review of Chinese Christian Periodicals, Continue from the Last Issue and End). *The True Light Review* 37: 6–8.

Wang, Guohua. 1931. Ru Ye Mo Yu Wo Jiao Zai Ren Sheng Zhe Xue Shang De Bi Jiao Guan (A Comparison of Philosophy of Life in Confucianism, Christianity, Moism and Our Religion). *Yue Hua* 3: 8–12.

Wang, Zhengshan. 1939. Yue Hua Bai Sui (Hundred Years, Yue Hua). *Yue Hua* 11: 14.

Meng, Yang. 1929. Hui Jiao Yu Zhong Guo (Islam and China). *Yue Hua* 1: 1–2.

Yang, C. K. 1961. *Religion in Chinese Society: A Study of Contemporary Social Functions of Religion and Some of Their Historical Factors*. Berkeley: University of California Press.

Yu, Yishan. 1934. Wei Fu Xing Zun Kong Jin Yi Yan (An Advice for Reviving the Veneration Confucius). *The True Light Review* 33: 1–2.

Zhang, Wenkai. 1921. *Qu Jing Chu: You Ming Du Chen Huanzhang Bo Shi Kong Jiao Jiang Yi Bian Miu (Destroying the Thistle)*. Canton: The China Baptist Publication Society.

Zhang, Yijing. 1924. Sui Gan Lu: Ren Zhi Huan Zai Bu Zhi Zi Fan (Reflection: The Problem of People Is That They Do Not Turn round upon Themselves). *The True Light Review* 23: 90.

Zhang, Yijing. 1925. Tao Lun Ye Yu Fo Ji Ye Yu Kong (Discuss Christianity and Buddhism, and Christianity and Confucianism). *The True Light Review* 24: 80–1.

Zhang, Huaide. 1934. Hui Jiao De Jing Ai Zhu Yi (The Doctrine of Veneration and Love of Islam). *Yue Hua* 6: 20–24.

Zhao, Zhenwu. 1936. San Shi Nian Lai Zhong Guo Hui Jiao Wen Hua Gai Kuang (A Survey of Chinese Muslim Culture in the Last 30 Years). *Yu Gong* 5: 15–28.

Article

Shakespeare in Chinese as Christian Literature: Isaac Mason and Ha Zhidao's Translation of *Tales from Shakespeare*

Dadui Yao

Department of Chinese, Sun Yat-sen University, Guangzhou 510275, China; yaodd3@mail.sysu.edu.cn

Received: 31 May 2019; Accepted: 25 July 2019; Published: 26 July 2019

Abstract: The introduction of Shakespeare to China was through the Chinese translation of Mary and Charles Lamb's adaptation of Shakespeare's plays, *Tales from Shakespeare*. The Western missionaries' Chinese translations of the Lambs' adaptation have rarely been studied. Isaac Mason and his assistant Ha Zhidao's 1918 translation of the Lambs' book, entitled *Haiguo Quyu* (*Interesting Tales from Overseas Countries*), is one of the earliest Chinese versions translated by Christian missionaries. Although Mason was a Christian missionary and his translation was published by The Christian Literature Society for China, Mason adopted an indirect way to propagate Christian thoughts and rewrote some parts that are related to Christian belief. The rewriting is manifested in several aspects, including the use of four-character titles with Confucian ethical tendencies, rewriting paragraphs with hidden Christian ideas and highlighting themes closely related to Christian ethics, such as mercy, forgiveness and justice. While unique in its time, such a strategy of using the Chinese translation of Shakespeare for indirect missionary work had an impact on subsequent missionary translations.

Keywords: Shakespeare; *Haiguo Quyu*; Isaac Mason; Ha Zhidao; Missionary in China

---

1. Introduction: Western Missionaries and Shakespeare in Chinese

"Will the clumsy five or seven syllables which go to make a Chinese line convey any idea of the majestic flow of Portia's invocation of Mercy? We trow no."[1] This is a question from an anonymous author's article, "Shakespeare in Chinese", published in the newspaper *The North China Herald* in 1888. In this article, the author states that he/she has heard the news regarding the translation of Shakespeare into Chinese from an American press in Peking. It reads as follows, "An Imperial Mandate directs the President of the Academy to translate Shakespeare into Chinese for the benefit of the young Princes."[2] The author indicates that this message does not clearly state either which "Academy" was being referred to, or who the "President" was. After making a series of invalid speculations, the author proposes that perhaps W. A. P. Martin (1827–1916), an American missionary in China, would be the best candidate to complete this project. In August 1898, Martin was appointed by Emperor Guangxu 光緒 (1871–1908) as the inaugural president of the Imperial University of Peking京師大學堂. Martin himself was a prolific translator, but he did not engage in any project of translating Shakespeare into Chinese. Meanwhile, there is no way of knowing the result of this Imperial project.

While it is true that it is challenging to translate Shakespeare into a classical Chinese poem of either five- or seven-character lines, there are several translations of Shakespeare into classical Chinese in narrative form. The earliest was rendered from Mary and Charles Lamb's *Tales from Shakespeare*[3]

---

1   See (Anonymous 1888, p. 295).
2   See (Anonymous 1888, p. 295).
3   See (Lamb and Lamb 1973). The following citations of this book record the page number only.

(Henceforth "*Tales*"), a collection of stories for children adapted from twenty of Shakespeare's plays. This is a fascinating cultural phenomenon: when Shakespeare's plays were introduced to modern China, they were transformed into other genres such as short stories, to the point that Chinese readers themselves wondered if Shakespeare was really the one who had written them. The first two Chinese versions of *Tales* were rendered into classical Chinese, the *Haiwai Qitan* 海外奇譚 (*Bizarre Remarks from Overseas*) by an anonymous translator in 1903 and *Yinbian Yanyu* 吟邊燕語 (*Chatting Next to the Place Where the Poets Write Poems*) through the cooperation of Lin Shu 林紓 (1852–1924) and Wei Yi 魏易 (1880–1930) in 1904.[4] We do not know who translated the 1903 translation. Judging from his/her skill and mastery of both Chinese and English, the translator was no ordinary literatus. Although Lin Shu's translation achieved great success and was the one that made Shakespeare widely known in China, the 1903 translation is more elegant in terms of its usage of classical Chinese.[5]

In this area, we also find that Western missionaries played a pivotal role in introducing Shakespeare to Chinese readers. There are at least three understudied Chinese translations of Shakespeare produced by Western missionaries in China. These missionary translations are important since these texts involve cultural exchanges, religious conflicts, and cultural re-production. The earliest Western missionary translation of Shakespeare was by Miss Laura White (1865–1937), from the American Methodist Episcopal Mission. White's abridged translation of *The Merchant of Venice*, entitled *Wanrou Ji* 剮肉記 (*The Story of Shedding Flesh*), was made for a students' performance in a girls' school where White served as a teacher. Categorized as "xiaoshuo/novel," White's translation was serialized from 1914 to 1915 in *Nu Duo* 女鐸 (*The Woman's Messenger*), which was a magazine for foreign missionaries and Christian women in China.[6]

In 1918, British Quaker missionary Isaac Mason[7] and his Chinese assistant Ha Zhidao 哈志道worked together to translate twelve stories from *Tales*, entitled *Haiguo Quyu* 海國趣語 (*Interesting Tales from Overseas Countries*),[8] which turned out to be the first of its kind published by a Western Christian missionary. Although not much is known about the Chinese assistant Ha Zhidao, it has been established that he was a Muslim who was later converted to Christianity, possibly by Mason. Together, the two produced some pioneering works on the study of Chinese Muslims.[9] It is possible that Mason had read the 1903 anonymous Chinese translation of *Tales* when he started his translation project, because the titles of the two translations in Chinese, *Haiwai Qitan* (*Bizarre Remarks from Overseas*) and *Haiguo Quyu* (*Interesting Tales from Overseas Countries*) are quite similar. Moreover, at the time, Mason was in Shanghai, where the 1903 translation *Haiwai Qitan* was published, and he might have been able to acquire a copy before starting his translation.[10]

---

[4]　See (Lamb and Lamb 1903; Lamb et al. 1904). Subsequent references to this book cite the page numbers only. Lin Shu is considered as a conservative reformer who upheld Confucian doctrines and acknowledged the translations of foreign works as vital to save China from further decline. See (Chen and Cheng 2014, p. 1205). Lin Shu was once misidentified as the first translator of the Lambs' *Tales*, and his translations are considered as an "ideological manipulation of the religious materials of the source texts (*Uncle Tom's Cabin* and others)." See (Huang 2006, p. 13; Cheung 1998, pp. 127–49).

[5]　This issue is left to be discussed elsewhere due to the present limitations of space. For a discussion of the popularity of Lin Shu's translation, see (Wong 2018, pp. 42–43.)

[6]　See (White 1914–1915).

[7]　Isaac Mason (1870–1939) was a British missionary to China, from a special denomination, Quakers (The Religious Society of Friends). Quakers "affirmed an 'inner Light' within all humanity, including the pagans. They gave greater esteem to the Word in their midst than the Word in Scripture..." (House 2018, pp. 649–50). Also, Quakers place special emphasis on the goodness shared by all human nature. Mason was a scholar specializing in Western China and the history of Chinese Muslims. In 1892, he came to Chongqing as a missionary and also participated in educational work. He moved to Shanghai in 1915 and returned to the UK in 1932. During his stay in Shanghai, he worked for a publishing house, *Guangxue Hui* (The Christian Literature Society for China), editing magazines and translating Western books. He published dozens of religious books and pamphlets and helped compile a Chinese dictionary of the Bible. The Western literary works he translated into Chinese, including Lambs' *Tales* (1918), and two adventure novels translated for young readers, *The Swiss Family Robinson* (1920) and *The Adventures of Robinson Crusoe* (1923), were only a small part of his output. He was elected as a fellow of the Royal Geographical Society in 1921.

[8]　See (Lamb et al. 1918).

[9]　See (Israeli 2018, p. 79).

[10]　There is no evidence to prove that Mason was influenced by Lin Shu's Chinese translation.

The third Chinese translation of Shakespeare's plays by Western missionaries in China was a re-translation of Mason's work by Madge D. Mateer (1860–1939) and her assistant Wang Do K'wi 王斗奎 in 1929. Mateer's translation was reprinted several times after it was published. Mason's classical Chinese translation includes twelve stories, while Mateer's version consists of fifteen in modern vernacular Chinese.[11] These Chinese translations were produced by Christian missionaries and published by the same press in Shanghai, *Guangxuehui* 廣學會 (The Christian Literature Society for China).[12] The crucial question in this regard is: How did these missionary translators deal with the religious elements in the *Tales* when translating for Chinese readers in the Chinese context? Alternatively, how were Christian elements in Shakespearean stories transformed and localized in the target language? Yang Huilin once noted that Laura White deliberately excluded Christian information from her translation, and used a non-Christian tone to convey Christian significance.[13] Since Mason himself was an erudite scholar with a prolific publication record in both translation and original work, he should have been familiar with the religious implications in the *Tales*. When Mason translated Shakespearean stories, how did he deal with the religious information in the texts? The following discussion focuses on Mason's Chinese translation of Lambs' *Tales* and leaves out Mateer's version because the latter is quite similar in content to Mason's translation.

2. The Chinese Title and its Confucian Implication

The Lambs' *Tales from Shakespeare* was an adaptation of the original plays for young readers (especially girls) which aimed to inspire exploration of the original works. To make it easier for young readers, the Lambs changed the verse and poetic expression of the plays to prose and adopted a narrative form to summarize the play's plots.

Mason used classical Chinese and expressions for his translation, which indicated that he preferred to give Shakespeare a familiar image and an easily understood voice for the Chinese audience. Mason's translation includes twelve stories, with each one having a four-character Chinese title following the original English one. The titles of each story (with my back translation) are as follows: (1) *Pianyu Zheyu* 片語折獄 (*Half a Word Settles Litigation*) [*The Merchant of Venice*]; (2) *Tianlun Qibian* 天倫奇變 (*A Weird Change in Heavenly/Natural Ethics*) [*Hamlet*]; (3) *Zhicheng Weixiao* 至誠為孝 (*The Most Devout of Filial Piety*) [*King Lear*]; (4) *Yewai Tuanyuan* 野外團圓 (*Reunion in the Wild*) [*As You Like it*]; (5) *Qing yu yu Chou* 情寓於仇 (*Love is Hidden in Hatred*) [*Romeo and Juliet*]; (6) *Yanshi Youren* 厭世尤人 (*Aversion to the World and Bearing a Grudge Against Men*) [*Timon of Athens*]; (7) *Hufeng Yinlei* 呼風引類 (*Summoning the Wind, and Recruiting the Same Kind*) [*The Tempest*]; (8) *Yaoyan Guhuo* 妖言鼓禍 (*Heresy Brings Disaster*) [*Macbeth*]; (9) *Xinchan Shaqi* 信讒殺妻 (*He trusted in Slander and Tried to Kill His Wife*) [*Othello*]; (10) *Juechu Fengsheng* 絕處逢生 (*Finding a Way Out in a Dangerous Situation*) [*Pericles, Prince of Tyre*]; (11) *Xiangjian Ruchu* 相見如初 (*Meet Again as Before*) [*The Winter's Tale*]; and (12) *Baigui Kemo* 白圭可磨 (*Spots on the White Jade can be Ground Off*) [*Cymbeline*]. Half of these twelve stories are from Shakespeare's comedies (like 1, 4, 7, 10, 11 and 12) and the other half are from his tragedies.

Mason not only translated the stories into classical Chinese but also used elegant Chinese four-character symmetrical titles. These four-character titles that summarize the story-line of each play allude to some classical Chinese texts and include the translator's extended interpretation. The Chinese

---

[11] See (Lamb et al. 1929).
[12] *Guangxuehui* (The Christian Literature Society for China) was one of the most influential publishing institutions in modern China, publishing many Chinese works of Western learning, both religious and secular, through the cooperation of Western missionaries (from different denominations) and Chinese scholars (some of them are anonymous). In the second half of the nineteenth century, many European and American missionaries who came to China realized that in order to encourage the Chinese to accept Christianity, they had to transform the social and cultural foundations of China. Therefore, they published many works of Western learning to disseminate useful knowledge, and Christian messages are implicit in these works. As Tiedemann mentions, "It became the principal means of the Christian Literature Society to disseminate useful knowledge." See (Tiedemann 2010, p. 23).
[13] See (Yang 2015, pp. 82–90).

title for *The Merchant of Venice* is *Pianyu Zheyu*片語折獄 (*Half a Word Settles Litigation*), which is derived from Confucius's *Analects*. Confucius once praised his disciple Zilu 子路 by saying, "子曰：「片言可以折獄者，其由也與歟？」子路無宿諾." [Legge's translation] "The Master said, 'By one party's rhetoric, he can settle the litigation. Only Zilu has such a talent? All the things that Zilu promised will be done, never overnight.'"[14] The Han 漢dynasty scholar He Yan 何晏 (196–249) once commented, "此章言子路有明斷篤信之德也." ("This line is to say that Zilu has virtues of clear judgment and integrity.")[15] That is, Confucius appreciates his disciple Zilu, who can use unilateral testimony to settle litigation. People tend to tell Zilu the truth directly because he is a model of virtue. The line emphasizes Zilu's credibility, integrity and reliability, rather than simply underlining his clear judgment. He Yan's explanation was considered by the Qing Dynasty Confucian scholar Ruan Yuan 阮元 (1764–1849) to be an accurate explanation in *The Shisanjing Zhushu* 十三經注疏.[16] One of the Confucian scholars in the Qing dynasty also mentioned, "This line is to praise Zilu who has the talent to convince others, rather than to praise Zilu who has the talent to settle litigation."[17] Some of these commentaries were generally accepted and canonized in some textbooks by the Qing court, so a Chinese scholar like Ha Zhidao would have been familiar with *the Analects* and their interpretation. If this is the case, what the Chinese titles refer to here is not only Zilu's quick and fair judgment (that is, the wisdom of quickly settling litigation), but more important his *duxin*信 (steadfast faith). There is another line in the *Analects* regarding the word "*duxin*", "子曰：篤信好學, 守死善道."[18] ([Legge's translation] "The Master said, 'With sincere faith, he unites the love of learning; holding firm to death.'")[19] The main idea is that a gentleman should stick to his faith, be diligent and eager to learn, and firmly protect the faith (good way) until death.

Why did Mason and Ha use this title with a Confucian moral implication for *The Merchant of Venice*? *Pianyu Zheyu*片語折獄 (*Half a Word Settles Litigation*) illustrates Portia's eloquent speech and her excellent judgment, but its reference to the *Analects* shows that it has some religious implications. *The Merchant of Venice* is one of the most obvious Christian texts among Shakespeare's plays, in which "Shylock and Antonio embody the theological conflicts and historical interrelationships of Old Law and New."[20] The play shows the theme of Christianity's triumph over Judaism by portraying the greedy Jewish Shylock and enjoining him to convert to Christianity. Therefore, the Chinese title *Pianyu Zheyu* is borrowed from the Confucian canon but refers to Christian content. Moreover, this story in the original *Tales* was not placed in the first part of the entire book, but Mason moved it to the forefront and turned it into the opening story. It means that, at least for Mason, this is the most important story in the entire collection. Perhaps the reason is that this story not only has a fascinating plot but also highlights Christian faith and virtues.

The titles of the other stories have similar ethical themes. For instance, the Chinese title of *The Hamlet, Tianlun Qibian*天倫奇變 (*A Weird Change in Heavenly/Natural Ethics*), which has a peculiar Confucian tone, where the word "tianlun" (natural ethical relationship) refers to natural bonds and ethical relationships between family members. In *Hamlet*'s story, King Claudius murders his brother

---

[14] See (Cheng 1990, pp. 857–59). This line illustrates more than Zilu's decisiveness, intelligence, and loyalty. As Cheng Shude mentions, "Zilu is faithful and decisive. Therefore, whenever he speaks, people are convinced." (子路忠信明決, 故言出而人信服) In James Legge's translation, "The Master said, 'Ah! it is Yu, who could with half a word settle litigations! Tsze-loo never slept over a promise.'" See (Legge 1861a, p. 121).

[15] See (He and Xing 1990, p. 108).

[16] See (He and Xing 1990, p. 108). Please see *The Shisanjing Zhushu* 十三經注疏 (*Commentaries and Explanations to the Thirteen Classics*). Modern Transcription of He, Yan and Xingbing's *Lunyu zhushu*論語註疏, see (He and Xing 2016, p. 191). The *Shisanjing Zhushu* is an edition of the Thirteen Confucian Classics that includes all relevant commentaries from the Han 漢 (206 BCE–220 CE), Tang 唐 (618–907) and Qing 清 (1644–1911) periods. It was compiled by the Qing period scholar Ruan Yuan 阮元 (1764–1849) and became a canonical text for the study of Confucian classics.

[17] See (Cheng 1990, p. 860). This is from Wang Fu汪紱's commentary in the book *The Interpretation of Four Books*四書詮義. His commentary in Chinese reads, "此稱子路有服人之行, 非稱子路有斷獄之才也." Wang was a scholar of the Confucian classics in the early Qing Dynasty. His interpretation and commentary on the Four Books are close to the school of Zhu Xi's commentaries on the Confucian classics which was officially accepted by the Qing court.

[18] See (Cheng 1990, p. 539).

[19] See (Legge 1861a, p. 76).

[20] See (Lewalski 1962, p. 334).

King Hamlet, marries the Queen, his sister-in-law, and ascends to the throne, while Queen Gertrude marries her brother-in-law shortly after the death of her husband. All these acts are severe violations of Confucian ethics. In this way, the translator assumes the target reader's perspective and criticizes the violation of Confucian ethics.

The Chinese title of *Cymbeline* is *Baigui Kemo* 白圭可磨 (*Spots on the White Jade can be Ground Off*), which relates to a classical allusion that comes from *Shi Jing, The Book of Poetry* 詩經. *Baigui* 白圭 (the white jade) is not a general white jade, but a ritual tool used by ancient kings and princes in some sacred ceremonies such as sacrificial offerings to heaven. The original line from *The Book of Poetry* reads, "白圭之玷, 尚可磨也；斯言之玷, 不可為也." ([Legge's translation] "A flaw in a mace of white jade, May be ground away, But for a flaw in speech, Nothing can be done.")[21] This play has a happy ending, with the villain Iachimo confessing his misdemeanors, the resolution of all misunderstandings and the reunion of lovers. Imogen forgives her father King Cymbeline and her husband Postumus, who mistakenly believed the slanderous claims that led to all the misdeeds. The Chinese title of the story, *Baigui Kemo*, uses the opposite of the original meaning, in that it highlights repentance and forgiveness.

The Chinese title of *King Lear* is *Zhicheng Weixiao* 至誠為孝 (*The Most Devout of Filial Piety*). An important theme that runs throughout King Lear's story is the parent–child relationship, in which Shakespeare (and the Lambs) focus on the discussions of human nature, morality, and even philosophical thinking. However, Mason emphasized Confucian filial piety in the Chinese translation. After being rejected by his two daughters, King Lear does not want to stay in the palace anymore and runs into the wilderness amidst a storm.

In this passage, the Lambs' story reads, "Not that a splendid train is essential to happiness, but from a king to a beggar is a hard change, from commanding millions to be without one attendant; and it was the ingratitude in his daughters' denying it, more than what he would suffer by the want of it, which pierced this poor king to the heart; insomuch, that with this double ill-usage, a vexation for having so foolishly given away a kingdom, his wits began to be unsettled, and while he said he knew not what, he vowed revenge against those unnatural hags, and to make examples of them that should be a terror to the earth!" (p. 133)

Mason's translation focuses on the fluency of reading, but it also covertly emphasizes filial piety. For example, the paragraph above is translated as, "(King Lear) 愈思兩女辜負親恩, 愈有忿恨之意, 以致腦筋病發, 口出狂妄之言. 又謂將兩女不孝之行, 顯揚於天下, 因此負恩之女, 實為天地所不容." (p. 16) "The more King Lear thought that his two daughters had failed his parenting, the more resentful he was. His mind soon became ill, and his mouth spoke frenzied remarks. He added that the unfilial behavior of these two daughters should be announced to every one under heaven so that these two unfilial children ultimately be unacceptable to heaven and earth (the world)."[22]

Lear becomes crazy and swears revenge at the ending part of Lambs' adaptation, while in Mason's adaptation, Lear vows to expose the unfilial behaviors of his two daughters to the general public. The translator presupposes that the entire story takes place in the context of a Confucian society, wherein unfilial behaviors such as Lear's two daughters' misdemeanors is condemned. In many places, the translators' settings of the cultural background reflect the realities in a Confucian society. Hence, it is no exaggeration to state that the translator rewrote Shakespeare's stories, especially the social and cultural setting in these stories, for the target audience. To attract more readers, Mason deliberately changed the title of Shakespeare's plays to Chinese four-character titles and interspersed Confucian ethical themes throughout the text. It can be said that Mason adopted a localization strategy that fully considered the reader's context even at the expense of sacrificing the spirit of the original plays. However, I argue that, while Mason's localization strategy is premised on the use of a common Confucian vocabulary, the translation itself also implies some Christian ideas. Therefore,

---

[21] See (Legge 1871, p. 513).

[22] This and subsequent English versions following Chinese quotations from Mason's translation have been made by the author of this article, translating the Chinese translation back into English.

we still need to examine how Mason's translation deals with the overt Christian religious message in Shakespeare's plays.

3. Portia's Invocation of "Mercy" and Christian Thought

Mason and Ha's cooperation in the translating of *Haiguo Quyu* aimed to persuade people to do good deeds for others, guide readers to "civilized" life and promote acting for the benefit of humanity. As Mason stated in his preface (in Chinese), "因其（莎劇）文筆雋雅, 意義深厚, 中間亦具良好之教育, 善惡之報, 釐然不爽, 更指導世人講公義、嫻禮義、尚忠厚, 以及一切人類有益之舉." (p. 1) "Shakespeare's plays are elegant in style and profound in connotation, which produces a good educational effect on readers. The karma for good and evil should not be absent since this also guides people to adhere to the principle of justice, be acquainted with etiquette, admire loyalty and kindness, and be willing to do everything for the benefit of humanity." Although Mason was a Christian missionary, he did not directly promote Christian doctrine in the translation. Each of these twelve Shakespeare stories has a different focus, but Mason's Chinese translation highlights two major themes:

(1) Sin and redemption/forgiveness. In his view, all faults are caused by the complete depravity of human nature, while redemption relies in Christianity as a transcendental power.

(2) Good, evil and righteousness. Wicked people will be punished, and good people will eventually obtain justice. Mason's text is, however, quite similar to some exhortation novels (勸懲小説) guided by Confucian moral tenets and quite popular in the Ming and Qing dynasties. Though the starting points and the footholds of the two belief systems, namely Christianity and Confucianism, are different, the literary representation of these two types of work is somewhat similar.

Mason praised Shakespeare's plays, stating that they "are elegant in style and profound in connotation." His translation strategies, including changes in the narrative perspective, the usage of free-verse style, and literal translation, are intended to convey to readers the twists and turns of Shakespeare's stories. In *The Merchant of Venice*, some parts of the play, such as the love story of Portia and Bassanio, and the plot of law and benevolence, are controversial. In his preface to the adaptation, Charles Lamb said that the purpose of their own rewriting was to improve the moral quality of the stories for child readers and to mitigate the individual's tendency toward selfishness. The Lambs' adaptation thus proved to be an excellent textbook that laid the foundation for moral education. To make it easier for younger readers, the Lambs included judgments of good and evil deeds in their translations. When describing the characters' behavior, they included psychological descriptions to distinguish morally noble from corrupt acts that could not be found in the original play.

The adaptation of *The Merchant of Venice*, in which there were deletions of some episodes such as Portia's choosing among suitors, and Shylock's daughter Jessica's eloping with her Christian lover Lorenzo, was made by Mary Lamb alone. She kept one story-line, that is, Antonio's borrowing of money from the Jew Shylock and Antonio's trial. Mary Lamb tends to use adjectives with opposite meanings to enhance the difference of personality between characters. For example, she portrays Shylock as a greedy, insidious, cruel Jew, while Antonio is a charitable and merciful Christian. In the opening paragraph of the story, Mary Lamb says that the wicked Shylock is a "covetous", "hard-hearted man" who is "disliked by all good men," while the "generous" Antonio is "the kindest man that ever lived." The images of these two characters are sharply contrasted starting from their first appearance in the stories. In the trial scene, Mary includes several descriptions of Shylock's character, some of which were not in the original play, to strengthen the portrayal of his sinister intentions, describing him as a "cruel," "merciless Jew," who is "unfeeling," with "no mercy," and the "cruel temper of a currish Jew."

Mary Lamb used Shylock as a counter-example to sway readers toward Christian values like mercy, kindness and battling avaricious desire. In Shakespeare's original work, Antonio and Shylock have several disputes that epitomized the conflict between Judaism and Christianity. Mary Lamb simplifies this conflict into personality clashes between an avaricious Jew and a benevolent Christian.

At the end of the story, Shylock is asked to convert to Christianity to rectify his evil ways. Lamb's moral judgment is so straightforward that it has lost the complex discussion of the differences between the Old and New Testaments as found in the original play.

Aside from simplifying the conflict between Judaism and Christianity, Mary Lamb also turns to the "worldly" conflict between Antonio and Shylock. Jews are here depicted as greedy and cold, while Christians are merciful and kind. As already mentioned, Lamb's moral judgment did not anymore showcase the elaborate exposition of biblical comparisons in Shakespeare's plays because these were shifted toward cultural conflicts. In contrast, Mason did not wish to convey the differences between these two religions. He removed the plot regarding theological conflicts and racial contradictions between Antonio and Shylock and kept the plots simple. He believed that his mission was to convey the meaning of the story and provide essential moral instructions for readers. In order to truly understanding Shakespeare's plays, young readers would need to read the original texts.

By rewriting some critical plots details, Mason purposely minimized religious contradictions in his Chinese translation. For instance, almost all of the sections that include the word "Christian" in the original text were deleted. Only the word "Jew" is retained, to highlight Shylock's identity. When Shylock makes an appearance in the story, Lamb writes, "Shylock, the Jew, lived in Venice: He was a usurer who amassed an immense fortune by lending money at great interest to Christian merchants" (p. 92). Lamb's depiction of Shylock's lending money to Christians for usurious profits was omitted from Mason's translation, which simply reads, "(夏洛克)系以錢借出而求重利者, 家成巨富." (p. 1) "(Shylock) is a person who seeks to make a profit by lending money." In the scene of the trial, Portia says that according to the contract, the Jew Shylock can take a pound of flesh from Antonio's body, but cannot take even "one drop of Christian blood." (p. 102) Mason translated this sentence into "a drop of blood when the flesh is cut off," (p. 5) and also deleted reference to Antonio's identity as a Christian, which was highlighted in the original play. From the scene of the trial in the Chinese translation of *The Merchant of Venice*, Mason deleted almost all negative adjectives describing Shylock, the Jewish money lender, so the ethnic conflict is omitted. Therefore, in Mason's translation, Shylock is no longer a Jew who deliberately exploits Christians, but a wicked man by nature.

Mason's translation also changed the theme of the story. Shylock's hatred for Antonio is no longer an intense and intractable religious conflict, but a mere battle of interests. As a result, the contradiction between them is easier to resolve. If Shylock listens to Portia's exhortation and forgives Antonio, forgetting the grudge and giving up revenge, the conflict between the two can be ultimately resolved. In Mason's translation, the conflict between the two cultures or two religions that Shylock and Antonio represented is absent. Nevertheless, the purpose of this Chinese translation is to promote indiscriminate forgiveness and mercy, which is quite different from the Confucian emphasis on mercifulness in the literal meaning of the Chinese translation.

In Lamb's adaptation, Portia's exhortation to Shylock is taken closely from Shakespeare's original. Let us take a look at Portia's famous speech on the topic of Christian mercy.

In Lamb's text, "She spoke so sweetly of the noble quality of *mercy*, as would have softened any heart but the unfeeling Shylock's; saying, that it dropped as the gentle rain from heaven upon the place beneath; and how mercy was a double blessing, it blessed him that gave, and him that received it; and how it became monarchs better than their crowns, being an attribute of God Himself; and that earthly power came nearest to God's, in proportion as mercy tempered justice; and she bid Shylock remember that as we all pray for mercy, the same prayer should teach us to show mercy." (pp. 98–99)

Mason's abridged translation is as follows, "上帝慈恩待人, 故人應效法, 彼此施恩. 我等獲罪於上帝, 若求上帝寬待, 上帝必赦免之, 人若獲罪於我, 若求我寬待, 我亦當饒恕之." (p. 4) "God is kind to others, so people should imitate the law and give each other grace. We all transgress against God. If we ask for God's mercy, God will forgive us. When someone offends me and later asks for my mercy, I shall also forgive him." In Lamb's adaptation, the purpose of Portia's speech is to open the possibility that Shylock will give up insisting on the terms of the contract and show compassion since it would be ruthless to enforce the contract strictly in accordance with the law. This way of dealing with the trial embodies the Christian perspective of the Old and New Testaments, wherein mercy and forgiveness prevail over cruelty. In Mason's translation, he removed some parts of Lamb's adaptation that discuss the relationship between law and compassion.

Judging from Mason's translation strategy, Shylock's hatred of Antonio is no longer foregrounded by historical and religious worldviews. Whether or not the contradiction between the two can be resolved will depend on the presence of compassion and mercy. Moreover, the value of mercy does not only hinge on kindness towards others but also on offering forgiveness to those who offend oneself. The primary purpose of Mason's translation is to encourage people to forgive each other. At the end of the story, the Duke of Venice forgives Shylock's attempt to murder a Christian and returns his property upon his conversion to Christianity. The Duke says, "余當表明慈愛之性情, 以寬恕爾命, 與爾不用慈愛之心異." (p. 5) "I should show the nature of my kindness (mercy), and forgive and save your life, which differs from your hard-heartedness without mercy." This is quite different from Lamb's adaptation, wherein the Duke's forgiveness of Shylock is to show "the difference of Christian spirit."

The idea of persuading people to do good deeds in Mason's translation is rooted in the principle of universal love that relates to mercy and kindness, and which has a broader meaning compared with Lamb's adaption. Mason changed the theme of religious conflict by omitting characters and sections of plot and "softening" the impact of these conflicts in his translation. Mason believed that, for young Chinese readers, topics such as religious and ethnic conflicts should be avoided. The more critical issue that Chinese readers needed to learn was forgiveness and mercy. Mason worked for The Christian Literature Society for China, where he was tasked with introducing Western knowledge to Chinese readers on one hand, and disseminating Christianity in China by means of these Western classics on the other. He needed to reach Chinese readers, which was why the translation sought common ground with Chinese experience. The Western background, which was puzzling to some Chinese readers, was eliminated, and the concept of universal Christian love was instead introduced.

This kind of discourse of benevolence and mercy closely relates to the translator's aim of moral education. While both the original and the adaption of *The Merchant of Venice* forced Shylock to believe in Christianity, the Chinese translation stresses the need to do good deeds, and to be kind and merciful. In these twelve stories, the translator repeatedly highlighted acts of mercy and kindness as a way of overcoming sinful behavior caused by jealousy, cruelty, and the wickedness of human nature.

Although each of Shakespeare's plays has a particular focus, several of these stories, when rewritten, are based on the common themes of suspicion and jealousy. Such is the case of Chinese adaptations of stories like *Othello* and *Cymbeline*. These stories end with all disputes being settled, the wicked person either forgiven or punished, and, most importantly, the virtuous characters obtaining their reward. The translators used these techniques to demonstrate that forgiveness and kindness "cure" evil in human nature. In the Chinese translation of *Hamlet*, the translator added this comment at the end of the story: "因哈太子夙為慈愛性質、温柔品格之人, 並非偏好殘忍者可比. 故衆人因其死而惜之, 倘能久存於世, 則丹麥之王位可就, 國其庶幾矣." (p. 12) "Prince Hamlet has always been kind and gentle, and he is different from those who like cruelty. Therefore, everyone is deeply saddened by his death. If he could survive in the world for a long time, he would be able to sit on the throne of Denmark, and the country would be better." Hamlet is a controversial figure because he also has negative traits like indecisiveness, hastiness, and brutality. In the Chinese translation, however, he becomes a kind and gentle prince. Mason preferred to use the Chinese word "ci-ai" 慈愛 (literally meaning "kindness and love" or "mercy") in the translation of twenty stories in describing his favorite characters. The word "ci-ai", however, is not appropriate for describing Hamlet. When using this word "ci-ai" in other stories, Mason described how some characters, especially those who were merciful and compassionate, could bridge God's attributes, particularly his love, to Chinese sensibilities.

4. The Reconfiguration of Themes

Haiguo Quyu reveals that Mason reconfigured themes highlighted in the Lambs' *Tales*. Quite similar to *The Merchant of Venice*, there are other stories in *Haiguo Quyu* which are related to themes of mercy and forgiveness. The purpose of such kinds of stories is to show "the mercy of God." The ultimate implication is that God forgives sinners and justice prevails. Even though there are some Christian references in the original plays, Shakespeare hardly uses a direct religious tone, let alone putting doctrinal issues to the fore. Among the twelve stories in Mason's Chinese translation, many places emphasize on "tianli" 天理 (the Heavenly/Natural Truth) or "*gongdao*" 公道 (Justice or Fairness), meaning that there is a God who maintains justice in the world. Therefore, although there are many injustices, and good people might not obtain their recompense immediately, there is justice in the end. Whether good or bad, everyone gets what they deserve for their deeds.

At the end of the story of *Zhicheng Weixiao* [*King Lear*], Mason comments on the outcomes of good and evil deeds. When narrating the tragic fate of King Lear's third daughter Cordelia, Lamb describes, " . . . the lady Cordelia, whose good deeds did seem to deserve a more fortunate conclusion: but it is an awful truth, that innocence and piety are not always successful in this world." (p. 139) In Mason's Chinese translation, "可德理亞在監內病故, 以此德孝兼備之人, 竟遭惡人之毒手, 但善者為惡者所致死, 世界亦所常有. 然善惡之報自在, 非不可信者也." (p. 17) "Cordelia died of illness in prison. A person like her who has both virtue and filial piety is killed by a wicked man. However, good people are sometimes murdered by wicked ones, and this often happens in this world. Nevertheless, the reward for good or evil, as found in nature, is trustworthy."

In Lamb's adaptation, the phrase "an awful truth" acknowledges the difficult reality of a good person not rewarded for his/her goodness. In Mason's translation, this is translated as "this often happens in this world." After this, Mason attaches his own comments, "Nevertheless, the reward for good or evil [善惡之報], as found in nature, is trustworthy." This sentence persuades people to be kind, and that the "reward for good and evil" will surely come in the end, and that the world is still fair.

Shakespeare, the Lambs, and Mason all have sympathy for Cordelia, and also condemned the other two daughters of King Lear. After King Lear's two elder daughters have received the punishment they deserved, the Lambs' adaptation concludes, "Thus the Justice of Heaven, at last, overtook these wicked Daughters." (p. 139). Mason's translation reads, "此乃天神懲罰兩不孝之女, 為罪惡之報應云." "This is tianshen (the God of heaven)'s punishment of these two unfilial daughters as retribution (baoying; 報應) for their sinful behaviors." Mason re-emphasizes that King Lear's two wicked daughters are unfilial, and their behavior would eventually reap the punishment they deserve from the God of Heaven. The word "baoying" is derived from the Buddhist philosophy of karma, which was widely accepted in the Ming and Qing dynasties. Here, the word "Heaven" in Shakespeare's original or the Lambs' adaptation refers neither to "tianshen" nor to Buddhist karma. Mason added the idea of karma so that Chinese readers could easily understand it and translated "heaven" into "tianshen" 天神 rather than "tian" 天 or "shangdi" 上帝 (the Supreme God), deliberately avoiding being too straightforward in referring to Christian thought.

At the end of the story of *Qing yu yu Chou* (*Romeo and Juliet*), the translator adds his comments. The Lambs' adaptation reads, "And the Prince, turning to these old lords, Montague and Capulet, rebuked them for their brutal and irrational enmities, and showed them what a scourge Heaven had laid upon such offences, that it had found means even through the love of their children to punish their unnatural hate." (p. 261) This sentence has been shortened and translated as, "本城之王, 對二族長言, 兩家夙仇, 於理不合, 故上天不忍視之, 特以此法譴罰, 俾爾等消釋怨尤." (p. 27) "The king of this city says to the patriarch of these two families, 'it is unreasonable for your two families to have been enemies for a long time, so God cannot bear to see this situation and punish your two families in this way in order to dispel your resentment and complaints.'" (p. 27). Here, the phrase "God *buren*/has commiserating mind" (上天不忍)[23] does not exist in the adaptation. The phrase "God has a

---

[23] The phrase "上天不忍" comes from "先王不忍" in *Mencius*. In James Legge's translation (Legge 1861b, p. 77), "Mencius said, 'All men have a mind which cannot bear to see the sufferings of others. The ancient kings had this commiserating mind...'" (孟子曰：「人皆有不忍人之心. 先王有不忍人之心...)

commiserating mind" shows that there is a personal and merciful God here who presides over the administration of justice.

The original theme of Shakespeare's play *The Tempest* is forgiveness. Its Chinese translation *Hufeng Yinlei* sticks to the original theme and magnifies some religious content. The deposed Duke of Milan Prospero's anger and resentment at the beginning of the story later becomes forgiveness and mercy and, eventually, he is restored to his title and returns to his territory. In the concluding paragraphs of the Lambs' version, the King of Naples and Antonio ask for forgiveness from Prospero.

"'Then I must be her father,' said the king; 'but oh how oddly will it sound, that I must ask my child forgiveness.' 'No more of that,' said Prospero: 'let us not remember our troubles past, since they so happily have ended.' And then Prospero embraced his brother, and again assured him of his forgiveness; and said that a wise over-ruling Providence permitted that he should be driven from his poor dukedom of Milan, that his daughter might inherit the crown of Naples, for that by their meeting in this desert island, it had happened that the king's son had loved Miranda." (p. 15)

Mason's translation reads, "(The King of Naples says,) 惟前已招怨於其父, 應請其父恕我. 泡氏聞之曰：舊惡不念, 前雖為禍, 後竟變為福, 吾儕宜喜之不勝. 又曰：慈悲之上帝, 能使憂轉而為樂, 且將來之樂, 較目前之樂更大." (p. 35) "(The King of Naples says) I had previously become her father's enemy, so I should have asked her father's forgiveness first. Prospero hears this and says, 'We should not recall the unpleasant things of the old days since though they were disasters, but now they have turned out to be blessings. We should all be happier, more than ever.' And he continued, 'The merciful God, he can turn worries into pleasures, and the joy of the future will be greater than that of the present.'"

In this part of the Chinese translation, most of the content can be identified with the text of the Lambs' adaptation, but the following text regarding "the merciful God," which cannot be located in the Lamb's text, is appended by Mason. The Lambs' text does not use words such as "God", but refers to "a wise overseeing Providence", which stands for the rulership of the Christian God over the world. The translator, however, directly rendered it as "The merciful God, he can turn worries into pleasures, and the joy of the future is greater than that of the present." This eschatological commitment in the text comes from Christian theology. Thus, we see a follow-up translation that says, "安脱略大哭認過, 求兄赦免, 王亦承認前過. 泡氏均恕之." (p. 35) "Antonio cried, acknowledging the faults he had committed before, and begged for his brother's forgiveness, and the King also confessed his previous faults. Prospero forgave them all."

Mason deliberately supplemented some Christian admonitions to make the whole text replete with Christian meaning. There is also a short paragraph at the end of the story, with some traces added by the translator. Mason's text reads, "故大眾登船返國, 泡氏恢復原有之公爵權位, 其女與太子在那破里城行婚禮, 更有團聚之樂. 先憂也如彼, 後樂也如此, 是亦天道無常也." (p. 35) "As a result, everyone boarded the ship and returned to the country, Prospero was restored to the original title of Duke, and his daughter and the Prince married in the city of Naples. They felt the joy of reunion. One has to go through so much sorrow to be able to get such happiness, which is also the uncertainty of tiandao (the natural/heaven's way)."

At the end of the Chinese translation, the translator comments on the entire story from a Christian perspective. The phrase "先憂也如彼, 後樂也如此" "One has to go through so much sorrow to be able to get such happiness" echoes to the aforementioned Chinese phrase "慈悲之上帝, 能使憂轉而為樂, 且將來之樂, 較目前之樂更大." "The merciful God, he can turn worries into joy, and the joy of the future is greater than that of the present." The term "tiandao" 天道 of "tiandao wucang" (The uncertainty of the natural/heaven's way) has profound meaning in Neo-Confucianism. "Tiandao" is an essential category in Song Ming Neo-Confucianism. Some scholars argued that Neo-Confucianism during the Song and Ming Dynasties further elaborated terms like 性 (Xin/Nature) and 天道 (tiandao/heaven's way).[24] Chen Chun 陳淳 (1159–1223), a student of the Neo-Confucian master Zhu Xi 朱熹 (1130–1200)

---

[24] See (Chen 1992, pp. 10–11; Chen 2014, p. 154; Hou et al. 1984).

defined these basic terms in his book 北溪字義 *Beixi Ziyi (Neo-Confucian Terms Explained)*.[25] Zhu Xi's interpretations of Confucian Classics were officially recognized by the Qing court. Scholars during the late Qing and early Republican periods like Ha Zhidao were likely to be familiar with terms such as "tiandao, or the natural/heaven's way".

The word "tiandao" in the story, which in the English text is "Providence", refers to God's rule over the world and everything in it, or "God's will", which has profound theological significance in Christianity.[26] Thus, Mason's comment may be regarded as a summary and moral reflection on the story. Mason wanted to show the Christian "God of Mercy", and that that God will administer justice and restore faith and a hopeful future to believers. Mason used these stories to demonstrate forgiveness and justice, and these two are mutual proofs of each other. In short, Mason and Ha Zhidao utilized the canonicity of Shakespeare's play in promoting Christianity in the Chinese context. Mason's preface emphasized that the purpose of the translation of the book is to highlight "the reward of good and evil." Nevertheless, the book is not a traditional Chinese book that exhorts people to be kind in the general sense. Instead, the translators' rewriting is supported by Christian ideas. In the translators' view, the purpose of the translation was to "persuade the readers to do good deeds for others, guide them to know civility and promote every good thing for the benefit of humanity." The generalized concept of exhortations, "for the benefit of humanity," is the cover of Mason's preaching of Christianity.

Quakers believe that everyone has "the Light of Christ" within them, so a missionary like Mason, when compared with Christians from other denominations, places special emphasis on human values such as mercy, pity, peace and love, and these noble ideas espoused in Shakespeare. Mason's translation is designed for Chinese readers who might follow Christianity after reading the translation, especially in the chaotic beginnings of the new Republic period when the old system (of the Qing Dynasty and Neo-Confucianism) that had been overthrown had failed in maintaining and promoting universal goodness. As for those Christian convictions, this translation will undoubtedly make them more convinced of universal ethics and the omnipresence and omniscience of the God of Christianity. In short, Mason's translation can be viewed as a missionary activity in the cultural sphere of China through his promotion of the ethical ideals in Shakespeare, which are at the same time Christian ideas.

5. Conclusions

When Shakespeare's plays were introduced to modern China, they first came in the form of Lamb's adapted stories. *Haiguo Quyu*, translated by Mason and Ha Zidao, was the first missionary translation of the Lambs' Shakespeare tales and thus had a unique value as a seminal form of cultural exchange between the East and West, and dialogue between Confucianism and Christianity. The purpose of making this Chinese translation was to introduce Western classics to young Chinese readers and to enhance their interest in reading the original Shakespeare plays. Despite the use of classical Chinese, the two translators used an intelligible expression, as well as an indigenous strategy, in translating Shakespeare stories. They did their best to convey the intent of Lamb's adaptation which, on the one hand, showed the characteristics of Western literary classics, while on the other hand persuaded people to be good and do more good deeds. Although Mason was a Christian and the book's publisher was The Christian Literature Society for China, Mason used a localized translation strategy, hiding Christian significations throughout the text. He thus rewrote Shakespeare's plays into Chinese Christian literature in the form of short stories. Mason's translation contains twelve stories, some of which adopted classical Confucian allusions. Behind the localized translation, however, are implicit Christian messages. Mason consciously veiled the Christian message, reduced the portrayal of characters with overt religious overtones, and diluted religious conflicts among characters. In turn,

---

[25] See (Chen 1983, pp. 38–41). As Chen Chun elaborates in the first chapter of his book, "天命, 即天道之流行, 而賦於物者, 乃事物所以當然之故也." [My back translation] Providence is the widespread dissemination of the Tao of heaven, and endows things with forms, which is also the reason why things become as such." See (Chen 1983, p. 1).

[26] See (House 2018, p. 623).

he emphasized mercy, forgiveness, and universal justice—all of which point to Christianity. Thus, it can be said that Mason used the Chinese translation of Shakespeare to spread Christianity, albeit indirectly. After the publication of Mason's translation, a certain impact of the translation may be seen. In 1929, Madge D. Mateer and Wang Do K'wi re-translated Mason's version into vernacular Chinese and published this under the title of *Shashibiya de Gushi* 莎士比亞的故事 (*Shakespeare's Tales*). As well as being a missionary, Mateer was also engaged in education. When she re-translated Mason's version, she did so for middle school students in the schools she founded. In other words, Mateer's re-translation was adopted as a textbook in some missionary schools.

Acknowledgments: The author would like to thank the two anonymous reviewers for their helpful and constructive comments that greatly contributed to improving the final version of this essay.

Conflicts of Interest: The authors declare no conflict of interest.

References

Anonymous, and 佚名. 1888. Shakespeare in Chinese. *The North China Herald*, September 15, p. 295.

Chen, Chun 陳淳. 1983. *Beixi Ziyi* 北溪字義. Beijing北京: Zhonghua shuju中華書局.

Chen, Lai 陳來. 1992. *Songming Lixue* 宋明理學. Shenyang瀋陽: Liaoning jiaoyu chubanshe 遼寧教育出版社.

Chen, Lai 陳來. 2014. *Chenlai Jiangtanlu* 陳來講談錄. Beijing北京: Jiuzhou chubanshe九州出版社.

Chen, Weihong, and Xiaojuan Cheng. 2014. An Analysis of Lin Shu's Translation Activity from the Cultural Perspective. *Theory and Practice in Language Studies* 4: 1201–6. [CrossRef]

Cheng, Shude 程樹德. 1990. *Lunyu Jishi* 論語集釋. Beijing: Zhonghua Shuju.

Cheung, Martha Pui-Yiu. 1998. The Discourse of Occidentalism? Wei Yi and Lin Shu's Treatment of Religious Materials in Their Translation of Uncle Tom's Cabin. In *Translation and Creation-Readings of Western Literature in Early Modern China, 1840–1918*. Edited by David Pollard. Amsterdam: Benjamins, pp. 127–49.

He, Yan 何晏, and Bing Xing 邢昺. 1990. *Lunyu Zhushu* 論語註疏. Shanghai上海: Shanghai guji chubanshe上海古籍出版社.

He, Yan 何晏, and Bing Xing 邢昺. 2016. *Lunyu Zhushu* 論語註疏. Beijing北京: Zhongguo zhigong Chubanshe 中國致公出版社.

Hou, Wailu 侯外廬, Qiu Hansheng 邱漢生, and Zhang Qizhi 張豈之. 1984. *Songming Lixueshi* 宋明理學史. Beijing 北京: Renmin chubanshe人民出版社.

House, H. Wayne. 2018. *The Evangelical Dictionary of World Religions*. Grand Rapids: Baker Books.

Huang, Alexander C. Y. 2006. Lin Shu, Invisible Translation, and Politics. *Perspectives: Studies in Translatology* 14: 55–65. [CrossRef]

Israeli, Raphael. 2018. One Century of Vain Missionary Work among Muslims in China. In *The Cross Battles the Crescent*. Newcastle upon Tyne: Cambridge Scholars Publishing.

Lamb, Charles, and Mary Lamb. 1903. *Haiwai Qitan* 海外奇譚. Translated by Anonymous. Shanghai上海: Dawenshe 達文社.

Charles Lamb, Mary Lamb, Lin Shu, and Wei Yi, transs. 1904, *Yinbian Yanyu* 吟邊燕語. Shanghai上海: The Commercial Press 商務印書館.

Lamb, Charles, Mary Lamb, Isaac Mason, and Ha Zhidao. 1918. *Haiguo Quyu* 海國趣語. Shanghai上海: The Christian Literature Society for China 廣學會.

Charles Lamb, Mary Lamb, Madge D. Mateer, and Wang Do K'wi, transs. 1929, *Shashibiya de Gushi* 莎士比亞的故事. Shanghai上海: The Christian Literature Society for China廣學會.

Lamb, Charles, and Mary Lamb. 1973. *Tales from Shakespeare*. London: J. M. Dent & Son Ltd.

Legge, James. 1861a. *The Chinese Classic, Vol. I.*. London: Trubner & Co.

Legge, James. 1861b. *The Chinese Classic, Vol. II*. London: Trubner & Co.

Legge, James. 1871. *The Chinese Classics, Vol. IV. The She King, or the Book of Poetry*. London: Trubner & Co.

Lewalski, Barbara K. 1962. Biblical Allusion and Allegory in "The Merchant of Venice". *Shakespeare Quarterly* 13: 327–43. [CrossRef]

Tiedemann, Rolf Gary. 2010. *Handbook of Christianity in China, Volume Two: 1800 to the Present*. Leiden: Brill, p. 23.

White, Laura M. (亮樂月). 1914–1915. *Wanrou Ji* 剜肉記. *Nu Duo* 女鐸 (*The Woman's Messenger*), September 1914–November 1915, vol. 4, 5.

Wong, Jenny. 2018. *The Translatability of the Religious Dimension in Shakespeare from Page to Stage, from West to East.* Eugene, Oregon: Pickwick Publications.

Yang, Huilin. 2015. Christian Implication and Non-Christian Translation: A Case Study of the Merchant of Venice in the Chinese Context. *Studies in Chinese Religions* 1: 82–90. [CrossRef]

Article

The Gospel According to Marxism: Zhu Weizhi and the Making of *Jesus the Proletarian* (1950)

Zhixi Wang

College of Liberal Arts, Shantou University, Shantou 515063, China; zxwang@stu.edu.cn

Received: 31 May 2019; Accepted: 13 September 2019; Published: 19 September 2019

Abstract: This article explores the integration of Marxism into the Gospel narratives of the Christian Bible in Zhu Weizhi's *Jesus the Proletarian* (1950). It argues that Zhu in this Chinese Life of Jesus refashioned a Gospel according to Marxism, with a proletarian Jesus at its center, by creatively appropriating a wealth of global sources regarding historical Jesus and primitive Christianity. Zhu's rewriting of Jesus can be appreciated as a precursor to the later Latin American liberation Christology.

Keywords: The Gospel; Marxism; Zhu Weizhi; *Jesus the Proletarian*; Life of Jesus

1. Introduction

In recent decades, scholarly attention has been increasingly paid to Chinese intellectuals' rewriting in the early twentieth century of the Gospel narratives of the Christian Bible (Ni 2011; Wang 2014, 2017a, 2017b, 2019; Starr 2016; Chin 2018). Among these intellectuals—Zhao Zichen (T. C. Chao, 1888–1979), Wu Leichuan (L. C. Wu, 1870–1944), Zhang Shizhang (Hottinger S. C. Chang, b. 1896), etc.—stands out Zhu Weizhi (W. T. Chu, 1905–1999), who in addition to being first and foremost a preeminent literary scholar, also devoted himself within no more than two years to the recasting of two very different Lives of Jesus, one in 1948 and another 1950. Entitled *Yesu jidu* (Jesus Christ) and *Wuchan zhe yesu zhuan* (Jesus the Proletarian) respectively, these two biographies of Jesus (particularly the latter one) have drawn attention from scholars of various disciplinary backgrounds (Gálik 2007; Chin 2015; Liu 2016).

Having recognized some foreign influences on Zhu's composing of *Jesus the Proletarian*, however, scholars did not probe sufficiently into the extent to which he borrowed from global sources as follows regarding historical Jesus and primitive Christianity: Friedrich Engels' "On the History of Early Christianity," Karl Kautsky's *Foundations of Christianity*, Bouck White's *The Call of the Carpenter*,[1] Naozo Yonezawa's *Musansha Iesu* (Jesus the Proletarian), F. Herbert Stead's *The Proletarian Gospel of Galilee*, and David Smith's *The Days of His Flesh*. By "global" here we respectively mean American, British, Japanese, German and Czech-Austrian in terms of the aforementioned writers' nationalities. Equally under-explored are the ways these global sources have been creatively localized (*bentu hua*), or indigenized (*bense hua*), by Zhu through the lens of Sinicized Marxism. To capture the nature of this phenomenon, in this article I apply the discourse of globalization and its extended version, glocalization (Robertson 1995)—a discourse that has been adopted in analyzing the history of Christianity in China (Harrison 2013; Kilcourse 2016; Sachsenmaier 2018; Inouye 2019). The elucidation of the glocal entanglements in *Jesus the Proletarian*, the very first Life of Jesus (*yesu zhuan*) after the establishment by the Chinese Communist Party (CCP) of the People's Republic of China, will shed new light upon not only the ways social Christianity and Marxism were interlocked with each other in quest of a historical

---

[1] Zhu Weizhi in his preface to *Jesus the Proletarian* misspelled "Bouck White" as "Buck White" (Zhu 1950a, p. 2), which has been followed by scholars including Marián Gálik and Liu Yan (Gálik 2007, p. 1343; Liu 2016, p. 182). There is a high possibility that they did not consult Bouck White's *The Call of the Carpenter*—one of the most significant sources, as I argue in the following, for us to understand the origin of Zhu's conception of the Gospel according to Marxism.

Jesus by a progressive Christian intellectual, but also the ways Christian intellectuals like Zhu strove to remold themselves intellectually (*sixiang gaizao*) to the adaptation of the exclusively Marxist ideology under an avowedly atheist regime.

In what follows, I firstly offer a synopsis of Zhu Weizhi's life and literary career up until the year 1950 when he published *Jesus the Proletarian*, before moving to discuss in detail Zhu's borrowing from contemporary global sources for its composition. In this regard, *Jesus the Proletarian*, a Chinese historical novel falling under the genres of both Life of Jesus and leftist/proletarian literature (*zuoyi wenxue* or *wuchan jieji wenxue*), can be read as part of world literature. The last section examines the ways Zhu adopted Marxist viewpoints and the CCP's political terms to re-imagine a Gospel according to Marxism for New China (*xin zhongguo*). A Christian socialist theology underpinned Zhu's literary enterprise. Along with other Chinese intellectuals, the Christian intellectual Zhu Weizhi was grappling with the problem that modernity (in the forms of revolution, rationalism, secularization, and Marxism in this context) had posed for traditional (i.e., "feudalistic" and "capitalistic") conceptions of Jesus. In an epoch when all religions including Christianity were plunged into a precarious situation, Zhu's literary *apologia* might be doomed to fail, but what might be worth rethinking even until now is his very endeavor in quest of the relationship between Jesus and proletarity, religion and politics, literature and ideology, and spirituality and secularity.

2. Zhu Weizhi's Life and Literary Career

Zhu Weizhi was an offspring both of the modern Protestant missionary movement and the secular New Culture/Literature Movement. Born on 26 May 1905 into a "middle-peasant family" (*zhongnong jiating*, a Marxist-laden term used by Zhu in his later years) in a southern village of Wenzhou, China, a city that would later be called "China's Jerusalem" (Cao 2011), the boy Zhu enjoyed himself very much in Nature—"beautiful mountains and clear waters" and "the blue sky and white clouds" (Cui 1999, p. 46). There is little wonder that he would later identify affectively with a boy Jesus who "lies freely under a fig tree and watches clouds coming and going slowly" (Zhu 1941, p. 5).

There seems to be of no record as to when and why Zhu's peasant parents converted to Christianity, but their acquired faith (Liang 2000, p. 490; Zhu 2009, p. A22; Qu 2011, p. 92) played a decisive role not only in Zhu's primary and higher education, but also in his growing interest in the Bible—a religious *and* literary text Zhu would devote himself to studying for the rest of his life. For primary education, Zhu likely spent about four years in a China Inland Mission boarding school in Wenzhou city, where he started to learn English—a language to be essential in his later years for his academic pursuits, such as translating the works of John Milton. For higher education, after five years in a Wenzhou teachers' training school (secondary level), Zhu chose Nanking (Nanjing) Theological Seminary, partly because of its complete tuition waiver (Qu 2011, pp. 92–93, 95).

As important for his future literary career as education was Zhu's enduring interest in the Bible since his childhood in a Christian family. As he recalled, "At that time [when he was still a middle school student in the early 1920s], there was nowhere to make inquiries about Christian literature, and nobody studied the Bible from a literary point of view. In my childhood, however, I loved myths, legends, and folktales in [the Bible]; during my middle school, I loved poetry in it." By "poetry" he meant at least Psalms and the Song of Songs in the Mandarin Union Version of the Bible (UVB, 1919), arguably the most influential Chinese Bible in the twentieth century. Two other beautiful books in the UVB singled out by Zhu were the Book of Job and the Gospel of Matthew (Liang 2000, p. 490). His then love for the Bible as a literary text was assured by a well-known and beloved lyrical prose writer of the May Fourth era, Zhu Ziqing (1898–1948), who happened to be Zhu Weizhi's middle school teacher for only about one year (1923–1924) (Liang 2000, p. 490; Zhu 1992).

Even before Zhu Ziqing's arrival in Wenzhou, the middle school student Zhu Weizhi had enthusiastically embraced the New Culture/Literature Movement, and his literary favorites included some renowned literati emerging from this movement: Guo Moruo (1892–1978) and the books and journals produced by the Creation Society (*chuangzao she*, one of whose founders was Guo), Bing

Xin (1900–1999, the pen name of Xia Wanying), Wen Yiduo (1899–1946) and, of course, Zhu Ziqing. Now, since Zhu Ziqing was right before Zhu Weizhi, Zhu Weizhi's literary spirit was set aflame by Zhu Ziqing's intellectual spark. "Under Mr. Zhu Ziqing's teaching and influence," as Zhu Weizhi later put it, "my road to literature" was determined once and for all (Zhu 1989, p. 189; Zhu 1992). Therefore, during his three years of studies in the Nanking Theological Seminary (1924–1927), Zhu Weizhi immersed himself in the world of literature and came to publish academic articles on various topics such as Mozi, Qu Yuan, Li Bai, *Chu Ci* (Lyrics of Chu), the Bible as literature, nature poetry in Psalms, and the patriotic poetry in the Old Testament.

No less patriotic than the Old Testament poets was Zhu himself, whose nationalistic fervor could date back to as early as his very first year in middle school, 1919, when the May Fourth Movement concurrently broke out. The fourteen-year-old student Zhu participated in this movement by "propagandizing and lecturing," by "checking and banning and burning Japanese goods," and by "boycotting classes and opposing the schoolmaster." In the spring of 1927, Zhu exhibited his patriotism again, this time by *"toubi congrong"* (tossing aside the brush to join the military ranks), that is, by leaving his seminarian life and joining the General Political Department of the North Expedition army (with Guo Moruo as one of Zhu's superiors). Having then read the "Communist Manifesto" for the first time as an officer in the army, Zhu appreciated its "poetic language" without "a thorough understanding [of it]" (Zhu 1989, pp. 189–90; Qu 2011, p. 98).

After being in the army for less than one year, Zhu became an editor and translator for the Association Press of China (the national publishing arm of the Young Men's Christian Association in China), before moving south to join Fukien (Fujian) Christian University (FCU) for teaching a course about Chinese New Literature in its first decade, a topic on which he had published a research article. One year later, he was sent for in-service training by the FCU to Waseda University and Chuo University (both in Tokyo, Japan). Under the instruction of Professor Takeshi Yamaguchi (1884–1932) in Waseda University, Zhu conducted his research on the history of Chinese literary trends of thought (Zhu 1989, p. 190) in applying the Western dialectics of realism and romanticism.

Coming back from overseas, Zhu spent another four years in the FCU (1932–1936) before transferring himself to the Baptist-affiliated University of Shanghai, another well-known Protestant Christian college in Republican China. He stayed in Shanghai for 16 years until 1952, when he was redeployed north to Nankai University, Tianjin, for the rest of his life (Zhu 1989, p. 191). It was during the Shanghai period that Zhu had published most of his scholarly outputs in the first half of his life. Among them were the aforementioned two Lives of Jesus, *Jesus Christ* (1948) and *Jesus the Proletarian* (1950).

3. Global Sources for Zhu Weizhi's Composition of *Jesus the Proletarian*

Why did Zhu produce two Lives of Jesus within such a short two-year time span? There must be significant reasons in Zhu Weizhi's judgment that rendered the first one unsatisfactory and the second necessary; fortunately, he provided a brief explanation. In the preface to *Jesus the Proletarian*, Zhu described his most crucial task in this work as presenting Jesus "as he truly was" by "taking off the exotic costumes put on him for two thousand years by feudalism and capitalism." This task should be undertaken, Zhu continued, from a bluntly "proletarian viewpoint" (*wuchan jieji de guandian*), a viewpoint Zhu did not take two years ago when writing *Jesus Christ*, in which Jesus was represented as a "pure religionist" (*chun zongjiao jia*). Such a religionist Jesus, though not without a "revolutionary consciousness" (*geming de yishi*), was still colored by something "idealistic" (*weixin*). Since 1948, however, two things had taken place for Zhu personally and politically. For one thing, after reading, among other ancient histories and social histories, "On the History of Early Christianity" written by Friedrich Engels (1820–1895) and *Foundations of Christianity* by Karl Kautsky (1854–1938), Zhu "gradually came to understand Jesus' correct position and viewpoint."[2] For another, the post-1949 political reality in which Zhu lived had been "turned upside down," implying the defeat of the Guomindang (Nationalist) regime and the establishment of the CCP's. This historical turn was likened by Zhu as "a larger reference book" to help him "see more clearly [whom Jesus truly was]": a proletarian, as shown by the provocative title of his 1950 Life of Jesus (Zhu 1950a, p. 2). The 1948 image of Jesus had not taken into full account this proletarian aspect and hence was no longer sufficient; it needed to be refashioned in light of Marxism.

Zhu's explanation evinced both global (Engels and Kautsky) and local (the regime transition) influences on his worldview, and accordingly on the re-interpretation of Jesus and the Gospel accounts. To begin with, in chapter 1 of *Jesus the Proletarian* Zhu quoted from Engels' "On the History of Early Christianity" in its very first sentence: "The history of early Christianity has notable points of resemblance with the modern working-class movement" (Engels 1990, p. 447). This quotation was intended to draw young Chinese readers' attention to "come and see" the ways Jesus would be endowed with proletarity in the following chapters (Zhu 1950b, p. 3). Whereas the observation made by Engels did generally embolden Zhu to investigate a proletarian image of Jesus, "On the History of Early Christianity" itself cared nothing about the issues of the historical Jesus and the four Gospels, which would have been essential for the reconstruction of any Life of Jesus. As a matter of fact, Engels' piece unfolded the history of early Christianity in analyzing, instead of the historical Jesus, the Revelation of John, a book Engels dated as the earliest one in the New Testament (Engels 1990, p. 454). Therefore, Engels did not specifically exemplify for Zhu the ways the "marriage" of Jesus and proletarity could be consummated.

In this regard, another figure mentioned above, Karl Kautsky, was not helpful either. One of the authorities on Marxism, in *Foundations of Christianity* Kautsky applied the materialistic conception of history to the rigorous study of the beginnings of primitive Christianity. Kautsky admitted that "Christianity in its beginnings was without doubt a movement of impoverished classes of the most varied kinds" (Kautsky 1925, p. 9). Yet in following the German biblical higher criticism of his time, Kautsky treated the Gospel accounts not as sources for a Life of Jesus but as testimonies of faith in Jesus, holding that "it is impossible to say anything definite of the alleged founder of the Christian congregation" (Kautsky 1925, p. 326). It was thus by no means possible for Kautsky to project the proletarity of primitive Christianity onto the historical Jesus.

Having said that, *Foundations of Christianity* did have influences in some respects on Zhu's composition of *Jesus the Proletarian*, chapter 4 of which was a most conspicuous case in point. In this chapter, entitled "Jewish Society Under the Roman Rule," Zhu gave a Marxist analysis of both the class distinctions constituting Jewish society during the time of Jesus and the class antagonism therein. Three classes—the proletarian, the bourgeois, and the patrician—were said to be represented by Zealots and Essenes, Pharisees, and Sadducees, respectively (Zhu 1950b, p. 8). I would suggest that Zhu borrowed this framework of classification directly from *Foundations of Christianity*, in which Kautsky's longer version of a counterpart analysis of Judaism was clearly grounded upon these class distinctions. Where Kautsky noted that "the contrast between the Sadducees and the Pharisees was not at bottom a religious one, but a class opposition, a hostility that can be compared with that between the nobility and the Third Estate before the French Revolution" (Kautsky 1925, p. 273), Zhu translated the same point, with several minor deletions and additions, into *Jesus the Proletarian* (Zhu 1950b, p. 11). More borrowings from Kautsky, and even a host of verbatim extracts, could also be evidenced by a parallel reading of chapter 4 from *Jesus the Proletarian* with chapter 2 on "The Jews After the Exile" from part 3 of *Foundations of Christianity* (Zhu 1950b, pp. 8–14; Kautsky 1925, pp. 272–320).

---

[2]   Zhu, though generally apolitical since 1928, stood as a sympathizer of the communist movement towards the late 1940s, as evidenced by his covering in 1948 of an ex-student of the University of Shanghai and underground communist party member (Ding 2014, pp. 10–14).

However, in many significant respects, the dominant influences on Zhu's literary production of the first post-1949 Chinese Life of Jesus came not from Engels and Kautsky, but from Zhu's reading of some other global sources. Here we identify three such sources. One was *The Days of His Flesh* written by David Smith (1866–1932), Professor of Theology in Magee College, County Londonderry, Northern Ireland. It contributed to Zhu's composition, particularly regarding the arrangement of the sequences of what Jesus said and did. For example, in line with Smith for harmonizing the Synoptic Gospels and John's Gospel, Zhu had Jesus cleanse the temple twice (Zhu 1950b, pp. 4, 35–37, 95), which is almost unparalleled in contrast to "Jesus novels" produced in the English world (Crook 2011, p. 505).

Another two closely related sources that left a more indelible imprint on Zhu's composition of *Jesus the Proletarian* were Bouck White's *The Call of the Carpenter* and Naozo Yonezawa's *Musansha Iesu*.[3] *The Call of the Carpenter*, written by the American socialist and Congregationalist minister Rev. Bouck White (1874–1951) (Kenton 1998), was regarded by Zhu Weizhi as the earliest Life of Jesus that was written from a proletarian point of view. White's work was also the one upon which the Japanese socialist and Congregationalist minister Rev. Naozo Yonezawa (1876–1936) (Kasahara 1978) substantially based his Life of Jesus.[4] Zhu Weizhi recalled in 1950 that, among several Lives of Jesus written from a proletarian perspective, Yonezawa's work, *Musansha Iesu*, stood out as both the first one Zhu read eighteen years ago (quite possibly during his stay in Japan) and "the one impressing him most" (Zhu 1950b, p. 2). Zhu did admit in general that he "drew significant inspiration" from works like White's and Yonezawa's (Zhu 1950a, p. 3), but in *Jesus the Proletarian* there was no citation of such contemporary works whatsoever, which increases the difficulty in differentiating between Zhu's original ideas and his borrowings.

That said, it is still evident that not a few of the contents and ideas in Zhu's *Jesus the Proletarian* should be attributed to the influences from White's *The Call of the Carpenter*, either directly or indirectly through the detouring of Zhu's reading of Yonezawa's *Musansha Iesu*. Take for instance chapter 3 on "A Ruthless but Crafty Exploitation" from Zhu's *Jesus the Proletarian*. In this chapter, Zhu depicted the rule of the Roman Empire from an economic standpoint. According to Zhu, Rome governed the colonies, not by the policy of utter political conquest, but by tax collection through its local allies—for instance, the aristocracies in the conquered Carthage or Palestine. The exorbitant tax collection of Rome, Zhu wrote, "oppressed the [colonized] people out of breath" (Zhu 1950b, p. 5). This depiction should be seen, however, as a borrowing—a conspicuous paraphrase that stemmed initially from *The Call of the Carpenter* and *Musansha Iesu*. On the one hand, it was precisely from the tax-collecting viewpoint that White and Yonezawa described the Roman ruling. On the other, even Zhu's examples concerning the Roman collaboration with the upper class in Carthage or with the native princes in Palestine were identical to what White and Yonezawa had written (White 1911, p. 9; Yonezawa 1928b, p. 4). Another of Zhu's obvious borrowings from *The Call of the Carpenter* appeared when in illustrating the Roman slavery system he cited a statement made by Edward Gibbon (1737–1794), which was also cited by White and Yonezawa, that across the Roman Empire there were sixty million slaves, accounting for almost half of the Empire's entire population (Zhu 1950b, p. 6; White 1911, p. 13; Yonezawa 1928b, p. 5).

Zhu's Jesus was not always in line with White's (and Yonezawa's), however. For example, White straightforwardly broke up with both the "Christian socialism" camp and the "liberal theology" camp as far as the view of God is concerned. Whereas the Christian socialism movement "had for its

---

[3] I herein thank Dr. Yosuke Matsutani, church historian and pastor of the United Church of Christ in Japan, who made a copy of Naozo Yonezawa's work for me.

[4] In his preface to *Musansha Iesu*, Yonezawa notes that his work is not a total translation of White's *The Call of the Carpenter*, and he has done his own research by also consulting other books, including (1) the American leading social theologian and Baptist pastor Walter Rauschenbusch's three books about "social Christianity" (implying *Christianity and the Social Crisis*, *Christianizing the Social Order*, and *A Theology for the Social Gospel*), (2) the American sociologist Charles A. Ellwood's *The Reconstruction of Religion*, and (3) the British Baptist pastor and educator Theodore Gerald Soares' *The Social Institutions and Ideals of the Bible* (Yonezawa 1928a, p. 5). However, the stark commonalities between *Musansha Iesu* and *The Call of the Carpenter* can be identified by simply comparing the tables of contents. A majority of the keywords shown in chapter titles are exactly the same in meaning; this is particularly the case in the first eleven chapters, where Jesus' whole life is retold.

intellectual foundation the orthodox doctrine of a heavenly despot" and the liberal theology proponents "[had] been taught to believe that 'the father almighty' [*sic*] is the *sine qua non* of Christianity," White could not endure a "God the father [*sic*] almighty" (White 1911, pp. 292, 297–98). He firmly believed that fatherhood equaled despotism and brotherhood equaled democracy, and he would be all for brotherhood. In contrast, Zhu's Jesus did not bother with a father-like God and did not see a dichotomy between fatherhood and brotherhood. For Zhu's Jesus, the conception of the fatherhood of God for all human beings signaled a spirit of equality. The conception that "everyone is a child of God after all," Zhu opined, would "break the distinctions either between the propertied class and the unpropertied class or between those who toil with their minds and those their hands" (Zhu 1950b, p. 31). In this regard, Zhu's Jesus bore more resemblance to the Jesus in F. Herbert Stead's *The Proletarian Gospel of Galilee* (another biography Zhu had also consulted) than to White's and Yonezawa's Jesus. In his Life of Jesus, the British social reformer and Congregationalist minister Rev. F. Herbert Stead (1857–1928) prioritized "the Divine Fatherhood" as below: "Fatherhood is fundamental to Jesus. It is also fontal. Because God is Father to all men, therefore all men are brothers. The Brotherhood is based upon the Fatherhood. And there is no other foundation that can compare with this that is laid by Christ Jesus" (Stead 1922, pp. 31–32). Although the theme of "the Fatherhood of God and the Brotherhood of Man" was commonplace among the liberal Protestant circles (Richardson 1963, p. 311) and there was no need for Zhu to read Stead in order to come to this conclusion, Zhu's view at least resonated well with Stead's or was even reinforced by the latter.

In all, then, Zhu Weizhi had consulted the above contemporary sources to various degrees when portraying a Jesus in response to, and in harmony with, the CCP's ideology. These sources were read enthusiastically by such a progressive Christian in light of a brand new political reality. The global literary antecedents provided a model for Zhu's Marxist presentation of Jesus. As mentioned before, *Jesus the Proletarian* can be read in this regard as part of world literature (Duran 2018). Indeed, *Jesus the Proletarian* should not be considered a completely original biography; it bears the stamps of global socialist movements (as one aspect of modernity) and their literary reflections in the first half of the twentieth century. Yet the contributions that Zhu made through his creative localization of the globally produced Lives of Jesus cannot be ignored. Zhu executed his intellectual and literary creativity when rewriting the Gospel narratives. From these glocal entanglements emerged a Gospel according to Marxism. I now turn to this Gospel itself.

4. The Gospel According to Marxism

Zhu Weizhi's Life of Jesus did not emerge from a socio-political vacuum. As mentioned previously, Zhu in post-1949 China sought to reconstruct a Gospel story in harmony with the *zeitgeist*, the spirit of the time. What is immediately striking about Zhu's *Jesus the Proletarian* is that the events and characters in the Gospel accounts were now placed in a Marxist frame of interpretation. Simply by a random reading of *Jesus the Proletarian*, one can identify the following widely-used terms that either were adopted from Marxist literature or were fashionable in the CCP's propaganda of the time: exploitation (*boxue*, used 23 times in the whole text); inequality (*bu pingdeng*, 1 time); the people (*renmin*, 5 times) or the masses (*dazhong*, 24 times); socialism (*shehui zhuyi*, 2 times) or communism (*gongchan zhuyi*, 2 times); revolution (*geming*, 22 times); "overturning the body" (*fanshen*, 3 times), liberation (*jiefang*, 17 times), or liberation movement (*jiefang yundong*, 7 times); political program (*gangling*, 10 times); class interest (*jieji liyi*, 1 time), class consciousness (*jieji de yishi*, 1 time), class struggle (*jieji de douzheng*, 1 time), or class antagonism (*jieji duili*, 1 time); the privileged class (*tequan zhe* or *tequan jieji*, 20 times), the propertied class (*youchan zhe* or *youchan jieji*, 4 times), or the bourgeoisie (*zhongchan jieji*, 6 times); the proletariat (*wuchan zhe*, *wuchan jieji*, *wuchan dazhong* or *puluo lieta liya*, 55 times), the working class (*laodong zhe*, *laodong jieji* or *laodong dazhong*, 6 times), or the oppressed class (*bei yapo zhe*, *bei yapo jieji*, or the like, 13 times); proletarian solidarity (*wuchan jieji tuanjie*, 1 time) or unifying the masses (*tuanjie qunzhong*, 1 time); comrade (*tongzhi*, 12 times) and cadre (*ganbu*, 2 times); social sin (*shehui de zui'e*, 3 times); public servant (*gongpu*, 2 times); democracy (*minzhu*, 11 times); human right (*renquan*, 16 times);

internationalism (*guoji zhuyi*, 1 time); social existence (*shehui cunzai*, 1 time); and dialectic (*bianzheng*, 5 times). Zhu's Life of Jesus therefore arguably operated within a Marxism-oriented context. As far as I know, there is no single Chinese Life of Jesus—not even *Jidu jiao yu zhongguo wenhua* (Christianity and Chinese Culture) by Wu Leichuan (Wu 1936) or *Geming de mujiang* (The Revolutionary Carpenter) by Zhang Shizhang (Zhang 1939)—that has made such extensive use of Marxist terminologies as Zhu's.

All these terminologies aside, we may also adopt a thematic approach to examine the extent to which Marxism was integrated into Zhu's narrative. *Jesus the Proletarian* tells its story in 26 short chapters, drawing from all four Gospels as narrative materials in a typically harmonizing way. It opens its very first chapter with describing the contemporary Chinese dichotomy thinking of Christianity, seeing it either as downright superstition or as pure religion ("religion for religion's sake"). In a polemical manner, in *Jesus the Proletarian* Zhu tried to transcend the conflict by arguing (against the Chinese young atheists) that the founder of Christianity was no less revolutionary and socialistic, while holding (against the pure religionists) in the meantime that the core of Jesus' mission was not religious but socio-political ("religion for life/society's sake") (Zhu 1950b, pp. 1–3, 31–32). In the following, I would like to draw attention to six facets of the unfolding story of Zhu's Jesus to illustrate the ways Zhu attempted to justify this two-fold argument by adopting Marxist viewpoints and CCP's propaganda terms.

The class opponents of Jesus. From a literary perspective, not unlike Mark's Gospel (Telford 2011, p. 21), one of the major strands of Zhu's storyline or plotting is the conflict between Jesus and his opponents. Jesus had as his class opponents not only the Roman Empire who exploited Palestine and the aristocratic classes like the Sadducees as Rome's local collaborators, but also the bourgeois Pharisees. As regards Pharisees, on the one hand they opposed the aristocrats' loyalty to Caesar and committed themselves to "preserving the national essence" (*baocun guocui*), as Zhu puts it, while on the other hand, it is their class status as the bourgeois intelligentsia that brought "two-sidedness" (*liangmian xing*) and "wavering in determination" (*youyi xing*), thus "alienating themselves from the masses." As Zhu remarks in the middle of the work, given their class nature, Pharisees "despise the proletarian masses and support the distinction between classes because they want to maintain their class privilege." There is little wonder then that through a loose quotation from Matthew 23: 13–27, Zhu characterizes Pharisees as severely accursed by Jesus due to their collaboration in secret with the ruling class (Zhu 1950b, pp. 10–12, 46–48; cf. White 1911, pp. 96–99).

The dependence of social consciousness upon social existence. The class distinction between Jesus and his opponents further exemplifies Zhu's understanding of this classical Marxist thesis. Two stories illustrate this point. One story concerns a narrative originally from John 3: 1–21—namely, the dialogue between Jesus and Nicodemus, the latter being one of few (in Zhu's terms) "progressive" and "open-minded" patricians. However progressive and open-minded, it is nonetheless because of "being blinded by class prejudice" that the patrician Nicodemus still could not grasp what Jesus meant by "regeneration" in the sense of remolding oneself. In a similar vein, Zhu tells another story about a well-known conversation between Jesus and the young rich man. This story ends with Jesus' parabolic statement that "It is easier for a camel to go through the eye of a needle than for a rich man to enter into the kingdom of God" (Matthew 19: 24). Zhu then makes a Marxist implication out of this narrative: "The living condition, social relations and social existence of an individual determine his consciousness, and class interest influences his standpoint. It is almost a mission impossible for a rich man to join a revolutionary community" (Zhu 1950b, pp. 38–39, 89–90).

Women as the liberator and the liberated. Much ink has been spilled by Zhu depicting the roles that women play in Jesus' life and public ministry. Jesus' mother Mary typifies one type of women as the liberator. The portrayal of Mary as a "revolutionary, laboring woman" makes up the whole fifth chapter of *Jesus the Proletarian*. In stark contrast to a Mary "born into a distinguished family" (*xichu mingmen*) in Zhu's 1948 Life of Jesus (Zhu 1948, p. 17), two years later Mary in *Jesus the Proletarian* is reconstructed as someone "born into a humbly laboring family" (*shengyu beiwei de laodong zhe zhi jia*) (Zhu 1950b, p. 14) so that her proletarian-class background is well established. Along the same line with Luke's Gospel (1: 46–55), Zhu refashions a progressive Mary partly through the message in her Magnificat—"an unparalleled, proletarian-revolting song" that "exudes class consciousness, revolutionary mood, and democratic thinking" (Zhu 1950b, p. 15). In this song, Mary is expecting that her future child would liberate the oppressed and the weak not from sin, but from their oppressor—the Roman Empire—even though the Magnificat itself does not mention the Romans by name. It is very likely that Zhu here borrows some critical insights from Bouck White, such as: "Heaven is not on the side of privilege and oppression, she [Mary] affirms, but is rather on the side of the trodden" (Zhu 1950b, p. 16; White 1911, p. 22). One more affirmation of Mary's revolutionary character emerges when Zhu re-interprets what Jesus intends before his death in connecting his mother and the Apostle John (identified by Zhu as the disciple whom Jesus loved in John 19: 26–27). As opposed to what has been commonly assumed, in Zhu's judgment, Jesus' purpose is not that John should take care of the pitiful Mary, but that such a staunchly revolutionary woman as Mary would maintain the immature John's faith (Zhu 1950b, p. 18; cf. White 1911, pp. 197–98). We may term Zhu's characterization of Mary as a proletarian/revolutionary Mariology, which, not surprisingly, fits quite well into the CCP's representation of "progressive women" that dedicate themselves to the revolutionary cause.

Another type of women concerns those seen as the liberated ones due to Jesus' public ministry. One such woman, Mary Magdalene, is identified by Zhu as the woman in Luke who lived a sinful life (7: 36–38). According to Zhu's account, whereas Simon the Pharisee, on account of his class prejudice, withheld from Jesus the customs for inviting distinguished guests, the "promiscuous" Mary Magdalene anoints Jesus' feet with the ointment. Seeing through the hearts of fellow guest Pharisees who despise Mary Magdalene for her moral sins, Zhu's Jesus absolves her from responsibility because he deems Mary Magdalene's sinning out of not merely her own fault but also the society's (Zhu 1950b, pp. 62–63; cf. White 1911, p. 124). This discursive strategy of defending the female sinner and blaming the society is adopted again in Zhu's recasting of the narrative of a woman caught in adultery (John 8: 1–11). Zhu asserts that this woman works as a harlot simply because she "could not stand the economic oppression" and that Jesus sees these "social sins" as "far more severe and obstinate than the personal ones" (Zhu 1950b, pp. 97–98). Zhu thus constructs these biblical women as the liberated ones, for whose iniquities society at large is to blame. This theme of women's liberation in Jesus' time also resonates well with the CCP's propaganda discourse of the time.

The class nature of Jesus. As has been stated previously, Zhu's *Jesus the Proletarian* is a work revolving around the class nature of Jesus. To achieve his aim, Zhu primarily presents a fully human Jesus. It can be said without reservation that Zhu's Jesus is positioned in exclusively human terms. Jesus' birth from a virgin, divine nature, working of miracles, resurrection from the dead, and *Parousia* (second coming)—all these elements are missing from *Jesus the Proletarian*. In this non-miraculous framework, Zhu makes his attempt to justify a Jesus who belongs to the proletariat in at least three ways. First, in chapter 2 of *Jesus the Proletarian* Zhu contrasts ancient official history (*zhengshi*) in antiquity to the four Gospels. The near absence of Jesus in ancient official history, which tells of stories only concerning "princes and marquises" or "emperors and aristocrats," is highlighted by Zhu to manifest Jesus' proletarity. Only in the four Gospels, which Zhu attributes as "the people's history recorded by the people," can we find the trace of Jesus as a proletarian (Zhu 1950b, pp. 3–4).

Another way Zhu used to refashion a proletarian image of Jesus was to reconstruct the world into which Jesus was born. The Nativity narrative in Luke is appropriated by Zhu in chapter 6 to illustrate the contrast between a baby Jesus who "did not even own a cradle" on the one hand, and "the patricians and the propertied classes who lived a leisurely life" on the other. In contrast to imagining the Nativity story in *Jesus Christ* as "the most beautiful poem" (Zhu 1948, p. 18), two years later Zhu reconsiders the Nativity night, not as "a silent night," but as "a miserable and depressing night." This is the case because, according to Zhu, the poll tax that the Roman government collects from the proletariat such as Jesus' parents is abusive and the homeless shepherds in the field of Bethlehem suffer even more from the exploitative tax collecting. In a word, Zhu's Jesus was born "not so much on earth as on a living hell" (Zhu 1950b, pp. 18–19).

A third way of shaping the class nature of Jesus concerns an emphasis upon the labor work of Jesus as a carpenter. The labor work makes our young protagonist so conscious of the value of laboring (*laodong*) that he later would come to some truth claims such as "the laborer is worthy of his hire" (Luke 10: 7) or "my father [read here Joseph, Jesus's earthly father, rather than God, Jesus' heavenly father] worketh hitherto, and I work" (John 5: 17). Zhu then lauds Jesus for his thoroughgoing viewpoint about labor. "Labor creates the world and the universe," as Zhu puts it, "and since the universe is still unfinished yet and in the creating process, we need to labor to create a just world without oppression" (Zhu 1950b, pp. 22–23). Zhu's underlining of labor resonates again with both Marxism and the CCP's political discourse, and all these serve to render Jesus more attractive to the Chinese proletariat. In terms of theology, we may title Zhu's presentation of Jesus as a proletarian Christology.

The *basileia* (kingdom) mission of Jesus. In chapter 9 of *Jesus the Proletarian*, "The Program of the Liberation Movement," the mission of Zhu's Jesus is to advocate for "a movement of the kingdom of the heavens" (*tianguo yundong*)—that is, "a movement of new social construction" not only for liberating the slavery class but also for fundamentally remolding the lives of human beings. This movement of the *basileia* of the heavens, then, has little remaining religious connotation. In truth, the "maximum program" (*zuigao gangling*)—a conspicuously communist-style terminology—of Zhu's Jesus corresponds to that of communism and the CCP: "a new society where all human beings live, without class distinction and exploitation." In a nutshell, the *basileia* of the heavens equals a communist society.

Yet Jesus' maximum program cannot be achieved hastily. It needs to be accomplished step by step, and the very first step to take shall be the act of inculcating the masses with the "awareness of human rights": the proletarian class should have been equal to the propertied class because the former are as much the children of God as the latter. Rather than a revolutionary proper (as Bouck White has depicted) given the means he employs, Zhu's Jesus is more like a teacher or a prophet. The motif of awakening the masses on the part of this teacher-prophet figure, in line with White's narrative (see, for example, White 1911, p. 93), runs through *Jesus the Proletarian*. For example, although used to be despised abusively as "Galilean pigs" by Jerusalem's patricians, Zhu claims, the proletariat from Galilee where Jesus grows up are told by Jesus that "God is on our side" and that "God's wisdom is hidden from the wise and prudent and is revealed unto the lowly brothers" (adapted respectively from Matthew 1: 23 and 11: 25). The use of the term "Immanuel," meaning either "God with us" or "God on the side of us," "becomes a voice of liberation that makes a great impact on the lowest class" (Zhu 1950b, pp. 31–33). Theologically, the *basileia* mission of Jesus can be understood as an awakenment soteriology.

The passion of Jesus as the working out of dialectics. Finally, every Life of Jesus in history must find a way to come to terms with Jesus' death. Against basing the passion narrative upon the religious atonement theory, Zhu refashioned his Jesus as a firm adherent of Marxist dialectics. When his second year's public ministry begins, and another Passover approaches, Zhu's Jesus recalls the meaning of the festival and the agency of salvation: when Moses led Israel out of the hands of the cruel Egyptian despot (cf. White 1911, pp. 153–54), the Passover lambs as sacrifices were vital to the Israelite nation's very survival. Zhu's Jesus derives from this national story the dialectics of death and life and the significance of martyrdom (*xisheng*). It then makes sense for Zhu's Jesus in this context to state the following claim: "unless a grain of wheat falls into the earth and dies, it remains just a single grain; but if it dies, it bears much fruit" (John 12: 24). Jesus' resolution to become such a grain of wheat reflects, Zhu avers, his "dialectical views of the world, life, and society." Later on, in the district of Caesarea Philippi, Zhu's Jesus announces to his disciples "the most important manifesto": "If any want to become my followers, let them deny themselves and take up their cross and follow me. For those who want to save their life will lose it, and those who lose their life for my sake will find it. For what will it profit them if they gain the whole world but forfeit their life? Or what will they give in return for their life?" (Matthew 16: 24–26) This manifesto indicates, again, Jesus' "dialectical view of revolution" (Zhu 1950b, pp. 70–71, 76). The high praise of martyrdom, of course, was not alien to those Chinese who had just gone through the Anti-Japanese War and the civil war. Through Zhu's re-imagination,

Religions **2019**, *10*, 535

the Chinese readers, just as Wainwright claims for today's readers, "can read the passion narrative as providing a model for a life lived for the sake of justice and in fidelity to God, lived in a way that could lead to a martyr's death, especially in unjust imperial situations like that of first-century Palestine" (Wainwright 2011, p. 41).

5. Conclusions

To conclude, Zhu Weizhi's aim in composing *Jesus the Proletarian* is to provide a Marxist Jesus as equaling *the* historical Jesus, without the garbs of feudal and capitalist appropriations. Nonetheless, it is because of his Marxist framework that Zhu's Jesus—just as the Jesus in Mark's Gospel or any other Gospels—becomes another "Jesus of culture," "constructed by the literary or religious imagination and propagated in the interests of the believing community or society" (Telford 2011, p. 17). In keeping with Albert Schweitzer (Schweitzer 2001), New Testament professor Delbert Burkett remarks that "Ultimately humans have created Jesus in their images ... These images may not tell us a great deal about Jesus of Nazareth, but they do tell us about the people who conceived or imagined them" (Burkett 2011, p. 9). In a similar vein, the quest of the historical Jesus in Communist China may tell us more about Zhu the progressive biographer than Jesus the protagonist.

Moreover, our understanding of the Sinicization of theology should not be limited only to its "cultural" aspect, that is, something like the use of "the Chinese concept of yin and yang to understand the divine and human in Jesus" (Burkett 2011, pp. 6–7). Traditional scholarship in theological studies has attributed the development of what we now call "liberation Christology" overwhelmingly to the Latin American theological works under the influence of Marxism, without giving due attention to their Chinese counterparts such as *Jesus the Proletarian*, a work published more than two decades earlier than Leonardo Boff's *Jesus Christ Liberator* (1972) and Jon Sobrino's *Christology at the Crossroads* (1976) (La Due 2001, pp. 160–80). Globally speaking, Zhu Weizhi's Jesus stands as a precursor to his later Latin American counterpart. *Jesus the Proletarian* deserves to be appreciated as the Gospel according to Marxism in China that has long been forgotten and to which it is now time to pay heed.

Funding: This work has been supported by the STU Scientific Research Initiation Grant (Project No. STF19002).

Conflicts of Interest: The author declares no conflict of interest.

References

Burkett, Delbert. 2011. Images of Jesus: An Overview. In *The Blackwell Companion to Jesus*. Edited by Delbert Burkett. Malden: Wiley-Blackwell, pp. 1–9.

Cao, Nanlai. 2011. *Constructing China's Jerusalem: Christians, Power, and Place in Contemporary Wenzhou*. Stanford: Stanford University Press.

Chin, Kenpa. 2015. W. T. Chu's *Jesus, the Proletarian*. Sino-Christian Studies 19: 43–63.

Chin, Kenpa. 2018. The Image of Jesus in the Writings of Zhang Shizhang (Hottinger S. C. Chang). *Christianity & Literature* 1: 74–85.

Crook, Zeba A. 2011. Jesus Novels: Solving Problems with Fiction. In *The Blackwell Companion to Jesus*. Edited by Delbert Burkett. Malden: Wiley-Blackwell, pp. 504–18.

Cui, Baoheng. 1999. Zhu weizhi xiansheng jishi (A Chronicle of Mr. Zhu Weizhi). *Renwu (Personage)* 10: 46–53.

Ding, Jingtang. 2014. Enshi zhu weizhi yanhu wo (My Teacher Zhu Weizhi Protected Me). In *Zhu weizhi yu jiaren (Zhu Weizhi and His Family)*. Edited by Mingzhou Zhu. Unknown Publisher: pp. 10–14.

Duran, Angelica. 2018. Chinese Christian Studies and Anglophone Literary Studies: A Response to Chin Kenpa's "Chinese Marxist Biblical Criticism on Jesus: A Study on W. T. Chu (朱維之)". *Christianity & Literature* 1: 86–99.

Engels, Frederick. 1990. On the History of Early Christianity. In *Karl Marx–Frederick Engels: Collected Works: Engels: 1890–1895*. Translated by David Forgacs, Barrie Selman, John Peet, Joan Trevor Walmsley, and Veronica Thomson. New York: International Publishers, vol. 27, pp. 445–69. First published 1894.

Gálik, Marián. 2007. *Jesus the Proletarian*: A Biography by Zhu Weizhi (1905–1999). In *The Chinese Face of Jesus Christ*. Edited by Roman Malek. Sankt Augustin: Institut Monumenta Serica/China-Zentrum, vol. 3, pp. 1335–52.

Harrison, Henrietta. 2013. *The Missionary's Curse and Other Tales from a Chinese Catholic Village*. Berkeley: University of California Press.

Inouye, Melissa Wei-Tsing. 2019. *China and the True Jesus: Charisma and Organization in a Chinese Christian Church*. New York: Oxford University Press.

Kasahara, Yoshimitsu. 1978. From "Cultural" Christianity to "Social" Christianity: Naozo Yonezawa's Development of Thought (文化的キリスト教から社会的キリスト教へ――米沢尚三の思想的展開). *The Study of Christianity and Social Problems* (キリスト教社会問題研究) 27: 45–75.

Kautsky, Karl. 1925. *Foundations of Christianity*. New York: International Publishers. First published 1908.

Kenton, Mary E. 1998. Christianity, Democracy, and Socialism: Bouck White's Kingdom of Self-Respect. In *Socialism and Christianity in Early 20th Century America*. Edited by Jacob H. Dorn. Westport: Greenwood Press, pp. 165–97.

Kilcourse, Carl S. 2016. *Taiping Theology: The Localization of Christianity in China, 1843–64*. New York: Palgrave Macmillan.

La Due, William J. 2001. *Jesus among the Theologians: Contemporary Interpretations of Christ*. Harrisburg: Trinity Press International.

Liang, Gong. 2000. Zhu weizhi xiansheng yu jidu jiao wenxue yanjiu (Mr. Zhu Weizhi and the Studies of Christian Literature). *Jidu zongjiao yanjiu (Study of Christianity)* 2: 489–504.

Liu, Yan. 2016. The Rewriting of Jesus Christ: From the Saviour to the Proletarian: A Comparative Study of Zhu Weizhi's *Jesus Christ* and *Jesus the Proletarian*. *Asian and African Studies* 2: 173–90.

Ni, Zhange. 2011. Rewriting Jesus in Republican China: Religion, Literature, and Cultural Nationalism. *The Journal of Religion* 2: 223–52. [CrossRef]

Qu, Guanghui. 2011. Zhu weizhi: cong tiantang dao renjian (Zhu Weizhi: From Heaven to the World). In *Oufeng xinkan (New Series on Wenzhou)*. Edited by Fang Shaoyi. Hefei: Huangshan Publishing House, vol. 2, pp. 91–116.

Richardson, Alan. 1963. The Rise of Modern Biblical Scholarship and Recent Discussion of the Authority of the Bible. In *The Cambridge History of the Bible: The West from the Reformation to the Present Day*. Edited by S. L. Greenslade. Cambridge: Cambridge University Press, vol. 3, pp. 294–338.

Robertson, Roland. 1995. Glocalization: Time-Space and Homogeneity-Heterogeneity. In *Global Modernities*. Edited by Mike Featherstone, Scott Lash and Roland Robertson. London: Sage, pp. 25–44.

Sachsenmaier, Dominic. 2018. *Global Entanglements of a Man Who Never Traveled: A Seventeenth-Century Chinese Christian and His Conflicted Worlds*. New York: Columbia University Press.

Schweitzer, Albert. 2001. *The Quest of the Historical Jesus*. Edited by John Bowden. Minneapolis: Fortress Press.

Starr, Chloë. 2016. *Chinese Theology: Text and Context*. New Haven: Yale University Press.

Stead, F. Herbert. 1922. *The Proletarian Gospel of Galilee*. London: The Labour Publishing Company, Ltd.

Telford, William R. 2011. Mark's Portrait of Jesus. In *The Blackwell Companion to Jesus*. Edited by Delbert Burkett. Malden: Wiley-Blackwell, pp. 13–29.

Wainwright, Elaine M. 2011. Who Do You Say That I Am? A Matthean Response. In *The Blackwell Companion to Jesus*. Edited by Delbert Burkett. Malden: Wiley-Blackwell, pp. 30–46.

Wang, Zhixi. 2014. Yesu, shiren yu shi: dui minguo shiqi (1912–1949) jidu tu chuangzuo de kaocha (Jesus, the Poet & Poems: Focusing on Christian Writings in Republican China, 1912–1949). *Shengjing wenxue yanjiu (Biblical Literature Studies)* 9: 93–109.

Wang, Zhixi. 2017a. "Yesu zhuyi xuanchuan jia": jidu jiao shehui zhuyi zhe zhang shizhang de shengping, sixiang yu shidai ("Evangelist of Jesusism": Hottinger S. C. Chang as a Christian Socialist). *Logos & Pneuma: Chinese Journal of Theology* 46: 189–228.

Wang, Zhixi. 2017b. "Jiashi yesu sheng zai jinri de zhongguo": minguo jidu tu zhishi fenzi de fuyin shu quanshi yu yesu xingxiang de gonggong xing ("What If Jesus Was Born in Today's China": Protestant Intellectuals' Interpretation of the Gospels and Public Images of Jesus in Republican China). Ph.D. dissertation, The Chinese University of Hong Kong, Hong Kong, China.

Wang, Zhixi. 2019. Feizhan de yesu? weiai zhuyi, minguo jidu tu zhishi fenzi de fuyin shu quanshi yu yesu xingxiang de gonggong xing (A Non-Violent Jesus? Pacifism, Christian Intellectuals' Interpretation of the Gospels, and the Publicness of Images of Jesus in Republican China). *Sino-Christian Studies* 27: 93–139.

White, Bouck. 1911. *The Call of the Carpenter*. Garden City: Doubleday, Page & Company.

Wu, Leichuan. 1936. *Jidu jiao yu zhongguo wenhua (Christianity and Chinese Culture)*. Shanghai: The Association Press of China.

Yonezawa, Naozo. 1928a. Xu (Preface). In *Musansha Iesu (Jesus the Proletarian)*. Tokyo: Shunjusha Publishing Company.

Yonezawa, Naozo. 1928b. *Musansha Iesu (Jesus the Proletarian)*. Tokyo: Shunjusha Publishing Company.

Zhang, Shizhang. 1939. *Geming de mujiang (The Revolutionary Carpenter)*. Shanghai: Zhenli yu shengming she (The Society for Truth and Life).

Zhu, Minghai. 2009. Wo de fuqin zhu weizhi (My Father Zhu Weizhi). *Wenzhou dushi bao (Wenzhou City Newspaper)*, December 3, A22.

Zhu, Weizhi. 1941. *Jidu jiao yu wenxue (Christianity and Literature)*. Shanghai: The Association Press of China.

Zhu, Weizhi. 1948. Zhengzhuan (A Biography). In *Yesu jidu (Jesus Christ)*. Edited by Wang Zhixin and Zhu Weizhi. Shanghai: Zhonghua Book Company, pp. 17–98.

Zhu, Weizhi. 1950a. Xu (Preface). In *Wuchan zhe yesu zhuan (Jesus the Proletarian)*. Shanghai: Christian Literature Society, pp. 1–4.

Zhu, Weizhi. 1950b. *Wuchan zhe yesu zhuan (Jesus the Proletarian)*. Shanghai: Christian Literature Society.

Zhu, Weizhi. 1989. Zhu weizhi zizhuan (Autobiography of Zhu Weizhi). In *Dangdai wenxue fanyi baijia tan (One Hundred Contemporary Talks on Literary Translation)*. Edited by Wang Shoulan. Beijing: Peking University Press, pp. 188–92. First published 1982.

Zhu, Weizhi. 1992. Xiang peixian xiansheng xuexi (Learning from Mr. Zhu Ziqing). In *Zhu ziqing (Zhu Ziqing)*. Nanjing: Jiangsu wenshi ziliao bianji bu (The Editorial Department of Cultural and Historical Data of Jiangsu Province), pp. 145–49.

Article

A New Stream of Spiritual Literature: Bei Cun's *The Baptizing River*

Chloë Starr

Yale University Divinity School, 409 Prospect St., New Haven, CT 06511, USA; chloe.starr@yale.edu

Received: 30 May 2019; Accepted: 28 June 2019; Published: 30 June 2019

Abstract: This essay traces the emergence of new categories of "spiritual writing" in Chinese literature, before offering an interpretation of Bei Cun's 1992 novel *The Baptizing River* (Shixi de he 施洗的河) as an exemplar. Bei Cun's first novel as a "Christian author" attracted much critical attention, given the contrast with the author's prior works and its message of spiritual salvation at a time of political change and metaphysical searching. A psychosocial biography of its anti-hero Liu Lang, set in wartime China, the novel charts the protagonist's criminal livelihood, descent into moral depravity, and gradual questioning of life and purpose. This essay foregrounds the structure of the novel and explores how narrative form and theological meaning interact. To do this, it traces the course of the river journeys that mark the different stages of Liu Lang's life and which culminate in his unorthodox baptismal rebirth.

Keywords: Chinese Christian literature; spiritual literature (*shenxing xiezuo*); baptism; Bei Cun; *Shixi de he*; Shi Wei

---

1. Introduction

The resurgence of Christianity in China in the Reform era (1978–present) has garnered a great deal of academic attention and coverage in international media, but the revival of a Christian literature or Christian fiction in China has received scant scholarly consideration, especially in English-language research. The production of new writing by contemporary Christian authors and a broader reclamation of Christian tropes or vocabulary in literature followed naturally on from the upsurge in conversions of the post-Mao period. In the time-lag before the study and recognition of this literature by the academy, some authors themselves analyzed and promoted a new category of "spiritual literature," collating anthologies and publishing journals on the topic.[1]

"Spiritual literature" can be seen as both a sub-category of, and an alternative designation to, "Chinese Christian literature," and its key marker is a concern with an inner life, beyond the material and the interpersonal. Once Chinese-language scholarship began to take note of the phenomenon, various depictions of the new forms of writing emerged. Just as the catch-all term "Chinese Christian literature" provoked debate as to its parameters (does it, for example, include non-Christian authors writing on Christian themes?[2]), analyses of spiritual literature have yet to achieve consensus on form or content. The two major labels of "spiritual literature" *lingxing wenxue* 灵性文学 and "spiritual writing" *shenxing xiezuo* 神性写作 are not easily distinguished in English (the former relating to "soul" or spirit

---

[1] See, e.g., Shi Wei's 施玮 prose and poetry anthologies contained in her edited series *Spiritual Literature Anthology* (Lingxing wenxue congshu 灵性文学丛书); the prose collection entitled *Near Shore Far Shore* Bi'an ci'an 此岸彼岸 (Shi 2008) contained entries from 57 authors in China and abroad; or see poet Liu Cheng 刘诚's articles in the 2000s on the salvation of poetry itself through spiritual writing, or the journal entitled *Shenxing xiezuo* 神性写作 edited by poets of the Alliance of Chinese Spiritual Writers.

[2] See Liu Lixia's discussion of the "broad" and "narrow" definitions of Chinese Christian literature (Liu 2006).

and the latter to the "divine").[3] While the labels overlap, and much of their content may be subsumed into the broader category of "Christian literature," *lingxing wenxue* has been used of expressly Christian writing, whereas *shenxing xiezuo* has been used for a range of religious and metaphysical literature exploring the nature of life and meaning, without a necessarily Christian or theistic perspective. The term *lingxing wenxue* was used as early as 1940 by Lao She as he mused on why China had never produced a Dante, and has been popularized more recently by Christian author and émigré Shi Wei (Wang 2012). *Shenxing xiezuo* has become the more widely used term in scholarship, and been applied to the writings of Christian authors like Bei Cun or Shi Wei, to more philosophical works like the non-fiction of Shi Tiesheng, and to other religious fiction, including Buddhist novels (e.g., Zheng and Yan 2019).

The core facet of spiritual literature identified by many, the expression of an inner life, or soul, is differently articulated in different genres and oeuvres. He Guangshun suggests that the revival of spiritual poetry in contemporary China is seen in a return to wonderment, and in attention to the relations between humans and their creator, as exemplified in Huang Lihai's poetry collection *Who can run faster than Lightning?* where traces of creation and divine grace are seen in the writing of "small things." Such poems are, for He, "literary witnesses to the highest possibilities of humanity" (He 2018). Novelist and poet Shi Wei also valorizes a literature of the quotidian, arguing that spiritual literature is not found in the mysteries of nature or a renunciation of the world, but in ordinary life, a frown, a smile, in giving readers a pair of spiritual eyes with which to "let people see the beautiful light in the midst of a trivial and dull life; to let them see the image of the divine inside people in the midst of their own twisted, defiled lives; to see the dignity and glory that people had in the beginning" (Shi 2007, preface 3). In one of the most explicitly Christian analyses of spiritual literature (here, *lingxing wenxue*), Shi Wei contends that recourse to the spiritual is not a retreat or flight from life, but a liberation, a call to reflect on life, to listen to the soul behind life calling out (Zhang 2014). Literature lacking the spirit (which, as the ancients knew, is that which animates humans and separates them from other creatures) is for Shi blighted by its predilection for gloom and darkness and its constant recourse to the flesh and the senses, while key tenets of spiritual literature include self-examination, repentance, and dialogue between humans and God (Shi 2007, preface 2, 3). The difference between the two is encapsulated in a shift from "human-centred" to "God-centred" writing.[4]

For critic Yang Jianlong, *lingxing wenxue* is fundamentally concerned with "the salvation of the soul," and marks a new phase in Chinese Christian literature (Yang 2011, p. 20). Yang takes Shi Wei's short story collection *No 100 Xincheng Road* as representative of this category of spiritual writing, and shows how the collection foregrounds the values of love, repentance for sins, and the pursuit of the highest good. The anthology, like the genre more generally in Yang's estimation, focuses on the human spirit, on ultimate questions and on relations between humans and the world. Its main themes are Christian love, especially the cardinal commandment to love one's neighbor as oneself, seen in accounts of self-sacrificial or kenotic self-giving; a Christian sense of sin, explored in stories of people who realize their own wrong and put it right; the overcoming of challenges and dilemmas, possible because humans created in the image of God are endowed with a spiritual faculty; and tales of lives lived in the knowledge of death and judgement (Yang 2011).

A common denominator in discussion of Christian and spiritual literature is its social import, following a long tradition of hailing the moral and nation-building purposes of fiction. Critics frequently link the rise of religious-inspired writing to a perceived lack of "cultural values" in contemporary China (e.g., Wang 2012). Christianity offers a counterpoint, or supplement, to facets seen as lacking or muted in Chinese culture. Undergirding this is often a comparative discussion of "the West" and China, where Christianity is taken to represent a moral ethos, if not identity, derived from the modern west.

---

[3]   Yang Jianlong adds a third category of *lingxiu wenxue* 灵修文学, which he translates as "monastic literature" but we might
      call a literature of spirituality or spiritual growth/formation, written by and for believers (Yang 2011).
[4]   That is, from 人本写作 to 神本写作.

The specific counter-cultural traits ascribed to Christianity vary, but a transcendent focus is foremost. Religious interiority is taken to counter a lack of respect for the spiritual as well as the value of the individual. An engagement with the meaning of life counters the excessive materialism of a consumer era, while grappling with "spiritual questions" confronts a time of "desire and indulgence" (Wang 2012). Although novelist Bei Cun's early writings as a Christian predate much of the debate and language of "spiritual literature," his work blazed a trail, providing one of the strongest examples of the (re)turn to the Christian, and in its depictions of alienation, warped desires, and wrestling with the meaning of existence, exemplifies many of the themes critics have seen in the new spiritual literature. Bei Cun's writing speaks to the critics' debates on secularity and post-modern values, yet it also contributes an angle rarely discussed in the secondary literature: the theological.

2. The Baptizing River

The Baptizing River (Shixi de he 施洗的河) was written in two months in 1992, not long after the prize-winning young avant-garde author Bei Cun (1965–present) became a Christian.[5] First published serially in the magazine *Huacheng* in 1993, *The Baptizing River* attracted much critical attention, especially online, not just for the rarity of a Christian novel and the contrast with the author's prior works and reputation, but also because of its message of spiritual salvation at a time of political change and metaphysical searching.[6] The novel does not make for a particularly easy or edifying first read, and online critics noted the rather tortuous plot-line as the protagonist sinks from one depravity to the next, escaping death only to encounter some new folly or threat. As one editor noted, in this his first Christian novel, Bei Cun had yet to integrate the essence of his faith seamlessly with his creative art in the manner of Tolstoy or Dostoevsky (Wen 2016, p. 312). Yet the novel touched a raw nerve in society, and the shape of its trajectory and protracted examination of evil has much to say about the human condition.[7]

The Baptizing River is a psychosocial biography of its anti-hero Liu Lang, and follows him from a rural childhood lived in fear of a savage father, to his sexual awakening and self-loathing at university, through the turf-warfare of a business career in illegal commodities, to the apathy of middle age and the mental and physical decline of addiction. This first post-baptism novel of Bei Cun describes a life prior to baptism, and the individual and social sins that make that repentance and baptism necessary. We do not see beyond the first steps of the protagonist's new life in faith: we see nothing of the complexities of a developing faith journey, or of a Christian's changed relations with society that inspire Bei Cun's later novels; the focus here is the social malaise that fails Liu Lang, and the abject failure of his own many vices to bring satisfaction.[8] Baptism marks an emergence into light, and the confounding of death that meets every other character in the novel.

If literary fiction is writing that gains from a second or third reading, *The Baptizing River* stands the test of multiple immersions. It might be tempting for a critic to skip though a discussion of the protagonist Liu Lang's degenerate life and move to the "Christian" part at the end of the novel, the coda where Liu Lang struggles onto the riverbank and finds himself in a church community, taken under the wing of an evangelist—but this would be to ignore what Bei Cun is saying about life through the structure of the novel. Having spent years constructing abstruse, labyrinthine literary structures in his avant-garde phase, we have to assume the author understands form. Must we suffer through

---

[5] Examples of Bei Cun's avant-garde writings can be found in English in Wang (1998) and Bei et al. (2010). For discussion of Bei Cun's conversion and role as public intellectual, see Fällman (2016); on Cultural Christians, intellectuals and Christian publishing, including *Fangzhou* (The Ark), the magazine of Bei Cun's Beijing church community, see Wielander (2013); for a reading of Bei Cun's Christian fiction, see Faries (2010).

[6] Critics such as Wen Neng have argued that it was the "directive spiritual nature" and the fact that the novel coincided with the spiritual illness or spiritual void of the era that led to such a tide of debate; see, e.g., Wen (2016, p. 307).

[7] As critic Nan Fan noted, this may not be a "good" novel with the finesse of a mature writer, but it is an important one, a work that faces head-on the questions of its era and through which people can discuss the era, Nan (1995, p. 49).

[8] For a periodization of Bei Cun's post-conversion writing, and a three-stage movement from concentration on individual sin, to the complexities of a faith journey, to relations with society, see Zhai (2018).

all the abounding torture, the degradation, the putrefying corpses? Bei Cun's theological answer is yes. Liu Lang must reach absolute dissolution before he is finally willing to cede his life to the compunction of an inner voice, and its direction to the free flow of the current, the thalweg that lands him in a Christian community. It is not to paint a portrait of life in war-torn China that Bei Cun chronicles social evils for 250 pages, although the setting of the novel in the late 1930s or 1940s provides a chaotic backdrop and allows for levels of social criticism and introspection that might be problematic in a PRC setting—but to address the question of "why salvation?" and how the subjective "I" reacts to and processes the living of life.

The themes of the novel are important in themselves: backdrop questions over the status of women and gender relations; the city and its underworld; rural poverty and superstition; wartime deprivation; as well as themes relating to the psychology of Liu Lang, including childhood trauma; revenge; sexual addiction and self-hatred; psychosexual development and father-son relations; drug addiction. But these, and their interactions that form the focus of the novel, are all predicated on the tension that the reader knows from the outset, from paratextual features like title, cover illustration and epigraph, as well as hints throughout the narrative, that this is somehow a "Christian" novel, and that something is coming, something we take two hundred anfractuous pages to reach, that will change the meaning of the tale.

The form of narration offers one such teleological irruption. The narrative begins in the third person, and switches to a frame of first-person memoire shortly after Liu Lang's arrival in the city: the novel we are reading is ostensibly the narration of his life, as told ten years later to an evangelist in Du village. The actual framing device lasts only twenty pages, as the novel reverts to the third person for the remainder, but the proleptic interlude signals Liu Lang's future conversion, and sets the novel up as first-person testimony, or witness: a long mea culpa, more in Augustinian mode than the customary pre-baptism testimony demanded by contemporary churches. The nature of the story as testimony is underlined by Liu Lang's opening words in this section, "My evil began in the deep waters of the lower reaches," as he goes on to describe his triad business empire. But even in giving witness, Liu Lang's insistence that "the path I took was entirely due to fate, because I was not someone who wanted to do evil; I always wanted to be a doctor" alerts us to the possibility of an unreliable narrator: the self-delusion that characterizes our protagonist is not effaced in the early stages of conversion (Bei 2016, pp. 56–57). A second "Christian" element early in the novel is also fleeting, but creates a deep imprint. In medical college, Liu Lang admires and desires a young (and rather pious) Christian named Tianru ("heaven-like"), who quotes the psalms at him on every possible occasion, relates all natural phenomena and topics of conversation back to God, and disappears from his grasp as the war progresses. Her insertion into the novel offers the possibility of an alternative life, and the construct of an ideal which holds Liu Lang in its thrall, even as he is unable to respond to her entreaties to believe.

This essay foregrounds the novel's structure, and explores how the work as a whole leads to, and reflects on, baptism. To do this, it follows the course of the river journeys that mark the different stages of Liu Lang's life: childhood and adolescence, adulthood, and baptismal rebirth. Liu Lang's autobiographical testimony is far from the traditional Chinese genre of biography, but the course of Liu Lang's life is not just a prelude to baptism; it is too long, and too tortuous, not to harbour meaning in itself. Liu Lang's rise and fall is traced here through his power plays, relations to women, philosophy of life and recourse to superstition. The recurrent motif of the river, as literal transport and metaphor for journey, as bearer of sin and source of redemption, courses through the novel. The river that runs between the protagonist's hometown and the city where he inherits a business forms the boundary of his known world. It swallows up the young protagonist's brother when Liu Lang pushes him in; it is where he himself falls and is dredged up, clutching his gold, on arrival in the city. The eponymous river eventually guides him to the haven at Du village and performs its baptism as he is thrown into its waters, spitting him out on the bank. Like the Jordan today, the river is "a filthy place where dead rabbits, waste and industrial effluent floated by the dock" (Bei 2016, p. 56), an absorbent channel for human detritus.

The novel was a form of baptism for Bei Cun himself, as he entered the stream of writing anew as a Christian novelist. The repeated use of "transformation" (转型) by critics to describe Bei Cun's writing after 1992 carries overtones of metanoia, and points to the about-face in life and literature that characterized his conversion, when the meaning, form, shape and purpose of writing changed starkly for him. This novel is the first expression of a re-emergence into a new way of literature: in six months Bei Cun went from an "extreme formalism," from seeking meaning through form (or pointing to the impossibility of coherence in either), to possessing a meaning and wanting to transmit it. As one critic wrote, "Bei Cun is still Bei Cun, Bei Cun has changed" (Nan 1995, p. 50). Literary structure, once symbol of that search for meaning, was now a means to an end, and an ambivalent one at that.[9] Literature, to which Bei Cun had dedicated his life, now seemed to him more like something Eve encountered in Eden (see Bei 1995, p. 65). On conversion, his relation to literature paradoxically changed from a "holy pursuit" to a means of making a living and a source of vocational anxiety and doubt. According to Bei Cun himself, this stemmed from a reaction to the vision of despair that so many writers of his literary education had offered (from Hemingway or Faulkner to Kafka, Goethe and Camus) and their inability to articulate any way forward, coupled with a growing belief that literature itself could not perform the task. All literature could do, he surmised, was to diagnose the problem a little more accurately. It could not offer a prescription or cure; its utopia was "a fabrication."[10] *The Baptizing River's* epigraph, "Repent, for the kingdom of God is near," not only acts as a commentary on the life (and eventual penitence) of its main character, and as a warning to readers, but also as an enigmatic comment on the author's own profession.

Doubts aside, Bei Cun did continue to write, and critics have read his turning-point novel as part of a broader shift in the literary landscape, as the avant-garde movement of the 1980s began to splinter, freighted under the weight and unfulfilled expectations of its formal experimentation.[11] In Xie Youshun's explanation, Bei Cun, along with select other writers of his generation like Yu Hua or Ge Fei, chose the path of "spiritual depth," transcending the secular world, as an escape route. Other contemporaries such as Su Tong headed towards new realism, while a third group, including Sun Hanlu and Lu Xin, sought to develop a new independent aesthetic. The emptiness of an excessive attention to "technicalism" was countered by Bei Cun with a very plain surface expression, a type of "spiritual reportage literature" (Xie 2016, p. 317). The notion of a spiritual literature was a challenge to literary critics of the 1990s, and debates over Bei Cun's work opened up questions of the purpose of literature, just as his characters open up for readers' questions on the purpose and meaning of life. The intensity of Bei Cun's desire to evangelise through fiction is evident in the articles and interviews discussing *The Baptizing River* included as appendices to the 2016 edition.

3. Childhood

A growing body of data warns us of the dangers of adverse childhood experiences (Aces), and the links between the toxic stress they cause and poor health outcomes later in life (Felitti et al. 1998; Zanolli 2018). Continuous exposure to domestic abuse, poverty or neglect can cause malfunctioning responses to stress, and resultant elevated cortisol levels are associated with altered brain functioning, immune system and DNA damage. Given that children raised in households with multiple indicators of poverty and violence have higher addiction rates, Bei Cun's portrayal of the life course of his protagonist Liu Lang, from medical student to opium addict, via addictions to sex and to self-sufficiency, has strong scientific ballast. Liu Lang's childhood was, by any standards, terrible. Conceived in rape, plied with

---

9   The novel can be read as metanarrative on authorial conversion; while the degree of change in Bei Cun's life and writing may mirror that of his protagonist, this does not invite an assumption of parallels between the novelist's experiences of life and Liu Lang's, as some have suggested.

10 Bei (1995). Like his counterparts, Bei Cun had embraced aesthetics and poetry as the way to find meaning, but suicides among friends and in literary circles tested this belief, and contributed to the paradoxical drive to express (new-found) meaning through literature while questioning the possibility of this.

11 See Xie (2016) or Xie (1993).

abortifacients in utero, his early years were punctuated by violence and loneliness. The pathos of a child's eye view as he navigates a countryside populated by ghosts and evil spirits is one of the strengths of the narrative. The acuity of the psychological depiction of characters and their interactions throughout the novel is notable, and chimes with Bei Cun's interest in subjectivity and dreams.

The childhood years of *The Baptizing River* are important because they set not only the scene, but the direction of the protagonist's whole life. This life, together with Liu Lang's musing on it, forms the central plotline, and the subjectivity of life as plot accounts for some of the ponderous pace and seemingly directionless narrative later in the story. The novel takes on the qualities of a Greek tragedy in the first few chapters, with fratricide and attempted patricide, but other grand, mythic themes stem from the family nexus too: generational sordidness and the sins of the father visited on the son; the journey quest to leave a hometown and become a man in the world; ageing parents, and dealing with decay, dementia and their portent of one's own future. The spatial landscape, the rural-urban divide and the setting of war-torn China under Japanese invasion form background themes, but these are subservient to the interior, or psychic landscape of the characters. The two great boat journeys of the novel: Liu Lang's journey to town in his late twenties to follow in his father's footsteps, and the eventual rudderless floating to the riparian Christian haven, frame his adult life, but, suggests, Bei Cun, the traveller is already formed by his early experiences. This privileging of childhood is rare in Chinese literature, and offers a modern and holistic concept of personhood.

In the first three chapters of the novel, we see the protagonist at eight, and then in his twenties at medical school. The eight-year-old boy is taciturn and regarded as "weak" by his family and playground bullies alike, yet is the sole one to venture out on Ghost Festival day when other villagers are hiding indoors. His pale face and slender torso unman him in his father's eyes, and are linked, in his parents' eyes, to his birth (Bei 2016, p. 21). One of the many injustices in Liu Lang's life is the manner in which his conception—in a field, at which his mother was at work spreading manure—is held against him. "If we can fuck a child out in that sort of place stinking to high heaven, he's going to be rotten!" exclaims his father, while his failure to succumb to strenuous attempts to abort him lead his grandmother to exclaim that he seems to be "an evil spirit reincarnated." Liu Lang's father, Liu Chengye, utters the first of many dark premonitions: "if this child is born, my life's at risk" (Bei 2016, pp. 9–10).

Peasant superstitions surround Liu Lang's early life, and he himself is held to have second sight when he predicts a local death. Liu Lang's father is alternately absent and forcefully present in his life, and his returns to the village bring fear to life. The coarseness of Liu Chengye's language is shocking, and its repetition wearisome. When the child is brought in with a gash to his head from a fall, his father's "violent, frenzied expression" floats in front of him:" "Crying? Still crying? Cry-dick!... howling at a cut that size—your old man had his chest blown open and didn't make a sound—are you ever going to grow any bollocks?" (Bei 2016, pp. 5–6). Liu Lang's fear of his father is so great that he stops crying, although fresh blood spurts out after his father thumps him. Even as a child, Liu Lang only ever refers to his father as "he" in conversation with his mother.

Liu Chengye's foreboding over his son is fulfilled in the first of many episodes with Oedipal overtones, when Liu Lang, who has been given a Daoist charm to drink following his injury, appears at his father's bedside in the middle of the night, cocked revolver in hand. "Your eyesight's off," is his father's sardonic comment when his gun fires a blank (Bei 2016, p. 13). This incident remains "both clear and confused" in Liu Lang's later memory, but a second attempt twenty years later is perfectly lucid. His father's return to the family home triggers a traumatic response in Liu Lang, and the medical student returns to his father's bedroom at night, "as if possessed"—but cannot pull the trigger. "If you want to live, you have to fire it," offers his father darkly, surprised by his son's new-found facility with a firearm. Liu Chengye's revenge is cold and clinical: he shoots his son's right ear lobe off, and then argues with him over his claim not to have touched a gun: "Liar—you did when you were eight. Now we're even. You can go downstream [to town] now." (Bei 2016, pp. 18–19). The wound remains with Liu Lang throughout his adult life, and displays a visceral effect: when he meets his father by chance, his ear throbs and threatens to split open.

In his final year in his childhood home, waiting for his ear to heal, Liu Lang watches his father's slow senescence. We trace the change-over between father and son, as Liu Lang no longer hides from his father, but his father hides from the light of the son. We see glimpses of the future, as the paranoia that leads Liu Chengye to have a coffin and shroud prepared for himself—because no-one else will—is also reflected in the suspicion that his children will "give his body to the dogs." (Bei 2016, p. 29). Neither son does, in fact, care about their father's welfare. One night after empathising with his father and trying out his coffin, Liu Lang dreams that he chops his father up with an ax, but discovers that the corpse has his mother's face, with maggots crawling out of the eye sockets. Liu Lang gradually understands his mother to be both victim of his father's violence and complicit in it, but her mutilation severs the thread to his childhood. Woken in the night by a burst of gunfire as troops attack their compound, Liu Lang and his brother hide in their furnace until morning; when they emerge and discover a stray bullet has pierced their mother's breasts. Liu Lang's stomach turns at the thought that the breasts which nurtured him have been shattered by an iron bullet, and "things that had seemed so sacred were so fragile" (Bei 2016, p. 38). The last violent episode in Liu Lang's adolescence reifies the sexualised nature of his childhood suffering and sets up a confused and discontented adulthood.

4. City Vice and the Adult Self

One of the difficulties of sustaining a long narrative with an antisocial and increasingly unstable protagonist is in engaging readers. There is a certain fascination in the criminal underworld that Bei Cun depicts in the central section of the novel, and he does not flinch from its seedy side and violence. The very earthy nature of the stories sets up the conditions for the cleansing of baptism. Liu Lang's adult life is a litany of violations of the Decalogue: theft, adultery, murder, covetousness, unfilial acts. Moments of humour and wry understatement lighten the narrative, while an obstinate hope continually resists the pathos. If the first half of Liu's adult life is an excess of pleasurable vices and competitive skullduggery against his business rival, and the narrative skips along briskly, the second half is a time of introspection, depression and searching for meaning. Turpitude cedes to torpor, and the narrative slows to the pace of a blocked drain, as Liu Lang's mental processes are hampered by depression and opioids. For many Chinese critics, this exposure of a soul, and close-up view of a character's inner development is the centre-piece of the novel, its sense of a "lack of any existential significance" embodying the spiritual crisis of the times. (Xie 1993; Nan 1995).

Liu Lang arrives by boat in Zhangban with his father's parting advice ringing in his ears: "You shouldn't trust anyone, only trust gold and guns ... " (Bei 2016, p. 40). The advice is short-lived, as Liu Lang is mugged and robbed of his gold strands at the dock, a baptism into city life that convinces him "he has already entered a different world." Even the metaphors are bloody: as his first urban day dawns, "the skies were gradually lightening, the colour of the city like the dark red that seeps from a wound." (Bei 2016, p. 43). Norms are upended here: the violence against women of the rural world extends its reach as Liu Lang's nostrils are forcibly pressed into the ground and he smells the fresh earth, terrified at the sound of a gun clicking. Liu Lang, the aspiring medic who has been forced to give up his career plans and who now sees himself as a "sacrifice," understands on day one of his new life in the city that death is a physical reality and a metaphysical threat. Money may be the root of evil and the immediate cause of death, but "he knows that each step neared death, and whether you ended up thrown into the river feeding the fish or staring up the barrel of a gun, the result was the same." (Bei 2016, p. 43).

It does not take long after his initiation for Liu Lang to be infected with the power play and cruelty of his environs, once he has absorbed the shock that his inheritance is effectively an opium business, and that his father was a multiple murderer, some of whose corpses lie rotting in the stone cellar of the premises. Workplace violence in triad feuds inures him to cruelty, which is then played out in domestic abuse. In the first of many revenge incidents that spatter the novel and show the inescapable nature of childhood trauma, Liu Lang plays with his mugger-cum-servant A Jin, cruelly fiddling with a gun, wanting to enact humiliation "like a dog" until the employee can't stand the tension and pleads "just kill me!" Liu Lang shoots off his ear-lobe, an exact toll for his father's damage to his own ear.

The former medical student takes a certain aesthetic pleasure in discovering that "flesh opens like a flower." (Bei 2016, p. 52).

One of the more disturbing traits as the novel unfolds is Liu Lang's sudden and sometimes irrational violence, bouts of which were already present as a student, when he smashes a friend's head against a column "like a Japanese bandit" for an insensitive comment, or pins down and half-throttles a girl whose make-up and clothing bespoke falsity.[12] Later, when Liu Lang rolls over and wretches after intercourse, and the woman, Ruyu, asks him why, his response—that it is his first time—elicits a surprised exclamation of disbelief. Liu erupts in fury at not being believed, and throws her to the ground, pushing her head down so that her teeth are pressed into the mud, and she "emits sorrowful cries of fear, like a hen about to die" (Bei 2016, p. 91). His disproportionate outburst comes just after he has killed for the first time, putting a gratuitous bullet through the head of a hapless girl mistaken for Ruyu. Liu Lang is shocked by his experience of murder, and by the ontological change in someone alive a moment ago who is now suddenly named "corpse," and he vows not to do so again—but the act of killing gives him a graphically described sexual release nonetheless.

If the change in Liu Lang's character stretches credibility, the portrayal of domestic violence in the novel is disturbingly credible. Liu Lang's relations with women are central to the novel, and reveal many of his insecurities as well as self-imposed disconnect with society. This was, the narrator tells us, a time of male domination, when "whipping or insulting women seemed normal occurrences," and Liu Lang is caught between a father whose view of women is that "when you're close to them you think they're all bitches, and it's no fun—you might as well feel yourself to your heart's content" and a best friend in medical school whose running commentary as he dissects a female cadaver combines physical and moral violation, sending Liu running out of the room to vomit (Bei 2016, pp. 76, 74, 72). The depiction of women is sometimes more redolent of late imperial courtesan world than the 1940s, but the psychology of relations between the sexes is convincingly described. After Liu Lang has installed himself as boss of the snake triad, he wastes little time in engineering a meeting with Ruyu, the wife of his rival, and seducing her with his gaze and gallantry right under the nose of her husband, Ma Da. Once he has had sex with Ruyu, and she has endangered her life in helping him overcome is virginal impotence, he is searingly honest about his priorities: "I don't want to marry you. What I want to marry is Ma Da's wife; my dreams are all about possessing her." (Bei 2016, p. 93). Insensate to the pain he causes others, as her romantic fantasies are disabused and the reality of her disloyalty looms, Liu's instrumentalising of women borders on sociopathic.

Before Ruyu appears in the novel, there is a twenty-page flash-back to university days, narrated as Liu Lang's confession testimony, and recalling the one woman whom he does not regard as an object. The interlude is telling. Liu is captivated by Tianru's gentle manner, although their worlds of reference are far apart. He does not understand her references to a heavenly father, and points out he does not want to be anyone's father, and that hardly any sons love their fathers (Bei 2016, p. 58); his warped view of relationships militating against an easy reception of the Christian message (and its "father God" language). While Ruyu and other women in the novel frequently offer a sharp-tongued retort to Liu Lang, Tianru's repartee as she parries in dialogue shows her an equal partner, and his delight at her brings tears, even as he struggles to accept her claims that the word of God can teach him how to live or his "need to be saved" (Bei 2016, pp. 62, 64). As Liu pines for Tianru, his friend Tang Song introduces him to another girl, whose shapely form induces his first lascivious dreams, and the beginning of a masturbation habit that torments him with shame. Liu Lang is aware of the power of association with Tianru—he feels "as though his heart had been cleansed" after she responds to a touch of his hand and speaks of his need for God—but is also challenged by her. The tension between his carnal desires and his infatuation with Tianru increases as he begins to see himself through her moral compass, and becomes paralyzing when

---

[12] Bei (2016, pp. 67, 70). Nan Fan suggests that in depicting this irrational, sudden evil, Bei Cun is pointing to original sin, the flaring up of the evil of human nature, or instinctual nature itself. Nan (1995, p. 50).

he fears she might have caught sight of him doing his "dirty" act. Liu's inability to escape his own lusts sickens him, and in a moment of extreme self-loathing Liu prepares to take a surgical knife to himself, in the belief that "one knife stroke can solve it" (p. 69). Tang finds him with a sanitized knife before any irreversible damage is done.

It does not take long for Liu Lang to tire of the woman he steals as a wife. When Ruyu caresses him, he compares her touch unfavourably to his mother ("you're as different as heaven and earth; you're a bitch, my mother was a woman")—yet wants a wife to mother him and cradle him. (Bei 2016, p. 99). Liu Lang's arrested development would give a Freudian a field day, and his conscious musing that his mother's avoidance of him as an older boy was linked to his longing for her breasts provokes sadness as he recalls her comment that he would need to take a wife—"but I never thought I'd have a different woman lying beside me." Family relationships and well-being are threatened by increasing isolation. Liu's natal family is dispensable: he hesitates to open a letter from home, and when he does read its tale of destitution, he uses the letter as toilet paper. Liu rationalizes his lack of empathy and filial capacity as stemming from villagers thinking him a freak as a child, and his mother choosing to love his father. One of Liu's most egregious acts against kin marks a turning-point in the novel and the beginning of decline. Liu has been told that business rival Ma Da has captured his brother and is about to use him as a human shield in a deal. Having taken a mistress, the girl he once lusted for on campus, Liu is loath to leave her and go to see if Ma Da's threat is real. When he goes out to Du village to weep over his brother in the dead of night, it is too late. As even Ma Da thinks he is terrifying for not freeing his brother, Liu retorts, echoing Cain: "what's a brother?" In a game of rivalry where the most callous is victor, Ma Da concedes: "you're more ruthless than me. You'll win" (Bei 2016, p. 124).

Physical and mental decline progress in tandem over the second half of the novel, beginning with nightmares and lassitude. Liu sleeps cocooned between wife and mistress for safety, replacing them at one point with a stockade of books. Fearing retribution (报应), he withdraws from active leadership in the business, where armaments and wartime industries had added to healthy opium profits. As the racy living of pleasure-seeking pales, and having repelled family and friends, Liu retreats to his own drab inner life. Life and plot run out of options. As Liu's life begins to meander, so does the narrative pace.[13] Liu becomes photophobic, and paranoid that his food might be poisoned; his fear is somatized in vomiting. Mood swings persist: Liu takes delight in a new dog, then shoots it. He feels trapped by being locked into competition with Ma Da. Lethargy prevents him from working, but when Ruyu takes charge of caring for him, he sees her actions (tidying his clothes, tipping out the chamber pot) as violating his freedom, a freedom that values its own autonomy above all else. The thought of being beholden or dependent, or having to show gratitude is "worse than having a long spear roughly plunged into his belly" (Bei 2016, p. 165). The follies of the father are repeated in every possible way in Liu, as he builds a lavish tomb for himself, aware that no one will mourn his passing. Liu retreats to his anti-earthquake, bullet-proof tomb, taking his valuables with him. Literally self-enclosed, entombed, Liu at his lowest regards his life as completely without significance, lamenting his ageing body and loneliness (Bei 2016, pp. 174–75). The vapid sterility of life confronts him as he pursues "his dream ever since childhood: independent life, with no disturbance." As the narrator reminds any reader who has missed the point, an entirely autarchic life is selfish and cowardly, and requires expelling all kith and kin.

The physical decline of mid-life also engenders a metaphysical turn and consideration of ethics and meaning. A central dilemma of Liu's life is concretised exactly mid-way through the novel in the myth of self-determination. "Our poor protagonist," we are told, "always wants to be master of his own fate, but also thinks everything is already decided by destiny" (Bei 2016, p. 159). The return of his

---

13 Xie Youshun makes a similar point in suggesting that the narrative in *Baptising River* follows the "spiritual logic" of the character, Xie (1993, p. 39).

medical-era friend Tang Song provides a lifeline in a benign sparring partner, and their conversations skim across questions of goodness, deontology and religious belief:

> *People like you, said Liu Lang, will only ever eat coarse grain and wear cotton; in times like this there aren't things which we should or shouldn't do, there's only things you can or can't do. If you're savvy, you get to eat two bowls of rice while someone else starves to death ... What I can't stand most is sitting and discussing morality, the more we talk about it the more guilty I feel ... forget it.*(Bei 2016, p. 147)

As Tang tries to rescue and retrieve Liu from his self-enclosure and web of doubts, he discovers that their friendship, that cardinal Confucian relationship, is built on a foundation of sand. When Liu Lang mocks Tang for suggesting they are close friends, "he understood for the first time that Liu Lang had never trusted anyone, that his own advice was wholly unreciprocated, and that Liu Lang had kept him by his side for a while merely to dispel his loneliness" (Bei 2016, p. 176). This realization that his trust, and dependence on his companion were mere "soap bubbles" marks a downward turning point for Tang himself. Liu's response encapsulates the sentiments of many of the "spiritual void" generation (the term translated "believe" could equally be rendered "trust"):

> *When I was small I believed that there was a creator, then I believed in my parents, and believed in other people, after I grew up I believed in myself, and later discovered that I was unreliable too, and so believed in chance—and see, now I can practice divination, and I calculated that you would come here today and talk a load of rubbish.*
>
> *Now you only believe in your own doubts, said Tang Song.*
>
> *It's the only way, said Liu Lang, absently. To believe in doubt is more reliable than believing in oneself. Look, why should I believe what you say is true? How can I tell you're not about to shoot me in the back?* (Bei 2016, p. 176)

Bei Cun is prescient in pointing to a lack of trust as critical in society, before contaminated food scandals severely damaged consumer confidence in China and long before "belief" or "faith" (信仰) became a key term in Xi Jinping's rhetoric and a core political value. Tang cannot bear his friend's "cold, unfeeling" gaze, and the absurd end-point of his position—since without trust, there can be no human relationship—and leaves. Two teardrops fall from Liu, who now sees that he and Ma Da are the two most lonely and timid people in Zhangban.

The man-cave fails to provide solace. In his recovery from this mental breakdown, Liu becomes addicted. In the inward gaze of the second half of the novel, conversations with Tang rehearse snatches of the major themes of twentieth-century life: individual liberty and the totalitarian state, solipsism and socialism, utilitarian vs consequentialist ethics, freedom vs conformity. If Tang is a foil for Liu Lang, it is important for the impending baptism and conversion that the question 'but what of a good person?' be pre-empted. In a somewhat clumsy and directive passage, Tang, acknowledges that he is not so different from Liu Lang, that he too is "completely in the dark," and has no way of extricating himself from the wrong he has done. One night Tang wakes bolt upright to the question: if I were in Liu Lang's place, would I be like him? His own inner filth troubles him, as does the dissonance between what others see and his inner reality. While people regard Tang as a gentle and good medical teacher, he knows that he has had thoughts of raping young girls, even if he has not acted on them—thoughts that nauseate him and provoke him to gentleness. While others say he is a good person, Tang concludes that "trying to be a good person in this world is just a type of self-deception" (Bei 2016, pp. 190–91). Unable to achieve goodness, and with no Tianru to show him any other way, Tang takes solace in chess, and later *qigong* and *fagong*. The question of human nature recurs periodically. When Liu Lang has temporarily taken Ma Da's mother hostage to entice him to visit, he wonders "How can such a kind, good woman raise such an evil son?" Liu Lang answers his own question by positing a father like his own as the cause, while the narrator suggests that further thought would give an alternative reading: "human nature is evil" (Bei 2016, p. 214).

Existential fears of middle age lead the two triad bosses Liu and Ma to superstition and divination. As soon as Liu Lang achieved fame, the narrator reflects, "he discovered there was something he couldn't grasp—the future" (Bei 2016, p. 152). Having believed in his own capability all his life, Liu no longer bases business deals on acumen or intuition, but on divination prognoses. The most poignant, self-defeating episode of Liu Lang's superstitious turn comes when Ruyu is pregnant. The pregnancy draws together in a dense concentration many of the questions of Liu Lang's life as he contemplates fatherhood: his relationship with his own father, his relationship with Ruyu and other women; the notion of family; the nature of fear; his sense of transcendence and religion ("my son is my religion, in the past it was money, guns, women—now it's the turn of my son,") he tells Tang (Bei 2016, p. 235). The pregnancy triggers a strange illness in him, an intermittent deafness and piercing tinnitus, followed by visual hallucinations, a sort of prosopagnosia where he fails to recognize even Ruyu. When a fortuneteller refuses to divine, and Liu catches sight of his own pallid countenance in a mirror, he is terrified. "Abort it! Abort it! he roars at Ruyu, don't give birth!" (Bei 2016, p. 231). Ruyu's cries indicate her understanding of Liu's absolute control over her body, and the next month sees a succession of strenuous and bloody, but ultimately unsuccessful, attempts to kill off the foetus.

New depths unfurl as the protagonist spirals downwards. Ravenous and nauseous, the emaciated addict finds relief from a black fog of despair in the floating comfort of a morphine high. Opium offers a "ladder to heaven," but leaves Liu and Tang unrecognizable, prone to temper flares, extruding copious phlegm, and assaulting maid and servant alike. Opium becomes "absolutely more important than life" to Liu, and he sells his birthright to his business manager. In his opioid fug, Liu can no longer see the reason for enmity with Ma Da, something which "proves he has wasted his life" (Bei 2016, p. 252). When Tang dies, an event notable in its ordinariness, his death stands in for his friend's; it is the death Liu Lang deserves. In Tang we see the contradiction and fear that accompany an early death: seeming acceptance, followed by denial and resistance. "I've never so much as trodden on an ant in my whole life, why should I be punished? I'm a good person, what sin have I committed?" Tang laments, before echoing the bitter cry of Job: "Why wasn't I allowed to die at birth?..." Like the eponymous protagonist of Tolstoy's *Death of Ivan Ilyich*, a novella similarly written shortly after conversion, Tang and Liu expend much energy attempting to justify their own goodness to themselves and the universe in the face of death, while their questioning points to doubts over the answer.

5. Rebirth

If traditional Chinese narrative arcs rise to an apex then fall in the second half of a novel, *The Baptising River* appears to trace such a pattern, with Liu Lang's rise in power and wealth as the head of an (illicit) business empire, and slow fall into ill health and mental decline.[14] As a Christian confession, however, the novel forms more of a U-shape, with a deep nadir in Liu's layered depravities at the height of his powers, and gradual rise as he questions life and its meaning, even as his health and cognitive powers falter, towards the crescendo of baptism and salvation glory. Baptism marks an act—even if unsought and not fully comprehended—but Bei Cun's story shows how the whole arc of life has tended to this moment. Liu Lang's life has been proceeding towards baptism long before he is tipped into the river a final time; baptism for him was indeed "the unfolding story of our entry into the life of God" (Radcliffe 2012, p. 111). Liu Lang's youthful sins, his cruelty, temper and manipulation of others—relatable as they are to the trauma of his upbringing—have produced their own wreckage in his life in its loneliness and broken relations, while the more metaphysical sins of his later years, his extreme self-sufficiency and his determined self-justification, have led to the questioning of life that is a prerequisite for his conversion. The eventual acceptance of brokenness and dependency which propels Liu to leave the city may be God-given, yet God has, as Nan Fan notes, been present throughout, enabling Liu in the second half of life to understand that "he can never extricate himself

---

[14] C.f. Plaks (1987). Liu Lang is not eliminated prior to the conclusion, however, as central figures frequently were.

from the swamp of his sins," a point Liu Lang himself comprehends when his spiritual eyes are opened (Nan 1995, p. 55; Bei 2016, p. 295).

Baptism "admits the reality of sin," (Williams 2018, p. 136) and the construct of the novel implies that this confession is both individual and corporate. The long central section of *The Baptizing River* that portrays the sins and brokenness of Liu Lang is also an indictment of society: its greed, violence (including gendered and domestic violence) and addictive behaviours, as well as its superstitions and abuse of the vulnerable. Society itself needs cleansing, needs to admit the reality of sin, the novel suggests. Liu Lang needs saving from deformed human life, from generational mis-nurture and the sins of his fathers as well as sins conditioned by the social chaos of war. Baptism is a means of salvation from the troubles of life as well as troubles for the individual, which inserts the novel into the broad channel of *jiuguo* (救国, saving the nation) discourse that was so pressing for the first generations of Chinese Protestants. This is not, however, a nationalistic soteriology, and before he professes his faith Liu Lang is roundly chastised for putting forward a theodicy argument with a nationalistic bent:

He suddenly posed a question: can he [Jesus] really save me?

He can. He knows people, and knows that they are seemingly respectable but their mind is teeming with worms and full of filth. Only he can save you.

Then why doesn't he save the Chinese who are being killed by the Japanese? Why is he so cruel and unfeeling? If you get God to apologize to me for this, I'll believe in him. (Bei 2016, p. 215)

While the nation is at war and imperilled in the novel, the lack of attention paid to wider social issues by the main characters is almost shocking; opium-addled brains and self-centred preoccupations render this intelligible within the storyline, while theologically the absence points to the perceived need for individual conversion prior to social salvation.

When Liu Lang hears a voice telling him to go by boat to Du village, he responds to the call, using the last of his money to purchase a boat. "He does not know where he is going, and has no grasp of the future course of this journey," but out on the river, Liu experiences an ethereal feeling of peace, and a sense that "a hand is stroking his heart," a sensation of "absolute safety" so comfortable it feels as though he is back in his mother's embrace (Bei 2016, p. 271). A moment later he is thrown back to a world of decisions, aware, like Nicodemus, that "it is impossible to retract himself back into his mother's womb," and yet also aware that he has reached an impasse, a dead-end where it feels as though he is physically disintegrating.

"Heaven! he cried: if there is a god, I want to ask you, why have you brought me to such a state—didn't I have great wealth and property? Didn't I live well?...why is your punishment falling on me?....Why do you want to destroy me?" (Bei 2016, pp. 271–72)

Before his Job-like tirade continues, Liu Lang's cry turns to self-recrimination: what if he had become a doctor, if he had married Tianru? He could have lived a peaceful, pain-free life. As the boat carries on inexorably forward, it passes a graveyard in a patch of barren wilderness, overgrown with wormwood. Counting up all of his dead family members, Liu Lang is struck by a sudden sense that "he himself is a ghost."

"Why am I left alone? Why wasn't I allowed to die when I came out of the womb? Why didn't my birthday become a dark night?...Why have all around me died? How come I don't want to live but can't die?" (Bei 2016, p. 273)

The thirty-three questions Liu utters express his anguish, but also the paradoxes and contradictions of life. "Why give me eyes and yet dark night? Why give a mouth and desire to eat good food but no taste for it?" Liu asks the creator of the faculties, swinging between plaint and confession. "I've done too much evil; are you going to account it to my body? Why don't you let me die?" The boat starts leaking and Liu flounders, struggling for breath, until he grasps some reeds and sees a figure on the bank, arm outstretched, and is plucked from the mud and reeds. As the sound of prayer reaches him, the person tells him to change his clothes, and the narrator tells us that morning brightness had arrived.

Although Liu's river baptism seems highly unorthodox from a contemporary Protestant point of view, and, with no priest or recital of Trinitarian formulae the reader might indeed miss, or contest, that a baptism has just occurred, yet major elements of the ritual are present. Liu has acknowledged his failure. Having heeded a call, Liu accepts the end of his mastery over his own life. He is fully submerged when his boat takes water in. There is a symbolic death and resurrection as Liu Lang struggles for his last grasp of air, drowning. The waters of chaos release him. He is pulled out of mud and reeds to the sound of prayer, and given a change of clothes by the evangelist who welcomes him, symbolically stripped naked before God.[15] If baptism is illumination or photismos, at the moment Liu emerges from the waters, the skies lighten (Bei 2016, p. 275; cf. Radcliffe 2012, p. 228). A surging wave of prayer welcomes him into the community of saints. He opens himself up to judgement and examination in narrating his life story, and while his catechesis follows baptism, it is exceptionally thorough (producing a rather tedious section of narrative), even if Liu resists or questions some of the requirements of his new-found faith. There is, of course, biblical precedent for a seemingly backwards or out-of-sequence conversion. As Timothy Radcliffe writes of another dramatic volte-face, "Paul did not weigh up the arguments for and against Christianity and then make a mature option for Jesus. God burst roughly into his life and threw him to the ground ... so God's choice of us precedes our choice of God;" faith is a *response* to the discovery of chosen-ness (Radcliffe 2012, p. 9).

In the brief after-life of Liu's baptism, we see that he has been liberated from violence, from his fatalism, and by extension, from the original sin of his innate nature (天性). In the final two chapters of the novel, a mere 25 pages out of 300, Liu hears the gospel message, engages with it, and returns to witness to his rival-turned-companion Ma Da. In his new immersion in Christian culture, hymns instruct his sleepy subconscious, while in his dreams a cross floats in a flooded landscape, forming an expanding life-raft and collecting all who are struggling in the water, like some Alice in Wonderland vision. In the cascade of waters in the novel, tears trickle down, the river flows, and the flood is redeemed by the cross. Christ as the "reversal of the flood" forms an ancient theme in Christianity (see, e.g., Williams 2018, p. 137). The trope of tears is a significant element in the depiction of Liu Lang. He is forever crying—as a child, on leaving home, at Tianru's gentleness, at the dissection formaldehyde, at his own words, at thoughts of his family, when cradling his dead brother, at the awareness of his poverty of spirit—while his inability to emote, to produce tears at events like his mother's funeral, and the performative tears of paid mourners, trouble him deeply. His life's tears are redeemed in his prayer of conversion; when he prays: "Lord! I didn't know of your grace; I was so obstinate and rebellious, but now I cry bitterly to you, I shed my tears towards you ... " The evangelist picks up on his tears in responding to his long prayer: "Today your tears have a use; because they are shed to him, he will remember your tears. The people of the world cannot shed tears; they are ashamed even to say the word "love." (Bei 2016, pp. 282–83).

If tears represent an overflow of interior emotion that cannot be contained, the river connecting childhood in Huotong, adult life in Zhangban, and rebirth in Du village, has been the site of many relational lows and highs in Liu's life. The title of the novel could be translated "The River of Baptism," but the verb-complement *shixi* (施洗 to carry out, to administer baptism) allows for the participle in English, and points to the active role of the river in the novel. The baptizing river again points back to older currents of Christianity, to Christ as Flowing Sea and Living Flood (in the terms of Ephrem the Syrian), and forwards to the river of the water of life in Revelation. The river raises long-debated questions about what happens in baptism, questions that run in parallel with arguments on paedobaptism as to whether the actor is God or human being, baptism a profession of faith or

---

[15] As Michael Green spells out, "Baptism is putting on a new suit of clothes;" see Galatians 3:27, "for as many of you as were baptized into Christ have put on Christ;" (Green 2017, p. 46).

justification of sinners, and whether the sacrament confers new birth or symbolizes it. Was Liu Lang's immersion-by-drowning a baptism, and if not, at what point in the narrative is his salvation effected? While Roman Catholic or Lutheran theology might hold that regeneration begins at baptism, Reformed theologians and Calvinists believe regeneration precedes faith, a stance that seems closest to Liu Lang's experience (the Anglican position as clarified by the Privy Council in 1850 allows characteristic leeway: "that the grace may be granted before, in or after baptism," while "baptism is an effectual sign of grace, by which God works invisibly within us, but only in such as worthily receive it."[16]). If the river is a channel of grace, Liu Lang catches up with evangelical orthodoxy by uttering a long prayer of repentance and commitment soon after, as he is taken into a church community. The symbolic change may have happened in the immersion into the waters of the river (no further baptismal ritual is described), but in the eyes of the evangelist catechizing Liu, salvation comes through faith, "you only have to believe in him and you will freely receive saving grace, and enter into his death and be resurrected together with him" (Bei 2016, p. 279) and it is Liu Lang's prayer of faith and repentance that marks the culmination of his faith journey, the point at which "everything before his eyes had changed" (Bei 2016, p. 284). Salvation, moreover, cannot be wrested back from him—when doubts resurface and Liu confesses "I feel as though I've not been saved, my mood is still bad, I can't do it ... " the evangelist retorts: it is not about feelings; feelings are most unreliable, "if he [Jesus] says it's done, then it's done" (Bei 2016, p. 287).

There is a surprising second current to the baptism narrative, with the suggestion that the narrative itself is the baptizing river. After Liu Lang's immersion in the river but before he prays his prayer of confession, it seems as if a great hand grasps hold of him, and will not release him. Liu continues:

> *I'm from Huotong, but I've spent the majority of my life in Zhangban, Liu Lang said to the evangelist—I want to tell you about some of the things that happened when I was there.*
>
> *... ... Liu Lang's narrative unfurled across this lengthy afternoon; his description was filled with horrifying elements, like a dirty river in which were drifting dead rabbits and rubbish, with murky foam floating on the surface, and he was sinking in this river, futilely struggling in the water. But from start to finish the evangelist maintained a mild expression.* (Bei 2016, p. 277; ellipsis in the original)

The repetition of the language of flotsam and filth from the beginning of Liu Lang's account to the evangelist (p. 56) re-introduces the frame to the novel, where the narrative is the text of his oral report—but with the twist that the narrative itself seems to be the river in which he floats; the long literary confession the baptizing river (and somehow instrumental in expunging his sins?). The physical river has the last word in the novel, however, as Liu Lang and Ma Da float on its moonlit waters, and Liu Lang tells him they are in Huotong. You can be baptized here.

6. Conclusions

What seems to be a long, godless biography of a disturbed life turns into an extended parable as Bei Cun's first well-developed Christian character sheds light on the human psyche and its many distortions. The fleeting nature of Christian elements in the book before the lustral dénouement allows the novel to build up as a story and as a picture of Chinese society, whether in its setting of the 1940s or in its reflection of contemporary life; the tale has to work as novel or narrative, before it can as act as a didactic metaphor. Chinese critics who have responded positively to *The Baptizing River* are united in acclaiming the importance of Bei Cun's writing for bringing Christianity to "cultural public space" in China. Nan Fan argues that the significance of the novel lay in exploring the "pressing nature of the link between faith and existence," and forcing readers to address a question latent in

---

[16] See, e.g., discussion on the Gorham Judgement in Green (2017, pp. 56–57). The latter clause is relevant in Liu Lang's case, since, as with a marriage sacrament that may be declared void if not consummated, a baptism that does not lead to faith or commitment is held by many Protestants to be ineffectual (see Green 2017, p. 90).

society. As Zhai Chongguang notes, the problem of evil is rarely addressed in Chinese fiction, although Bei Cun had earlier been interested in questions of ultimate meaning (Zhai 2018). The play between evil and superstition, and the many evils inherent in patriarchy and power relations are significant strands in the novel. For others, Bei Cun's novel pointed to a collective malaise that highlighted the absence of the spiritual in society; Xie Youshun described the novel as "a true representation of the defeated spirit of our times" (Xie 2016, p. 317) as he outlined the stages of transition in the human spirit that the protagonist undergoes from emptiness and fear, through anxiety and despair to redemption. The portrayal of a psychologically credible, damaged character, whose self-delusion and questioning of identity go hand-in-hand is at the centre of critics' responses.

Critics have also pointed to the significance of Bei Cun's answers, or Christian perspective, on the questions he raises, but have rarely followed this through with further analysis. Xie Youshun notes that Bei Cun created a "new model" of character for contemporary fiction, one whose interior life and spiritual journey is exposed to the reader, while critic Shen Xiayan makes the obvious but important point as she describes the great effect that reading Bei Cun had on her, that in his works of spiritual writing (神性写作) Bei Cun uses the lives of characters as a witness.[17] The fact that Bei Cun is also proposing a solution to the crisis he addresses needs taking seriously. Part of the problem in reaction to *The Baptizing River* is that the answer, the saving grace that the protagonist experiences, is one of the less successful literary elements. Since publication, critics have noted the suddenness of conversion in Bei Cun's early Christian writing, alongside a rather preachy style (the dialogue with the evangelist in the final chapter is practically a verbatim catechesis).[18] The simplicity and speed of baptism—and its power to wipe out a life-time of extreme suffering and evil—appears unrealistic, as does the seeming disjunction in Liu Lang himself: a taciturn, introspective character suddenly engages in a torrent of prayer, a monologic questioning of God, in the language of Hebrew scriptures he has not read. This too-sudden metamorphosis sits uneasily with Bei Cun's skilful depiction of the psychology of childhood, of abuse and addiction, and with the gradual nature of conversion conveyed in the narrative arc. For all Bei Cun's flair in portraying the interior life of his protagonist Liu Lang, the Christian character appears incongruous, with seemingly little continuity in voice across his conversion. This is particularly discordant since Bei Cun's point through the structure of the novel has been to emphasize God's presence and provision throughout the course of a life.

As the discussion of baptism above suggests, Bei Cun in this novel early in his Christian life offers both a straightforward evangelical perspective (through the post-immersion catechesis by the evangelist and the transcription of the prayer of conversion itself; and in the priority given to individual conversion at a time of great national need) and a more complex, literary-theological response in the manner of the baptism. This may not be incongruent with Bei Cun's own ecclesial position, as a member of an unregistered ("house") church that was a gathering point for Beijing intellectuals and writers. In his quest to find a way to speak as a Christian in an authentic, inculturated voice, Bei Cun resorts to copious stretches of biblical language in the final two chapters, some lifted almost directly, like the Job-like questioning and a long passage from Ezekiel reproduced verbatim at the conclusion of the novel. The dialogue with the evangelist or local preacher is stilted and formulaic; while this is a function of the need to convey the Christian message clearly to Liu Lang (and readers), it comes across more as catechism than conversation. In his new writing, Bei Cun is attempting two feats: to find a language for a modern Chinese Christian, and to find a narrative form in which to express a new comprehension of meaning, where life itself is no longer absurd. How to concatenate meaning and expression, which had become increasingly divorced from each other in the avant-garde

---

[17] (Shen 2007, p. 128). Shen describes how, on reading Bei Cun's *I have a Contract with God* (我和上帝有个约) she shut herself in her student room and did not eat or go to class, enveloped in a post-reading stupor.

[18] Cf. (Zhai 2018, p. 73). Shen Xiayan, writing of the rapidity of conversion from a murderer to seeking righteousness in Bei Cun's *Anger* (愤怒) notes "in terms of reader's experience, it seems to lack rationality" (Shen 2007, pp. 128–29).

Religions **2019**, *10*, 413

literature from which Bei Cun came, is the second strand in the struggle, as this very earthy novel seeks to describe a world made whole.

Despite these visible seams, there is also great subtlety in the novel, as this essay has shown. The depravity of human sin is counterbalanced by God's care throughout a life. The narrative arc of a human life, where the plotline is the self-awareness and growth of the character, is used to great effect. The waters in which Liu Lang commits his most heinous crimes are the same waters that wash him clean: the waters of tears, of the river that guides his life's journeys, of the flood that engulfs him. The natural waters of human life become tears of repentance, ablution and absolution in Christ, and a sign of God's covenant. Some of the literary effects that Bei Cun created in this novel as he discarded prior modes are highly efficacious. Time is used to effect, speeding up and slowing down the narrative in line with Liu Lang's mental state and well-being, but within a strongly linear setting. Narrative techniques which Bei Cun inherited from Borges et al., such as the recurrent narration of a single moment to show multiple perspectives,[19] are reduced, or subverted to make a point: here any sense of cyclical time appears only in superstitious or fearful minds, a cycle of false hope and of generational pain, countered by a unidirectional movement towards salvation. Liu Lang's baptism neither reverences western orthodoxy nor remains within one sign system. It is, however, highly effective, and the replay of Liu's obstinacy and conversion in miniature in the life of his friend Ma in the final chapter underlines the urgency of the process for readers.

Funding: This research received no external funding.

Conflicts of Interest: The author declares no conflict of interest.

References

Bei, Cun. 1995. "Wo yu wenxue de chongtu" 我与文学的冲突. *Dangdai zuojia pinglun* 4: 65–67.

Bei, Cun 北村. 2016. *Shixi de he* 施洗的河. Guangzhou: Huacheng.

Bei, Cun, Li Er, and Xu Yigua. 2010. *Stories from Contemporary China: Zhou Yu's Train by Bei Cun, The Sprinkler by Xu Yigua, The Crime Scene by Li Er*. Shanghai: Shanghai Press.

Fällman, Fredrik. 2016. Public Faith? Five Voices of Chinese Christian Thought. *Contemporary Chinese Thought* 47: 223–34. [CrossRef]

Faries, Nathan. 2010. *The Inscrutably Chinese Church: How Narratives and Nationalism Continue to Divide Christianity*. Lanham: Lexington Book.

Felitti, Vincent J., Robert F. Anda, Dale Nordenberg, David F. Williamson, Alison M. Spitz, Valerie Edwards, Mary P. Koss, and James S. Marks. 1998. Relationship of Childhood Abuse and Household Dysfunction to Many of the Leading Causes of Death in Adults: The Adverse Childhood Experiences (ACE) Study. *American Journal Preventative Medicine* 14: 245–58. [CrossRef]

Green, Michael. 2017. *Baptism: Its Purpose, Practice and Power*. Oxford: Monarch.

He, Guangshun 何光顺. 2018. "Dangdai shige shenxing xiezuo de fuxing" 当代诗歌神性写作的复兴——黄礼孩新诗集《谁跑得比闪电还快》的他在视域. *Hanyu Wenxue Yanjiu* 1: 120–28.

Liu, Lixia 刘丽霞. 2006. *Zhongguo jidujiao wenxue de lishi cunzai* (中国基督教文学的历史存在 *The Historical Actuality of Chinese Christian Literature*). Beijing: Social Sciences Academic Press.

Nan, Fan 南帆. 1995. 先锋的皈依—论北村的小说 [The Conversion of the Vanguard—On Bei Cun's Fiction]. *Dangdai zuojia pinglun* 4: 49–57.

Plaks, Andrew. 1987. *Four Masterworks of the Ming Novel*. Princeton: Princeton University Press.

Radcliffe, Timothy. 2012. *Taking the Plunge: Living Baptism and Confirmation*. London: Bloomsbury.

Shen, Xiayan 申霞艳. 2007. Zui, zhenxiang ji jiudu: tan Bei Cun de shenxing xiezuo 罪，真相及救度：谈北村的神性写作. *Dangdai zuojia pinglun* 2: 128–133.

Shi, Wei 施玮. 2007. *Fangsui yidian* 放遂伊甸 [Letting go of Eden]. Beijing: China Broadcasting and Television Press.

Shi, Wei 施玮. 2008. *Bi'an ci'an* 此岸彼岸 [Near Shore, Far Shore]. Beijing: China Broadcasting and Television Press.

---

[19] See, e.g., (Zhang 2007, pp. 273–74).

Wang, Jing. 1998. *China's Avant-Garde Fiction*. Durham: Duke University Press.

Wang, Benchao 王本朝. 2012. "Cong ling de wenxue dao xinling wenxue" 从灵的文学到灵性文学: 中国文学的神性资源问题. *Zhongguo nanfang yishu*. September 29. Available online: http://www.zgnfys.com/a/nfwx-32869.shtml (accessed on 28 May 2019).

Wen, Neng 文能. 2016. 一部小说和一个时代的精神坐标 [A Novel and the Spiritual Co-ordinates of an Era]. In *Shixi de he*. Written by Bei Cun. Guangzhou: Huacheng, pp. 303–13.

Wielander, Gerda. 2013. *Christian Values in Communist China*. Abingdon: Routledge.

Williams, Jane. 2018. *The Art of Advent: A Painting a Day from Advent to Epiphany*. London: SPCK.

Xie, Youshun. 1993. "先锋性的萎缩与深度重建: 兼谈北村的《施洗的河》 [The Retreat of the Avant-Garde and its Deeper Reconstruction—With a discussion of Bei Cun's *Baptizing River*]. *Dangdai zuojia pinglun* 5: 36–41.

Xie, Youshun 谢有顺. 2016. "写作能回家吗? —北村和他的《施洗的河》 [Can Writing Come Home? Bei Cun and his *Baptizing River*]. In *Shixi de he*. Written by Bei Cun. Guangzhou: Huacheng, pp. 314–29.

Yang, Jianlong 杨剑龙. 2011. Linghun zhengjiu de wenxue 灵魂拯救的文学———论灵性文学小说集 <新城路 100号>. *Xuzhou Shifan daxue xuebao* 37: 20–25.

Zanolli, Lauren. 2018. Can Children Be Saved from a Terrible Childhood? *The Guardian*, November 7.

Zhai, Chongguang 翟崇光. 2018. 北村 "神性写作" 的文化意义 [The Cultural significance of Bei Cun's "Spiritual Writing"—Interpreted through *The Book of Consolation* and *The Baptising River*]. *Journal of Fujian Normal University* 4: 68–77.

Zhang, Xuejun. 2007. Borges and Contemporary Chinese Avant-Garde Writings. *Frontiers of Literary Studies* 1: 272–86. [CrossRef]

Zhang, Lin 张林. 2014. Shi Wei tan 'Lingxing wenxue'. September 24. Available online: http://www.china.com.cn/opinion/female/2014-09/24/content_33604262.htm (accessed on 24 May 2019).

Zheng, Jian 郑坚, and Yuandan Yan 严远丹. 2019. "Wenxue de shijiexing yu shenxing" 文学的世界性与神性: 徐兆寿长篇小说《鸠摩罗什》. *Pinglun xiao ji* 评论小辑 2: 132–35.

MDPI

St. Alban-Anlage 66

4052 Basel

Switzerland

Tel. +41 61 683 77 34

Fax +41 61 302 89 18

www.mdpi.com

Religions Editorial Office

E-mail: religions@mdpi.com

www.mdpi.com/journal/religions